MOTHER STARTED IT

by Diana Steiner
Monica Hanna, Ph.D., Editor

To MARLENA
with All best wishes
Diana Steiner
6/10/10

FATROCK ink

LOS ANGELES, CALIFORNIA

TABLE OF CONTENTS

Prologue: Mother Started It   xii

Introduction   3

Elizabeth's Story in Her Own Words, Part 1   11
Elizabeth's Parents   11
Elizabeth's Grandfather & Alex van Straaten's Mother   15
Jewish Experience: Note from the Author   16
Elizabeth's Childhood: The Interview Continues   17
Elizabeth's Early Interest in Music, First Music Lessons   18
Studying Violin   21

Elizabeth's Story in Her Own Words, Part 2   25
The Beginnings of Elizabeth's Teaching Career, 1915   25
Teaching at Willamette University   30
Lena Belle Tarter   31
European Studies and Return to Oregon   32
Teaching in the 1920s, Oregon Music Teachers Association (OMTA)   33

Elizabeth's Story in Her Own Words, Part 3   39
Elizabeth's Paternal Family: Meeting Elizabeth Winkler   39
Meeting Alex van Straaten, 1926   41
The Depression, Elizabeth's Marriage, Solomon Levy's Death   45

Elizabeth's Story in Her Own Words, Part 4   51
Back to Oregon: Teaching and the Birth of Diana   51
Teaching Philosophy   53

Notes and Quotes from Elizabeth's Students, Colleagues and Friends   61
Letter from Lena Belle Tarter, a Friend of Elizabeth   61
Interview with Nathan Steinbock, a Former Student   62
Interview with Hortense Taylor Foster, a Former Student   62
Interview with Fay Mort, a Former Student   63
Interview with Margaret Hogg, Studio Accompanist for Elizabeth   65
Interview with June Director Nagel, a Former Student   68
Interview with Anne Berenson, a Friend   71

Oregon Memories of Mother   75
January 1, 1990, Lincoln Beach, Oregon   75

My Beginning, 1932-1940   91
  Our House   91
  The Depression   91
  Steiner's Music School   92
  My Imagination   93
  Early Talent   93
  Absolute Pitch   93
  My First Violin   94
  The Curtis Institute of Music   96
  Starting at Curtis   97

Life Changes, 1941-1942   103
  Father's Death, 1941   103
  Early Jewish Connection   104
  New York, 1941–42   105
  Childhood in New York   105
  Musical and General Studies in New York   106
  Otto Herz   107
  Friends in New York: Ruth Bradley Jones and Franklin Jones   107

Diana, 1943-1949   113
  Back to Philadelphia and Curtis   113
  Our Philadelphia Apartment   114
  Life in Philadelphia   115
  Student Days at Curtis   116
  1945 Philadelphia Children's Concerts   117
  Stage Door Canteen, 1945   118
  Miami Beach, 1945 (and 1951)   119
  More Student Days at Curtis   119
  Marcel Tabuteau   120
  Alexander Hilsberg   120
  Good Times at Curtis   121
  Mother's Suitors   122
  My General Studies   123
  World War II Memories   124
  Kennebunkport, Maine—Summer 1948   126
  Second Performance with the New York Philharmonic, Dec. 18, 1948   126
  From Student to Staff at Curtis   127
  Curtis Graduation, 1949   128

Veda Reynolds   131

Tanglewood, Summer 1950   139
    Leonard Bernstein   142

Performances and Competitions, 1950-1951   151
    Friday Morning Music Club Competition and Awards   151
    Philadelphia Orchestra, 1950   152
    Eugene Ormandy   152
    Baltimore Symphony Performance, 1950   153

Gregor Piatigorsky   157
    Piatigorsky's Performances   157
    Piatigorsky's Teaching Method   157
    Hollywood Bowl, 1955   158
    Grisha, Our Neighbor   160

Marlboro, 1951-1958 and 1990   163
    Fondue Party   164
    Adolf Busch   164
    Rudolf Serkin   165
    Peter Serkin   166
    Memorable Performances   166
    Alexander "Sascha" Schneider   167
    Marcel Moyse   168
    Other Fellow Marlboro Musicians   169
    Claude Frank   169
    Fun at Marlboro   169
    1990 Return to Marlboro   170

Competitions, Violins and Touring, 1952-1955   173
    Paul Whiteman's Radio Teen Show, 1952   173
    Borrowed Violins: Guadagnini, Hill Strad   175
    Naumburg Competition, Town Hall Debut, 1952   176
    Michaels Competition, 1952 and Chicago Symphony Solo, 1953   177
    Community Concert Touring Anecdotes: 1953–fall 1955 177
    Izler Solomon's Violin, Glen Burnie, Maryland   177
    Experiencing the South: The Carolinas   178
    Pekin, Illinois   180
    A Well-Meaning Presenter   181
    A Pianist's Nightmare, New England   181
    St. John's, Newfoundland   181
    Romance on the Way to Montreal   183
    Punxsatawny, Pennsylvania   184

Corning, New York and CAMI   184
Teaching   185
Concert with Yalta Menuhin, January 1955   185
1955, My First Fine Violin: Gagliano   186

Marriage, Awards, Festivals, 1956–1960   191
"And What a Damn Good Decision It Was": Ed and Diana in Love, 1956 191
NFMC Young Artists Award, 1959   194
1959–60 Concert Experiences as NFMC Award Winner   196
Brevard Festival, North Carolina, June 1959   196
Little Rock, Arkansas performance, 1960   196
Chautauqua, 1960, a Borrowed Stradivarius   196

Jascha Heifetz, 1960   201
Heifetz's Application for a Job at UCLA   201
Studying with Heifetz at UCLA, 1960   201
Heifetz's Teaching Philosophy   202
In the Studio   203
A Glimpse into Heifetz's Personality   204
Jack Benny Anecdote   206

Los Angeles Musical Community and a New Family, 1960–1969 209
Moving to Los Angeles, Summer 1960   209
Minna Coe and the National Association of   209
    American Composers and Conductors, 1960–61
Simon Ramo   210
Ed's Love of Music   211
A New Home and a New Baby   211
University of Southern California Years   213
The Steiner-Berfield Trio   215
Hollywood Bowl   216
Our Other Life: Foxhunting   217

1970s and 1980s   223
House in Lincoln Beach, Oregon   223
Margaret Hurley   223
Guadagnini   224
Recordings   224
Concertmaster   225
Curtis Alumni Association   225
My Stradivarius   227
Curtis Alumni Association, Continued   228
Adjunct Careers: Broadening the Horizon   229

Abram Chasins   229
Radio Broadcast Host/Producer   230
Mehli Mehta on "Air for Strings"   230
Magazine Editing   231
Finding a Brother   232

Trips for Fun and Music   235
First Trip to Hawaii, 1974   235
Alaska, 1978   235
Europe, September 1979   235
Japan, Summer 1982   237
Europe, Summer 1984   237

The Third Generation   259
Marcia and her Harp   259
The Debussy Trio Music Foundation   260
Salzburg Festival   261
Sallie   262
World Harp Congress Conventions   262
Copenhagen, 1993   262
Prague, 1999   263
Geneva, 2002   263
Other Notable Moments   263
A Multi-Faceted Career   264
Teaching   264
Fatrock Ink   265
Third Generation: To Be Continued   265

Conclusion, 2009   267

Appendices   273

Index   317

Fatrock Ink Music publishes a specialty catalogue focusing on repertoire with harp as well as other instrumental works by 20th and 21st Century composers. This catalog includes print music, books, recordings and MP3s.

Copyright © 2009 by Fatrock Ink
Published by Fatrock Ink
P.O. Box 492225, Los Angeles, CA 90049
www.fatrockink.com

Library of Congress Cataloging-in-Publication Data
Steiner, Diana.
MOTHER STARTED IT / Diana Steiner.
Includes references (Discography, Radio Broadcasts, Publications and Concerts) and index.

Library of Congress Control Number: 2009935966

ISBN: 978-0-578-05212-0

Book Design: Maureen Sautter
Set in Neutra Text and Baskerville

Printed in the United States of America

for
Edward, Sallie, Marcia,
Lena, Mattie and Austin

ACKNOWLEDGMENTS

Grateful thanks from the author and the editor to:

Naomi Graffman, Frances Cattermole-Tally (Ph.D, Co-Editor, Guide to the Gods) and Stewart Wade (writer, filmmaker) for their detailed, patient proofreading of the manuscript.

Charlotte B. Brown (UCLA University Archives), Norman Neblett (piano tuner to Heifetz et al.) and Susannah Thurlow (Archivist, The Curtis Institute of Music) for providing archival information and dates.

Parker Emerson (Emerson Music) for his technical advice and patience.

Our appreciation is boundless.

PROLOGUE: MOTHER STARTED IT

This book covers the lives of the three generations of the American women of my family who became professional musicians, each a pioneer in her own right in a particular area of classical music.

In order to follow a dream, it always takes the support and encouragement of some wonderful people. In my case it meant the honor and joy of working closely with and learning from some of the greatest musicians of the 20th century. These musicians included many famous names, but there were also those who were not the "big" names. Without these artist-teachers the rest of my musical growth could not have occurred. I am writing partly so they are not lost to history.

Then there are family influences, including my mother Elizabeth's mother, Dientje, my parents, Elizabeth and Ferenz, and my husband, Edward. Without them, my career probably would not have happened. They are my unsung heroes.

The story begins with Elizabeth Levy Steiner who was born in 1897. There were very few women who achieved the status of professional musicians at the time. A few did so on the East Coast and some in Europe, but they were frequently singers. It was quite unusual for female instrumentalists to succeed professionally. This was especially so for Elizabeth, who grew up primarily in the small rural communities of Oregon.

By the 1920s, she had already studied in Europe, earned a degree, played in concert and had a large class of pupils. In addition, she helped establish the professional requirements for music teacher certification in the State of Oregon. This removed the amateur status frequently ascribed to music teachers, especially women, and brought them into the professional realm.

In order to savor the experience of this highly motivated, vivacious, beautiful woman as she developed in spite of cultural and educational obstacles, I have chosen to reflect on her life by using the interview process and letting her speak in her own words.

When Elizabeth was nearing her 90th birthday, she frequently reflected on the numerous changes she had witnessed in nearly a century of life. Her experience as a child who loved music started during the time of the horse and carriage. As a grown woman and music teacher, she witnessed people engage in space travel. Women went from bustiers to mini-skirts, from cooking on a wood stove to running for president of the United States.

The next generation is my story and that of my sister, Frances. In many ways, I was breaking through what was a fairly solid glass ceiling for touring women violin soloists. The two women from previous generations who inspired me were Maud Powell and Erica Morini, who were really the only ones to achieve international careers.

By the time I arrived on the musical scene in 1938 as a violin prodigy, and had won national and international honors while in my teens and twenties, there were still very few women who were succeeding at that level. Most managers didn't want to take young women because they thought that by the time they became well-known, they'd "go off and get married and have babies." The two women who came before me didn't. In my generation, as women did begin to have families and major careers at the same time, it was a huge breakthrough. The other women I mention in my story, particularly Veda Reynolds, broke through primarily in the orchestral field.

I also became active in the contemporary music scene, both as a performer and promoter of late-20th century composers.

My sister Frances Steiner took a required course in choral conducting taught by the estimable Elaine Brown at Temple University in Philadelphia, which proved to be a turning point in her career goals. From age five, her life goal had been to become the "world's greatest cellist." However, conducting a movement of Brahms' Requiem for her final exam exposed her real talent and passion for conducting. A few years later, studying conducting with Nadia Boulanger in France, she received a great deal of praise and encouragement. However, at a time when women were not even accepted into the ranks of many major symphony orchestras, it seemed like an impossible dream. Yet, whenever an opportunity arose, she would happily lead. No ensemble was too small or too elementary. It was all experience that would lead to her making musical history as a woman in the field of symphonic conducting.

In 1977, Frances became the first woman to conduct a professional orchestra (the Glendale Symphony) from the stage of the Dorothy Chandler Pavilion of the Los Angeles Music Center.

My daughter, Marcia Dickstein, is a pioneer in establishing a whole new outlook for the harp as an instrument in chamber music with her group, The Debussy Trio. While maintaining an active career playing in other areas such as symphony, opera, film, television and commercials, as well as composing and arranging, her major focus over the last 20-plus years has been commissioning an extensive new harp repertoire. She has inspired composers from all over the world to look at the harp in a totally different way. Her story is interwoven with mine, especially the involvement with new music. It is a natural progression from my close interaction with many fine composers. Thanks to Marcia's inspiration, a whole new field of musical possibilities opened up for both of us.

I can appreciate the dedication and pride that Elizabeth had as she watched Frances and me succeed. She loved it as I love watching Marcia open new vistas for the world of music we all love.

This book is a very personal remembrance of what happened over a century of our lives.

–DSD

THE FIRST GENERATION: ELIZABETH

"I still believe that everything is destiny. I think I had a sort of charmed life. Maybe once in a while it flashes through my mind... I did a lot through music." Elizabeth Levy Steiner

1

INTRODUCTION

My mother, Elizabeth Levy Steiner, was born in Salisbury, North Carolina in 1897. She was the last of her mother's eleven pregnancies and six live births. Only three of those children survived to adulthood, which was not unusual in those days. She was the only one to attain a college education. She lived in the deep south for the first four or five years of her life. She told me that she had a "mammy." There wasn't slavery then, of course, but still the aftermath of slavery was apparent. After all, the Civil War had been over for only a few years.

As a five-year-old, she first moved to Montana and then in 1905, she moved with her family to Oregon where they lived a fairly rustic pioneer life. Her two brothers never finished elementary school and her father probably didn't either. All three were butchers. Though her brothers were not career cowboys, they were certainly able to ride horses and corral a cow when necessary.

Elizabeth's mother, Dientje (Diana) van Straaten Levy, was an educated woman from Dordrecht, Holland. The interesting thing about the Jewish people of Holland, which my grandmother always preached to my mother and her to me, was that they had not grown up in a ghetto. The Dutch Jews were free and had prospered in Holland for many generations following their arrival after the Spanish Inquisition. Dientje was a very proud lady, very aristocratic in her demeanor.

The German and Dutch Jews were educated and free-born people. One of the things Dientje always bragged about was that when she came through U.S. customs, she didn't have to sit on a bench at Ellis Island because she didn't come over in steerage; she came over first class. She was fluent in Dutch and Hebrew, and became relatively fluent in English after she came to the United States.

Despite her aristocratic manner, Dientje had a fairly difficult early life. As the only girl, with six brothers, and the oldest of the family, Dientje had to care for all of them after her mother died when the youngest child was still an infant. It was assumed she would be a spinster but she married at the age of 30, a fairly late marriage age for that era. Dientje was about 43 years old when Elizabeth was born.

Dientje was completely dedicated to Elizabeth. She wanted to make sure that her daughter was educated and that she would become, if possible, a professional woman. Perhaps as a result of her own difficult experiences, she wanted to ensure that her daughter was independent. At a very early age, Elizabeth showed musical talent and Dientje encouraged her. Even though they barely had a dollar to spend at times, Dientje managed to get Elizabeth music lessons and made her stick with it. She taught her daughter all of the practical things that she could and gave her every educational opportunity possible.

Elizabeth admitted that she was fed and pampered. Her job in life was to get an education. Her early motivation came from her mother. Dientje always told Elizabeth, "You never know when you are going to be on your own."

Elizabeth made good use of her education and talent. She was a very beautiful redhead, with hair so long she could sit on it. She studied very hard and had a winning personality on the stage, entertaining audiences with her flair for dramatic performance and lovely violin tone.

She became an excellent teacher. As she had to learn things the hard way herself, she decided that when she taught her students she would be more thorough and giving than her teachers of the previous generation had been. Those teachers thought that what they knew was a trade secret; students frequently learned in spite of them, not because of them.

Consequently, Elizabeth's early violin training was rather hit-and-miss. Her teachers varied widely in training, experience and philosophy. It took the combined determination of mother and daughter to achieve success. As a young adult, Elizabeth studied in Belgium with the famous violin pedagogue Cesar Thompson. Then she completed her degree at Ithaca College in upstate New York when Thompson came there as a visiting professor. Additionally, she studied with several other distinguished teachers for short periods of time, including Adolfo Betti.[1] In 1930, during a summer session at UCLA, she studied with Josef Borisoff while taking harmony and theory courses with Carolyn Alchin, a well-known professor who wrote one of the definitive theory books of the time.[2]

When Elizabeth returned to Oregon and became a leader in the Oregon Music Teachers Association, she helped to establish the certification requirements which led to music teachers being professionally well-respected.[3]

Elizabeth was a Jewish girl growing up in a state with very few Jews. In most of the places she lived, including Silverton, Tillamook, and even later in Salem, her family was often the only Jewish family. Her brothers strayed from the religion when they were young. They had to be active guys, and there were no Jewish boys with whom to pal around. They both married outside of the religion. Elizabeth, though, perhaps because of her mother, wanted to marry a Jewish man. It was difficult because most of the men that she did meet, either in Salem or Portland, were businessmen but not necessarily highly educated. Also, she wanted someone who was going to be interesting and sympathetic to her music.

She was close to 32 when she met my father, Ferenz Steiner. He came to Oregon from California, having been engaged by the Portland Symphony as

---

1   First violinist of the Flonzaley Quartet.
2   See Carolyn A. Alchin, Applied Harmony (Los Angeles: s.p., 1917).
3   See Notes from Students, Margaret Hogg.

principal cellist. He was a very good-looking, single young man. The manager of the Portland Symphony, Delta Spencer, loved him in this post. She was afraid that he would get bored and want to leave Portland, which was then a relatively small town (since he had previously been living in Los Angeles), so she endeavored to introduce him to a good-looking, eligible Jewish woman. Elizabeth was president of the Oregon Music Teachers Association at the time and was presiding over the association's state convention. Delta brought Ferenz to hear her speak. Elizabeth stood on stage in a beautiful Nile green suit which accentuated her gorgeous red hair. Delta used to say that if it weren't for her, I wouldn't be here. According to her, Ferenz fell in love with Elizabeth at first sight though it took him a year to convince her to marry him.

A year after their marriage, I was born. By the time I was eighteen months old, they discovered that they had a child with musical talent. I was already beginning to play a little on the piano and they learned that I had absolute pitch. Mother started teaching me along with the hundreds of other students my parents taught in order to make a living. By the time I was three and four years old, they discovered that I was extraordinarily talented. They realized how unique I was in the music world when Josef Hofmann[4] heard me and offered me a full scholarship.

Elizabeth and Ferenz gave up their home and life in Oregon, moving the family to Philadelphia so that I could attend The Curtis Institute of Music. There, Elizabeth continued teaching. Within three months of our arrival, Ferenz had a massive heart attack and was never really able to earn a living after that. He died a couple of years later, leaving behind a 44-year-old widow with a nine-year-old and a four-year-old just six weeks before Pearl Harbor. Elizabeth was left virtually penniless.

She managed to maintain such a positive attitude. She got some help from a very dear uncle, Alex, but very little from her brothers. She displayed the same grit and determination that her mother had. She wanted me to be able to finish my education, a desire she had for Frances as well, as she began showing considerable talent of her own on cello and piano. So Elizabeth decided not to go back to Oregon, which she felt had always hampered her musical education. By the time she'd gone to study in Europe and the East Coast, she was already too old to achieve the level of professionalism that she wanted as a performer. It was very important to her that we stay on the East Coast while Frances and I were young enough to develop. She gave up any opportunities to remarry in order to devote herself to keeping a roof over our heads and making sure that nothing would disturb our ability to take advantage of the fantastic opportunity that we had at Curtis.

As Frances and I grew up and moved away, she never complained that she was alone. She had her students and always made friends. She was very active in the Music Teachers Association in Philadelphia and became its president. She

---

4   Concert pianist and Director of The Curtis Institute of Music, 1927–38.

established herself as a very high-quality teacher and made a living for herself. She even saved enough money in case she might need it in her old age.

When Ed and I got married, she stayed in Philadelphia for a year and a half. As I tell elsewhere in the story, she was mugged, seriously injured and left to die in the snow. We insisted that she move to Los Angeles, which was a big jump since she already had established a life in Philadelphia. She had to start all over again at 68 years of age in a new city.

Elizabeth acclimated quickly. She went to the Marymount School of Los Angeles, a Catholic college in the Los Feliz area, and was appointed to the faculty.[5] She met a few friends in Beverly Hills and the next thing you know she had a class of pupils there, including the children of singers Steve Lawrence and Eydie Gormé.

She found herself a little apartment, got in touch with her Sigma Alpha Iota sorority sisters and started a bridge club. Her ability to make friends wherever she was seemed infinite.

Not only did she make new friends, but she was also wonderful at maintaining her relationship with old friends in Oregon. In 1971, when Ed and I bought our house in Lincoln Beach, Oregon, Mother reconnected easily with her former students and colleagues in the Portland and Salem areas.

For her 75th birthday, we threw her a surprise party in Lincoln Beach. She thought she was going to attend a dinner party with Fay Mort, one of her former violin students.[6] We invited Fay and her husband Loren to join us for a champagne toast before we headed off to a dinner in her honor. As far as Mother knew, it would just be the seven of us: her, Ed, me, the girls, Fay and Loren. All of a sudden, the doorbell rang and waiting at the door were two more former students, Hortense Taylor Foster and June Director (Nagel), who had driven down from Portland. A few minutes later one of her former piano teacher colleagues, Lillian Pettibone, came to the door. Margaret Hogg, her former studio accompanist, came from Salem. Before Mother knew it, there were ten of her closest friends who had all made the trip to Lincoln Beach. We all then headed to the Cedar Tree Restaurant at Salishan Lodge.

Fay Mort held a smaller birthday party in honor of Mother's 90th birthday in Lincoln Beach on August 23, 1987. Mother died in September, just a few weeks later.

Mother's affection for Oregon continued throughout her life. When she would go walking on the beach, she would get tired, so the grandkids would keep going while she would sit down on a log to rest. We used to laugh because even strangers would come by and sit and talk with her. She would tell them about the history of Oregon.

Her good friend Lena Belle Tarter, who lived in Corvallis, was in her eighties and she would get a ride to come visit at Lincoln Beach, as did Margaret Hogg,

---

5   Marymount merged to become Loyola Marymount University in 1973.
6   Fay was our neighbor in Lincoln Beach and helped us find the house.

who was about ten years younger. We maintained a close friendship with Margaret, who dedicated her life to teaching piano and taking care of her brothers, until her passing in 2007. All of these Oregon friendships continued throughout the years. They loved Elizabeth for her honesty, generosity and great spirit.

Mother's students were so devoted to her. The great affection that they had for her was incredible. They studied with her in the first few decades of the twentieth century, but their relationships kept growing as time went on. I always kid people that the day she died at age 90, I had to cancel a music lesson and a bridge club meeting.

Some say that if you truly want to understand a person, look at their relationship with their pets. Our dog, Rex, absolutely adored mother. She had always lived around animals while growing up and the dog apparently recognized this affinity she had for all living creatures. The last few years of her life, when she napped in the afternoon, Rex would forego being with us on the beach. He followed Mother and, with a big sigh, lay down at the foot of the bed to keep her company until she woke. The week after her ninetieth birthday when she may have had a minor stroke episode, she was not feeling well. Rex stayed with her throughout this time, never leaving her side.

She was a unique individual and certainly made a difference in the lives of hundreds of students across the country, from Oregon to Philadelphia to Los Angeles. Neither Frances nor I would have been the women we became, nor would we have been able to achieve the careers we have had, if it had not been for her unselfishness and steadfastness.

ELIZABETH'S STORY
PART 1

Elizabeth receives her first violin at
about age 8 in Forest Grove, Oregon.

ELIZABETH'S STORY IN HER OWN WORDS, PART 1

The following chapters, split into four parts, derive from interviews of Elizabeth Levy Steiner that took place during the summers of 1986 and 1987. My daughter, Marcia, and I both interviewed her.

Elizabeth's Parents

Elizabeth: My mother was born Dientje (Diana) van Straaten and my father was Solomon Levy.

I know only a little about my father's family, though I met my first cousin, Elizabeth Levy Winkler in a most unusual way in New York City, which I will describe later.

My father, born in Breda, Holland, on March 15, 1845, was his father's twenty-first child, born of his third wife, Elizabeth. I only knew one of his brothers–Wolfe–who, my mother [Dientje] later learned to her dismay, wrote my father's love letters to her. This did not come to her knowledge until they had been married several weeks and were living in London.

Solomon was 52 years old when I was born and he thought all the rest of his family might be dead as he had lost contact with them.

His mother often acted as a midwife. Once, she went to help with a birth in very stormy weather. As a result of this, he felt that she became paralyzed. Sol was very young when this happened and he took care of his mother, which caused him to miss quite a bit of school. He wasn't too impressed with book learning. Nevertheless, he matured very young and married at 18 to a very wealthy widow of 27 years of age who had fine family connections in London. They were married for 20 years and during that time came to America. She was buried in Philadelphia at the Sephardic Jewish Synagogue Cemetery. After her death, Sol returned to Europe. Somehow he met Dientje and fell madly in love with her.

She was an attractive redhead of 30, five feet tall and only 98 pounds. She wore high-heeled shoes and was quite fashionable and aristocratic in her ideas. She would say, "You might as well be dead if you're not in style." She lived in Belgium when she met Sol and dressed like a stylish rich lady. She often told me the story of how she didn't want to leave her relatives and go to America with Sol. So he told her that he would open a meat market in London, where he was well known, so that she could return often to see her relatives in Belgium and Holland.

Dientje was born in Dordrecht, Holland, the oldest and only daughter of Gertrude Debruyn and Harry van Straaten. She had five brothers: Jacques, Willem, Jacob, Maurice, and Herman.

My mother's mother died during a cholera epidemic when she was only 48 years old. Dientje took over as mother and head of the family with her father. Her youngest brother, Herman, was only three years old when their mother died. They had three servants in the home and Dientje became a very fine household manager.

Dientje kept house for three years. During that time, her father was lonely and started drinking. He wasn't taking very good care of his business and couldn't support them. Consequently, it was necessary for Herman and Maurice to be put into a Jewish orphanage. Dientje's uncles were all very successful and had no patience for her father's behavior. He was also in the meat business, but I have a clipping showing that he spoke seven different languages, and taught at Liege University in Belgium.

As a girl, Dientje could not just go out and live by herself. Instead, she went to live with her uncle for about eight years. She was called a jungfrau which meant she wasn't a servant, but she did an awful lot and was sort of the head housekeeper. They always worked upon her vanity, so she always had to do everything just right. She was very clever.

During the time that she raised her brothers, she said that she became a Hebrew scholar because she had such a quick, fine memory and her brothers couldn't get their lessons. Her father would beat them if they didn't do it just right. So, in order to spare them, she would teach them. By the time she got through, she knew the Torah very well.

It was while she was staying at one of her uncle's homes that Dientje met my father. When her uncle said that they had money in their business that her mother had left her for a dowry, Sol said, "Oh, I'm marrying the girl. I'm not marrying her for money. I don't need it. I'm going to take care of her from now on." Of course, she never did get the money which amounted to about 13,000 guilders, which was quite a sum in those days. In later years when they got to America, they could have used it.

While courting Dientje, Sol went back and forth to London, although it wasn't easy. When he lived in another city in Holland, it wasn't so hard. And he did supposedly write her those letters.[1] There was a law in Holland that you had to post banns if you wanted to get married. If anybody knew anything against you, like if you had been married before, that person could speak up now or never.

So the banns were posted for four weeks and then they married.

Sol opened a butcher shop in London as promised. He even got a music band to celebrate the opening of a beautiful market. He was showing off for Mother. But he had forgotten to get a kosher permit. Of course, he couldn't sell any meat in that neighborhood unless he had that. For some reason, his first wife's relatives were

---

1   As mentioned before, these were written by Sol's brother Wolfe.

very bitter against him. They fixed it so that he couldn't get a permit. They said that he had been converted to non-kosher by going to America. It became impossible for Father, so he closed the market and said, "Now I am going to America" and Dientje had no choice.

Dientje had seven trunks of the most wonderful wedding gifts from her relatives. She'd had a big wedding party in Rotterdam. But she was very bitter over this in later years and warned me, "Don't ever go spend all that money on a big wedding. It isn't worth the presents you get. You keep the money and go out and buy what you need yourself."

When they finally got to America, Father left Dientje with her own father who had preceded her to the United States and was living in Philadelphia. Her father had married a lady of about 40, though he was 60. At that time she (Dientje's stepmother) was pregnant with a little boy, Alexander van Straaten, my uncle who later became very prominent in my life. Mother was very nice to this little boy and his mother was very fond of her. Dientje was very handy with a needle and thread and made him a little white satin blouse with black velvet pants. Alex's mother thought that was just so sweet of her. Finally, Sol came back to Philadelphia for mother and they settled in Greensboro, North Carolina, where my oldest brother Harry was born.

Sol was quite successful in Greensboro. He earned a good living for the family. Dientje even managed to send her father $10 a month because he was having a hard time making ends meet. Her father stayed in Philadelphia until his death at 72, though he was buried in Charlotte, North Carolina and a window was dedicated to him at the Athens, Georgia Reform Synagogue where his son Jacob, Dientje's brother, lived.

Diana: What about Dientje's other brothers?

Elizabeth: Willem was next in line to Mother, the oldest boy. We stayed with him all the time we were in Europe, in Antwerp, Belgium. He owned several cafes on the waterfront but we never went to see any of them because it was too poor a neighborhood. But he made good money there. And he owned his house at 76 Rue Huybrechts.

Diana: In 1920, you and your mother went to Europe, partly so Dientje could reconnect with her brothers.

Elizabeth: We went every other night to dinner at Herman's. The alternate nights we had dinner at Willem's house. That was our agreement: that if we paid our way over, which was very expensive in those days from Salem, Oregon to Antwerp, they would house us.

Diana: How long were you there? Six months?

Elizabeth: Practically. We got there about the fourth or fifth of July and left in December.

Elizabeth: Then there was Uncle Maurice, who was a family outcast. He was one of the two brothers placed in the orphanage. Friends would come and see the children and give them money. It was put in the bank for them so that when they reached 18 or 21 and left the orphanage, they had a nest egg. Uncle Maurice swiped Herman's money. He drank heavily. He had never paid it back to Herman, so while we were in Europe, Mother got him to pay back with interest all this money he had stolen, which was quite a bit in those days.

Diana: What was Maurice's profession that he could afford to pay all that money back?

Elizabeth: He owned a hotel in Brussels for seniors and was president of the Catholic Alcoholics' League there. He also had worked as a spy for the Belgians. He was decorated by Cardinal Mercer and had a card that just gave him open sesame to everything.

So Maurice took me to Cesar Thompson at the Brussels Conservatory, who auditioned me when I got there. Thompson said he would take me and give me two lessons a week privately. We paid 25 francs a piece and he used to keep me for about two hours each time. I paid him by check and kept the receipts. I was so glad I had because later it was very important that I could prove that I had taken lessons from Thompson.

Diana: Did you actually study in the classes at the Conservatory?

Elizabeth: Well, I attended them. He said I didn't need to register. He would save me the 200 francs that a foreigner would have to pay to enter the classes. So he said, "You just say 'Je joue le piano' and make like you play the piano to the man at the gate."[2] I only had to do that once and after that they knew me with my red hair that came almost to my knees.

Diana: That could make you stand out.

Elizabeth: It was my American clothes. I was "la petite américaine." I had letters from Thompson's wife, and a card introducing me as a pupil of Cesar Thompson. When Mother wanted to leave, I couldn't continue because I couldn't stay at Maurice's hotel alone. He said if I walked up the stairs–and it was a grand stairway from the lobby–if I went there alone as a woman, and 10 or 15 minutes later a

---

2   This would indicate that she was a working accompanist for the class.

man walked up the steps, they would think he was visiting me. That would ruin my reputation, so I couldn't stay there. The classes were from 3 to 6 p.m. and I would have to go home at six o'clock alone. Any man could accost a single girl on the street alone after four o'clock. If Mother wasn't with me, they would come up and talk to me.

We had quite a time. We had to stay overnight at Uncle Maurice's when I had the classes because it was an hour's trip from Brussels to Antwerp.

Elizabeth's Grandfather & Alex van Straaten's Mother

Diana: What about your grandfather, your mother's and Uncle Alex's father?

Elizabeth: My grandfather was 72 when he died. He was visiting Mother in North Carolina.

Diana: Was Alex's mother still alive?

Elizabeth: Yes, but she didn't leave because she had to keep running their rooming house in Philadelphia.

Diana: So Alex didn't come either. He would have been just a youngster. Dientje was over 30 years older than Alex.

Elizabeth: My grandfather got gangrene from a blister on his heel. It was nobody's fault except in those days they didn't worry about something like that. They didn't know. In the South, gangrene was quite common. He died within three days and was buried in Charlotte.

Diana: Did he still follow the Jewish religion?

Elizabeth: Oh, yes. They were very strictly Jewish. He died in Salisbury and that was too small a town. But Charlotte had a Jewish cemetery which was just a few miles away.

Diana: Were you born already?

Elizabeth: Yes. I was 10 months old. I have that in a family Bible in Mother's own handwriting.

Elizabeth's Early Interest in Music, First Music Lessons

Diana: Do you remember your early interest in music?

Elizabeth: I was always trying to dance. I'd play my fingers up and down on the table pretending it was a piano.

Diana: How old were you?

Elizabeth: Between six and seven years of age.

Diana: Were you still in Montana?

Elizabeth: Yes. It was before I started lessons at Pacific University [Oregon], and that was in 1908 when I played in a recital. There were 25 pianists on the program. Only one violin, and I was number 26.

Diana: Where did you actually start to take the violin?

Elizabeth: I was in Forest Grove. I wanted to take piano, but my parents couldn't afford one. They moved so much, they wouldn't be able to carry it with them either. I heard some violin music coming out of a music store. It was Starr Music Store which was a few doors from my father's butcher shop. I thought it sounded so beautiful. They had a violin case open in the window. So we walked in to the store and Mama thought it would be a good thing to play because it was easy to carry around.

    The price was $5 for the violin, bow, and case. I still have it. That is that three-quarter I have now that is so beat up.

Diana: You paid $5 for the whole thing?

Elizabeth: Yes. We stopped and asked the girl in the store if she would give me lessons and she said she would be happy to. She taught me Nearer My God To Thee and Swanee River and other soul tunes.

Diana: Did she teach you how to read music?

Elizabeth: No, not much. I could read music and I knew the letter name of notes. But I did learn practically by ear. She would play it and I would repeat it.

    At that time I picked up the Merry Widow Waltz. We were always humming it and loved the tune. I was a confident "genius" when I had done that.

Then the girl said, "I can't teach you very long. I'm getting married." She told my parents, "She is so gifted, take her to Mr. Chapman, the head of the Music Department at Pacific University."

Well, he was a good pianist, but I don't think he ever took a violin lesson in his life. I had to pay him $1 a lesson, and I only paid her twenty–five cents. But she persuaded Mother it was worth it for me to go to the best, because I was so gifted.

Diana: What did he teach you?

Elizabeth: There was a little piece called Puss 'n Boots — it was the hardest thing I had ever learned.

Diana: Did anybody teach you how to hold the instrument?

Elizabeth: Oh, you just picked it up and copied them. Nobody ever taught technique or anything like that. But I had trouble keeping time. I played the tune, but I wouldn't keep a steady tempo. Nobody ever used the word "tempo" anyway.

Then we moved around a bit and I went to Portland for lessons. My next teacher, Mr. Betman, was a very fine musician but he didn't know the first thing about teaching a child. I took from him a year or so. He was concertmaster of the Orpheum Theater on the vaudeville circuit. And that was our extravagance when we were in Portland, that every Saturday Mother and I went to see the vaudeville show. Every once in a while they had a violinist on, but very seldom did women get to play. One woman did, and she would take her bow off with a flair. I copied that stage deportment, coming out, smiling and bowing. I was always practicing that. Mother said that was how you won your audience.

I quit taking lessons from Betman and began taking lessons from a man named Eichenlab, who was considered one of the best teachers in Portland. He taught me the Melody in F by Rubinstein and put me up in third position. That was the first I had ever heard there was such a thing. I was so proud, I just loved it and loved him for showing it to me.

Then I had to quit him after a year when I went to Tillamook. There, I didn't take lessons for the whole year. There was no one at all who was a musical professional. But I played a lot at school.

Then we moved to Silverton. When we got there, I took lessons again and again it cost $1 a lesson. Mother would try, somehow, out of the money that Daddy would give her for the household budget, to squeeze out my violin lessons. For her, that came first.

I went to the Mount Angel Academy and they thought I was very good. I helped dedicate the new building there in 1913. They made me principal violin, and there were six violins that played in that orchestra.

Diana: How old were you when you arrived in Portland?[4]

Elizabeth: I graduated in January 1911. There were nine grades in Portland as there was no junior high. Because of my transfer, they sent me to a school on Raleigh Street, but it was quite a bit north of where I lived, a good 20 to 30 minute walk.

    The teacher had us all line up and add a column of figures. After adding it up, we would turn around and not turn back because we could see other people's answers. So I turned around quickly. The teacher said, "Well, Elizabeth, aren't you going to add those up?" I said, "I've finished." There were only two other girls who had finished and got a correct answer. So at noon, I said, "Oh, it is so far for me to walk. Couldn't I go to school on Couch Street because that is only a few blocks from my house?"

Diana: Was that a high school?

Elizabeth: No. They did put me in the sixth grade, but to change schools I had to go to the ninth grade. And in the year and a half, I did make the ninth grade. I was in Miss Orchild's room, who became my devoted friend all the way through.

    For example, I got the chicken pox. If you were out longer than two weeks, you couldn't pass that grade. So Miss Orchild called Mother and told her that I should go to the city health officer and ask him to give me a certificate so I could go into her the minute that I came back the following Monday. Well, two weeks were all I had. If I missed a half a day that Monday to go get my certificate, that would throw me out for the year and I couldn't graduate in January. It was very important for me because of Father's business. We were going to leave Portland and I wanted to finish that school.

    I did finish and I was the youngest in the class. And the oldest was 19 years old because they didn't have adult classes for foreigners. I finished in the top ten out of about 30 in the classroom.

Diana: So, you left Portland in January and that was when you graduated ninth grade. Then what happened? Did you go back to Silverton or Salem?

Elizabeth: No, we moved to Camellias. It seemed Father had rented a farm so we could have a slaughterhouse to supply the meat. He went out of the retail business into the wholesale business and supplied meat to the men who were working and building the road across the mountain to Tillamook.

Diana: They were building a railroad?

---

4 She was probably about 11 years old.

Elizabeth: They had to break through the virgin forest, you know. They did lay the tracks for the train.

Diana: You lived in Tillamook for a while. Isn't that where he went bankrupt?

Elizabeth: Father went bankrupt when we left the farm because he couldn't afford to keep the farm. He was shortchanged a lot and the boys (my brothers) didn't know anything. They thought they knew a lot, but they didn't.

Diana: They were just in their late teens.

Elizabeth: Ben was only 19 or 20 when we went to Tillamook. Father opened a market there and Ben went with him. Ben did a lot of the slaughtering and Father did the buying. He was terrific with buying, so we got out of the financial hole.

That was where I first got to play violin solos for the kids at school. They just loved it. I wouldn't admit I was scared. One time, one of the boys said, "Oh, Elizabeth, you were scared because I saw your knees shaking." I just loved to show off. I played such things as Souvenir de Moscou, by Henryk Wieniawski.

Studying Violin

Diana: When did you study with William Wallace Graham?

Elizabeth: I didn't study with Graham until after we left Tillamook and we moved to Silverton where I studied with a lady. She taught me to be very careless and my counting was bad. But she used to play with me all the time during the lesson. Then I would go home and sometimes I'd play it a little worse or a little better. But I practiced hard at it.

Mother was always trying to elevate me and have me go to good people.

She took me to Mount Angel,[5] which was 5 or 6 miles, but the train used to stop there. It was very difficult to go, but we did. There was no car or any other way of getting there. I would go Saturday. Mother went to the head nun who said she was really a pianist and had taught the violin. There were very few violin players. She said that she thought I was a very gifted child and that Mother should take me to Salem.

Also, I had a neighbor who had played the violin in the movies in Silverton. He played for the dances, and things like that. So he told me, he said, "now listen. You ought to stop for those rests." And I said, "Oh, I'll remember." But I went through it so fast I didn't stop for all the rests. But that taught me a lesson and I

---

5 A Catholic school and convent.

went home and counted. I began to learn how important it was that I should be more careful with rhythm. In my efforts to do well, I just hurried and raced. I had no phrasing or anything like that.

Diana: You had no way of knowing what was correct.

Elizabeth: No. Nobody taught me anything.

Then Edna Stein[1] went to Salem and took lessons from a lady named Winifred Bird. Winifred had made a Town Hall debut in New York. Edna came home and stayed a year or two instead of going to New York. She had heard of this Mr. Graham who was coming to teach part-time in Salem.

Though I skipped a year or so, I did make marvelous improvement as Graham's student. He was very clever. He forbade me to play in public for a year. All the local groups wanted me to play, like the women's clubs and the Odd Fellows Club. They wanted me to play every time they had a social gathering. There were no radios and record players were few and far between. Anyway, I was a pretty lively young girl and everybody liked me. I went to Graham and I had to catch an 8 o'clock train in the morning, though it was only 16 miles to Salem. We would have to stop and wait for this little spur from Silverton to Salem to connect with the main line.

Diana: How old were you at this time?

Elizabeth: I was in high school in 1915. I was 17. I mended my ways of playing. Mr. Graham really was a very fine teacher and he was very demanding. He didn't make it interesting. He taught me like they taught him in Europe. For instance, for a whole half hour lesson, all I played was an introduction line. I went over and over it until I did it very well. I think that is one of the pieces I played for Thompson when I went.

Diana: He was probably doing you a favor. What you didn't realize was that if he let you go home, you would do it your old way. By forcing you to do it in front of him, at least you learned that much.

Elizabeth: I learned to count, too. And I improved. He said, though, that I couldn't play anywhere for a year. I was in the 11th grade because I know I was playing very well in the 12th grade when I graduated. I played the church service on the violin and did a beautiful job.

---

1 A friend.

ELIZABETH'S STORY
PART **2**

Courtesy Family Archives

ELIZABETH'S STORY IN HER OWN WORDS, PART 2

The Beginnings of Elizabeth's Teaching Career, 1915

Elizabeth: With Graham, I corrected myself to such an extent that the Women's Club, which was considered high society, invited me to play. There was a local widow, a very fine, cultured, educated piano teacher from the East, who was my accompanist. She was teaching a Lutheran minister's little twin girls; one was taking piano and the other wanted to take violin. So their parents wrote to Mr. Graham to see what he charged. He charged $5 a lesson. So they asked him if I was capable of teaching her. He said yes, that he couldn't recommend anyone any better than me if they didn't go to him.

So he started me teaching. I used to give the girl two half hours for a dollar. And that was high-priced because you could get all the piano teachers you wanted for fifty cents an hour. When I had a recommendation from Mr. Graham and had studied with him for about a year, this new student thought I was excellent.

I played very well, had corrected my bad counting and played better in tune. Before Graham, I didn't know there were eight tones to a scale and that there were two half steps in the major scale. I didn't know that until I was about 18! (That's part of why the work I did to change the music teacher accreditation system later was so important to me.)

Then Mr. Graham forbade me to play for nothing. He said charge a dollar for lessons or don't teach. If you didn't think your lessons were worth a dollar an hour, you must not teach. He taught me some very good things about becoming a professional. He said, "I don't care about these people. No matter how well you play and how well they like you, if you play for them twice for nothing, the third time they won't even ask you. They will get somebody else for nothing. So if they want you, they gotta pay you $2.50 or $5.00."

I didn't get quite as many calls. That was in 1915. Then Father wanted to expand his business. Ben started a little market in Salem called the Midget. It wasn't any bigger than a bedroom. They did all the slaughtering in Silverton and drove a team of two grey horses sixteen miles for the meat. They would kill the cows about midnight and at 2 or 3 in the morning, they would drive the wagon to Salem.

Salem was a big city: 14,000 people while Silverton had only 2,000 people. There were two butchers there. Father would get impatient. People would come in and say the meat was tough and then he would say it wasn't tough, they just didn't know how to cook it. That was probably true, particularly the people who complained the most were the people who really didn't know how to cook. However, there were enough people who liked it.

Ben got to doing so much business in Salem—he was a tall, good-looking boy—that he got somebody else to do the dirty work. But he did all the meat cutting. He was very capable and built the business. People would line up on the sidewalk. He sold cheaper and better meat.

I remember when I went from my lessons with Mr. Graham I used to have to go in to the Midget and take half the money that Ben made from 8 a.m. until before the banks closed. I took it to the bank because he was afraid people would come in and rob him because everything was cash. No credit.

Diana: You mean he gave a cheaper price because he was doing a cash business.

Elizabeth: Yes. Then Harry took over the other end. He did the slaughtering and Papa did the buying. They were doing so well that they rented a store next door and doubled the size. Then they put in a kind of ice box so the meat would keep and they wouldn't have to sell it right away. You see, that is one of the reasons meat was tough, because it wasn't aged at all.

But, nevertheless, they did sell a lot. Father was known for his honesty. Everybody said they were "the best damn Jews they ever heard of" because they were fair and didn't cheat.

Then we decided the whole family would move to Salem. They rented someplace else where they could slaughter so they didn't have to do that 16 mile trip with the meat. Then we moved.

Elizabeth: In 1915, I graduated from Silverton High with highest honors and had a school teacher's diploma as I had taken a teacher's training course. I got the highest grade in the class because our teacher posed questions like, "What are you going to do if some kid comes to you and asks, 'Why would that be the answer?'" No one knew what to answer a student who was asking foolish questions. I got up and said, "Why? It's a fact, that's why. White is white because it is white and black is black because it is black and this is the same. This is true because it is a fact." The teacher said, "Hooray!" and he gave me the highest grade in the class.

Also, while I was going to high school, I taught as a substitute. One of the teachers got sick and had to leave for two weeks. The principal was so fond of me that he gave me the job. I think teachers got about $3 a day and he gave me $1.50. He said the regular teacher had to have the balance for her living expenses. I would have done it for nothing, but he said I should get paid.

So I taught second and fifth grades. There were only boys in my classes because they separated the boys and girls.

The principal came over that first morning and couldn't believe his ears. There wasn't a sound coming from the classroom except my voice. So he listened a minute and walked in and it just about floored him. All the boys in the class were sitting there listening to me read them a story. I told them I would read that story for a half hour.

I had a big stick across the table with which I would hit them if they didn't behave. I had observed the regular teacher. She told me that a boy named Bjorn was the meanest one and he made all the rest bad.

So when I came in, I said, "Mr. Smith, (or whatever his name was) would you please close the windows for me." He jumped up and was so proud because I had addressed him as "Mister." He closed the window and was a good boy for me the whole two weeks. I had no trouble. The principal used to come over and check. He told the faculty the next day that he thought they were going to find Elizabeth dead on the floor!

I really had a knack for teaching and a quick understanding.

When I graduated, I was the leading lady in the class play. I just loved to act and mother was encouraging me all the time. She made me three costumes and it was really great. The most unfortunate thing was that Ben had left home and became very sick. He had a mastoid infection and Mother had to meet him in Portland. He was operated on that same day as the doctors said it had to be done immediately. He got over it, but I was the one child in the family that was graduating from high school and my mother missed the graduation. She missed the play and the opportunity of hearing me play the violin for the services held at the Lutheran church.

Through thick and thin I took my lessons and I practiced. Mother never had to urge me to practice. She never made me wash the dishes. She would wash and I would dry so I wouldn't get my hands soaked. Then when we got to Salem, my father had a better business, but he was still recovering from the bankruptcy in Tillamook.

But we always had plenty to eat and Mother always kept me in good clothes. She would buy remnants and make dresses for me so I always looked nice. At least I thought I did. I had a natural beauty because I had not only the red hair, but it was naturally curly and extra long. And my teeth were very good in front. I didn't have any split in my upper—of course, I should have had the lower teeth straightened. But when I smiled, my teeth were just like you see them today and I had two dimples and a slim figure. I just had a personality that everybody liked. I made friends easily.

Also, I was very honest and sincere. My brother Harry said, "Always tell the truth, kid. It's too damn hard to remember a lie."

I sort of followed that all of my life. If you can't tell the truth, don't say anything.

I had a large number of pupils in Silverton. By the time I graduated high school I would take a bus from Salem. It was only fifteen cents each way. The bus (we called it the stage) left about 8 a.m. and then I would come back at 5. I gave an hour lesson for a dollar and had a lot of good students who loved me. They learned to play well. I would show them by playing a piece and they would copy me. In fact, I was making more on that Saturday than they offered me for a full-time school position. I was offered $50 a month and they wanted me to work Saturdays and Sundays in the choir for nothing.

Meanwhile, I continued my lessons in Salem with Mr. Graham. He didn't teach any modern music or theory, so mother scraped together a dollar a week so that Mary Schultz could come to our house to teach me these things on the side. She was an excellent violinist and a very gifted girl. We didn't tell anybody that she was teaching me because Mr. Graham wouldn't have allowed it. Mary lived in Salem and was Mr. Graham's prize pupil. She had two church jobs which she passed on to me later when she went East to study. I didn't stay there very long because all the hymns were written in 5 or 6 flats and I didn't know how to play those keys in tune. I didn't know anything about scale formation, but I was the leader in the church orchestra and that is where I gave all my recitals.

Mary and I were good friends all the way through and she helped me greatly in my music. Mary played in the orchestra pit and every once in a while a road show would come through town. Mary was a good sight reader and she was the best violinist in town — man or woman — so she got the jobs.

There were a bunch of Christian ladies that thought she needed more teaching than Mr. Graham so they arranged for her to go to New York to study.

Before I went to Europe, Mr. Graham presented me in a recital, like a graduation recital. He was very influential in Salem. I didn't dare go to anyone else to get other ideas. But I felt I had gotten all I could from him.

Then there was a lady named Peachtree who was a very fine pianist. She taught me harmony and theory which I couldn't take openly.

When I went to Europe to study with Cesar Thompson, he asked me to play a four octave scale and I wouldn't have known how to do it if Mrs. Peachtree hadn't taught me. I played the four-octave G Major scale. I said, "I've never gone higher than three octaves." And he said, "Well, try it." So I played it.

Anyway, Mr. Graham lived in Portland and used to just come on Saturday and teach the violin in Salem. Because of me he got quite a few pupils. After I came back from Europe, I was in direct competition with him.

Diana: Do you have any idea what his training was, or what school of violin playing he taught?

Elizabeth: He was a quarter American Indian and very handsome. Like so many, he went to Germany to study. As far as I know, he never toured. He owned a big farm which he inherited from his father. He was supposed to be a graduate of a school in Berlin, though I never saw his diploma or anything.

We were always good friends. When I married Franz [nickname for Ferenz] he invited us to his house for dinner. It was my first introduction to wild rice. I don't remember if I was pregnant by that time, but I do know I didn't care for the dinner. And that was the end.

Diana: Did you ever see him again?

Elizabeth: I don't think I did. But when we left Portland, I sent my pupils to him to study.

Diana: He never knew about me being a violinist, did he?

Elizabeth: Oh, yes, I think he did. I had said, "The hard part is, just when you get students so they can play well, they leave you and go to college." He said, "Well the only thing is to have a child of your own and teach him or her."

Diana: Famous last words.

Elizabeth: That's it. I never thought about it. I knew he was just joking. He didn't have much success with his own children, though.

Diana: All these kids were taking lessons, why would they want to study the violin?

Elizabeth: Well, I don't really know. I never thought about it that way. People were attracted to me and they wanted to play like I did so their kids took lessons from me.

Diana: Did you have them play in an ensemble?

Elizabeth: My favorite was to have them play the Barcarolle from Tales of Hoffmann by Offenbach. That was quite easy. It was in the first position, and they sounded very well together.

Diana: You were the Salem version of Suzuki–you had all the kids playing something easy but they sounded great together.

Elizabeth: I was always pushing and thinking of new ideas. For instance, I don't know what gave me the idea to go to the Oregon State Fair. Mr. Lee, who ran the fair, liked my personality, I guess, and the fact that I had so much guts that I wanted to have my students play there. I thought that maybe he wouldn't consider doing it, but he said, "Well, sure. We'll book them as violins from all over the State." And that is the way we were booked: Elizabeth Levy's Violin Ensemble consisting of violinists from all over the state.

I had about 24 students. He said to dress them up a bit. So we bought red, white, and blue paper hats. It gave it a little color so that they were dressed alike. This brought me a lot of pupils and front-page publicity.

Mr. Lee wanted to draw a big crowd. If you have 24 young musicians, pa's and ma's, uncles and aunts and everybody who was related to them all came to the fair. So there was maybe an extra 100 people. He paid me $25 for two nights of the ensemble plus he had me be soloist with Tom Orsini's band.

I didn't have any printed arrangements so I played some popular pieces and the band accompanied me by ear. I got $100 for the two performances with the band and the two performances with my pupils. I had expenses, at least $5 or more for the students' paper caps.

We performed in the summers of 1918 and 1919.

Teaching at Willamette University

Elizabeth: In my freshman year in college, I was appointed head of the violin department at Willamette University. The university's president was so impressed with me, that I belonged to "the Hebrew religion," as he called it. People were very touchy about Jewish people–"Jewish" didn't sound as aristocratic as "Hebrew."

When I was a student there, one unit in Bible Studies was required for graduation. I didn't know anything about it and I didn't have time to read the Bible. I was practicing a couple hours a day and giving I don't know how many lessons a week. One of Ben's lawyer friends was a Methodist minister's son, so he wrote the essay for me. He said he would just love to write one of those papers. He typed it and I handed it in and signed my name. I didn't really understand it. It was such a good paper that the president called me to his office and asked me if there was anything in the chapel services that embarrassed me. They would not intentionally do anything, but was there anything I wanted to call to their attention? I said, "Oh, no. I enjoyed the chapel services." All of the students sat in the back and did their homework while the chapel service was going on.

Diana: Things haven't changed.

Elizabeth: Then the head of the music department at Willamette resigned. They appointed a new department head named Sites who was Jewish but wouldn't admit it. He started telling me what to do. He would come in and watch my classes and tell me how to teach. I came home and told Mother he was bossing me around. Mother said, "You've got to resign." Gee, I didn't want to because I had been so proud. Here I was: a professional, walking arm in arm as a colleague and professor of violin.

Diana: How old were you during your second year of college?

Elizabeth: I was about 19 or 20. Anyway, Mother said, "You resign tonight. You don't give one more lesson in that school. You quit before they fire you. You and that man will never get along." She was very smart that way. I wouldn't have even thought of it. I had to type my resignation. I wanted to be nice but Mother said the letter was too conciliatory. She said, "You mustn't admit that you have a problem." So I was up until about one o'clock that morning and Ben came down into the room. He said, "Oh, for god's sake, quit. You can't procrastinate like that. You've got to learn to make your own decisions and make them quick." Whatever it was I wrote, it was very short and to the point. I also had a bid from a little college in Albany. They put me in the violin department and I kept that position.

Lena Belle Tarter

Elizabeth: When Lena Belle Tarter came to Salem, she had just graduated from the American Conservatory in Chicago. Mother just adopted Lena Belle because she was such an honest, straight-forward person and we became very good friends.

I had recently been presented in recital by Mr. Graham with George Hoskis Street and his wife as my assisting artists on the program. Edgar Corsin, considered the smartest musician in Portland, was my accompanist.

I asked Mr. Corsin one time, "How can they know if a person is out of tune?" There were no recordings of my pieces. So I asked him how they do it. He said, "Well, most of the people don't know, but they know who does, like myself. They take my word for it and then present it as if they knew it."

I was trying to establish myself as a major teacher. Street told mother, "The music teachers are starting the Oregon State Music Teachers Association and we are trying to get new members. We'll bring your daughter in."

I was just about 20 when that happened. Anyway, at this point somebody came from Portland and started a chapter in Salem. Well, I was already a member, so I didn't get my name down as a charter member of the OMTA Salem District. But I was very active in it.

The funny thing was, Ms. Majors, the head of music at Salem High, was organizing the chapter. She had selected a lot of old piano teachers who were her friends. I came to the meeting and she said, "Well, you know we are not going to take inexperienced teachers like you, Miss Levy. I am very sorry. We don't feel that you should belong to this association." And I said, "Well, I'm sorry. I already belong to the Portland branch and I want to be transferred to here." She shut up then.

In the meantime, Lena Belle got a job singing at the Christian Science Church. She just barely made enough to live. She used to come over quite often for dinner at our house. Mother always said she needed a good meal. When Mrs. Majors resigned from Salem High School, Mother said, "Tarter, you have to take her place. Now you go and submit your resume. Since your father is a teacher in Corvallis, you graduated from the Chicago school and you had eight years of experience teaching regular school, you are the best qualified."

So Lena Belle tried, but still there were people that were for Ms. Majors who were holding out against Lena Belle. But there was a man named Simmons who was one of Harry's friends who was on the school board.

Mama said to Harry, "Harry, you go see that Simmons and you tell him he has got to vote for Tarter." And that was the winning vote. So Lena Belle became head of the music department at Salem High, which was quite the important post. So Mother felt she had done quite a bit to help Lena Belle.

Diana: They voted on a job like that?

Elizabeth: I don't know if it was five or three, but whatever it was, she just needed that one vote. If Simmons had voted for Majors, Lena Belle would have lost. Majors still wanted the job, but she wanted a raise. I don't know if they gave Tarter the raise, but she got $135 a month, which was a fortune in those days. So that was a big feather in Mother's cap.

European Studies and Return to Oregon

Elizabeth: In 1920 I went to Europe.

Mother wanted to make sure that I got a European education and I would be sitting on top of the world. Because Corsin, Street, and Graham, most of my teachers were European-taught, this indicated that they were good.

When I came back from Europe, I gave a program. A lot of people said they didn't think I played as well. They didn't like me as much because I was playing classical music. Thompson taught me the Vivaldi Concerto. Everything else was finger exercises, shifting, and scales.

But, nevertheless, I did play 100 percent better because I had been too careless for too long. Songs where I hit the highest popularity didn't sound bad, but I probably never would have passed on the critics' list. I went back and studied with Thompson another year at Ithaca College. Mother promised me that she would let me finish with him and I got my Mus.B. degree at Ithaca.

In the meantime, there was another upheaval. I had a lot of struggles, I'm telling you, with local politics. But my mother was sharp and she could beat any of them.

When I came back from Europe and said I had studied with Thompson, one of my competitors wrote to the Ithaca Conservatory and asked if I had ever registered. Just like he did in Europe, Thompson told me not to, so I probably wasn't on their books. So they wrote back and said that they had no record that Elizabeth Levy ever studied there with Thompson.

When I came back and was teaching in Independence, the woman showed that letter to the Irvins. Fay Irvin [later Mort] was one of my students but she had taken lessons from this other teacher while I was away and didn't like her at all. In the meantime, there was a man on the school board who was trying to get Lena Belle to marry him. She didn't particularly want to get married. I don't know why. Anyway, he was trying to gain favor with her and knew I was a friend.

Lena Belle talked to him and he asked her if it was true that I hadn't studied with Thompson. She said, "No, Elizabeth has all the papers." So I took my cancelled checks and all my papers to show him. Fay's father was on the board too, but he wouldn't have been as helpful. Lena Belle's friend said, "My God, I know that other teacher's father [they were both lawyers] and I'll tell him that she has got no case and that we will sue for libel if she comes before the school board with that letter. I've seen proof that Elizabeth has studied with Thompson." So that stopped it.

Teaching in the 1920s, Oregon Music Teachers Association (OMTA)

Elizabeth: When I became involved with the Oregon Music Teachers Association, I wasn't president right away, but I was chairwoman of a few committees and I got in touch with the President of the Association in Portland, which elected me Corresponding Secretary. I think we only had 100 teachers to start with. Portland and Salem were the two leading cities, but we got some of the teachers from Eugene. It was $3 a year. We did it to get more recognition for music teachers.

Diana: What year was this?

Elizabeth: When Thompson came over to Ithaca and I went back and took a whole year of classes with him in 1925.

Diana: Did you stay through the winter?

Elizabeth: Oh, yes. That was when I joined SAI,[1] the national music sorority.

---

1 Sigma Alpha Iota.

Thompson gave me what they call professional courtesy. Instead of paying $500 a semester, I paid $250.

Diana: You took other courses, too.

Elizabeth: Yes, I had technique courses. In the summer of 1922 I went to California and took lessons with Mrs. Alchin, the head of the UCLA music theory department. I got several university credits, which helped later when I got my degree.

Diana: What happened to your students while you were away that year? Did you lose them?

Elizabeth: No.

Diana: But you were there [Ithaca] the two semesters, right?

Elizabeth: The conservatory was able to give degrees through the University of New York.

Diana: What were some of the accomplishments you helped come about with the OMTA?

Elizabeth: By that time I had gotten up so high in the OMTA that I was on the State Board of Examiners as violin representative. Lena Belle was the voice representative as well as the head of the University of Oregon music department. We all sat down and made the rules for accrediting teachers. You see, OMTA worked out the requirements, so if a high school student took a 45-minute lesson and the student's teacher certified that he or she practiced at least 45 minutes a day for five days a week, the student could receive credit toward a minor in music for graduation.

The public schools went along with this and the students liked to do it. But when they got to college, the universities wouldn't accept the whole music credit. They had to have "the four r's" for basics like English, foreign language, math, etc. Students could only earn credits for two years, instead of the whole four years.

But it did help the music profession a lot. We had a lot of kids that never went to a university, so it helped them get through high school. By that time they were pretty good musicians. Some of them even became professionals.

Diana: So you got your degree. What did that do for you?

Elizabeth: It was a little bit like my French teacher at Willamette University said, "I've got four degrees and here you are making more money than I am." I was making about $40 a week which was almost as much as he was making on a yearly basis. He said, "What do you want a degree for? They aren't worth anything."

But it did help me with getting on the state board of the OMTA. They even kept me on two years after I went to Philadelphia. I continued to write the questions for certification tests.

I did a lot of pioneering to improve professional music standards in Salem and worked even after I got married as Corresponding Secretary of the OMTA. For social reasons, Mother wanted me to make a Portland connection and OMTA helped. She said I would never meet a Jewish man if I only taught in Silverton and Salem. She thought I might just accidently meet someone in Portland. And so I went and I did meet Ferenz through OMTA later on.

I started teaching at the Alameda School, which was right near where Ben lived. The PTA paid me $5.00 for an hour rehearsal. It was only about two and a half hours away from Salem, and I had my big car so I drove to Portland. I would stay overnight at Ben's and then come home. Then I got one or two private pupils, too. One PTA member told another and soon I had five schools there.

Then I took a studio in the same building with Ruth Bradley Kaiser (later Jones).[2] She used to practice 4 or 5 hours a day. I didn't. But I practiced some. I was making $5.00 an hour, which helped pay the rent, but I didn't meet any Jewish men to go with socially. I was just the same old teacher.

Around that time, in June of 1928, my mother died.

---

2   For more on our friendship with Ruth Bradley Jones, see Diana's biographical section, World War II years in New York.

ELIZABETH'S STORY
PART 3

Ferenz Steiner, Professor of Cello at Ellison White Conservatory
Portland, Oregon 1931

Courtesy Family Archives

ELIZABETH'S STORY IN HER OWN WORDS, PART 3

Elizabeth's Paternal Family: Meeting Elizabeth Winkler

Elizabeth: I said that I would relate how I met Elizabeth Winkler. She is my first cousin on my father's side, and the only paternal relative I know. She might have been the daughter of my Uncle Wolfe, on my father's side.

I went to New York to study at Ithaca College after my European trip. Mother said I could go back to school anywhere if I would leave Europe with her. I was very headstrong and wanted to stay in Europe by myself. And of course, I couldn't.

She said that I should make a connection with her brother Jacob's oldest daughter Gertrude van Straaten Janover who was married and living in New York. We had met her on our way to Europe. Mother even stopped and visited her brother Jacob in Athens, Georgia when we came back from Europe while I stayed in New York.

Before I arrived in New York, while on my way to Ithaca, Gertrude's mother and father were visiting her in New York. They were very anxious to hear me as they knew I was doing so much with my violin and was considered such a gifted concert violinist.

I took the train in September. There was no flying in those days. We were going through Salt Lake City on the Union Pacific and on to Chicago, but there was a wrecked freight train ahead of us, so they unloaded our passenger train. I was going Pullman (first class), with meals and a sleeping berth. They said we were going to be in Salt Lake City for six hours, until they cleared the track. So I went with a girl I met on the train to visit the Great Salt Lake. We took a sightseeing tour that guaranteed to get us back in time for the train.

I wired Gertrude in New York that I would be six hours late and would wire again when I got to Chicago. I didn't know what train I could get in Chicago because we had to change trains there. Gertrude's mother and father had been waiting for me and were terribly disappointed that they didn't get to see me. They were quite religious and had made all the arrangements to go back home to Georgia for their Jewish New Year celebration, so they left before I arrived.

Anyway, Gertrude had a little baby and a nurse maid who said, "You know, you keep talking about Elizabeth, Mrs. Janover. That is my name, Elizabeth. And I turn every time you say it." Gertrude asked, "Elizabeth, what was your maiden name?" And she said, "It was Elizabeth Levy." Gertrude said, "That's my cousin's name. Maybe we are related. I've got a picture of my Uncle Sol and my aunt. It was my father's first wife. Sure enough, Uncle Jacob immediately recognized the picture and said, "Yes, that is Sol Levy, Elizabeth's father." The nursemaid was delighted because she had had no relatives either from the Levy family. She said she had heard of her Uncle Sol a lot from her father.

Gertrude went to great lengths not to hurt Mrs. Winkler's feelings. The ad in the paper said she desired a very good woman to take care of her baby. Mrs. Elizabeth Levy Winkler answered that she wanted to get a home for her teenage son and she would work for small wages as a nursemaid if she could get a room for her boy.

So Gertrude broke this news to me very gently and with great pains. The van Straatens were all very aristocratic and high-minded in their ideas, so the thought of a relative working as a nanny didn't sit well. For instance, Gertrude had gone to finishing school and married a lawyer in New York. But I didn't care because I had found a first cousin on my father's side.

Marcia: So how old were you and Elizabeth Winkler then?

Elizabeth: It was 1923. I was 26 years old and she must have been in her late fifties.

I also met her stepdaughter-in-law, May Winkler, and May's husband, Oscar, who were terribly nice to me. They took me to the opera for which they had season tickets. We saw Meistersinger and Lohengrin during the Christmas vacation.

When Ferenz died, they just dropped everything and came over to see me in Queens. They were closer to me than my own first cousins.

During my student days, anytime I came to New York City, if I called Oscar, he would take me out to lunch on Fifth Avenue at a very swanky place. It gave me a feeling of not being alone in New York. Gertrude's husband was also nice to me when I called him and told him Ferenz had died. He was a lawyer and advised me that if I had anything in the safety deposit vault I should go take it. Also, we had a checking account with only about $160, but it took me months to get the money and clear the estate. Oscar Winkler was an accountant and he told me just what to do and what to say, and I didn't have to pay any inheritance tax because I didn't have anything.

Elizabeth: It was so unusual with billions of people that my two first cousins, truly blood relations, would meet one another in that strange way. Elizabeth Levy Winkler's husband had died and this stepson Oscar was very good to her. He was naturally a good man.

After Oscar got married, he wanted Elizabeth Winkler to live with his wife and him, but she and May did not get along and she had another, younger son. The only thing she could think of was to go and work as a nursemaid. She worked very hard and stayed with Gertrude for years. Eventually, the work became too heavy for her, so Oscar helped her get an apartment and contributed to her monthly income.

Meeting Alex van Straaten, 1926

Marcia: How did you meet Uncle Alex?

Elizabeth: It was the summer of 1926. My brother Harry belonged to several lodges like the Elks.[1] He would always contrive through them to get me a chance to play. This time I was to play in Philadelphia at the Sesquicentennial celebration. Mother said she didn't want me to go from Ithaca to Philadelphia and stay there alone.

She said she might have a half brother named Alex van Straaten who she bet was still living in Philadelphia. Harry couldn't get his address any other way, so he wrote to the Elks lodge and asked them if they would help him locate a lost relative, and they did.

Mother said, "You write a letter to your uncle." I was so busy getting off that I didn't write him until I got to Ithaca, where I had to do an eight-week summer course. But I did the eight weeks in six as I had earned most of my credits at Willamette University.

I wrote to Uncle Alex in Philadelphia. What I wrote, I really don't remember, but it was a very effective letter. Alex was just thrilled when he got it. He came home and told his wife (Leonore), "I've got a relative! I've got a niece and she's in New York and I just think her letter is terrific!" So he wrote me immediately and told me to get in touch with him as soon as I got to Philadelphia.

Well, I didn't want any favors. I was so independent. I went to the Bellevue Stratford Hotel. In those days, there was a floor for women who traveled alone, and men couldn't come on that floor. When my uncle wanted to come and see me, they wouldn't let him go to my room. He had to sit out on the sofa in the hallway where there was a receptionist. I came out and met him and we had lunch together on the roof garden.

He seemed to be at ease. Mother thought he would be quite a poor boy because he certainly didn't get anything from his father. I didn't know whether to offer to pay for the lunch. It was over $5.00. But I thought, I'd give him the $5.00 later, as a present or something.

He told me that he was delighted to meet me and would like to have me come to Atlantic City and visit his wife. They had a home in Oak Lane [an upscale suburb of Philadelphia], but it was closed because they had been living at the cottage in Atlantic City. He said he would have to go home and talk it over with his wife. He would call and let me know if I should come to Atlantic City the next day, which was the weekend.

---

1 Harry Levy was well-connected in Salem. In fact he was candidate for mayor between late 1922 and 1924.

So he called me and said yes, if I didn't mind sleeping in the same double bed with his wife's sister, who was a very nice young woman. I said, "Of course, I don't mind. I've been living in a dormitory where all the girls pile in with one another. That wouldn't bother me at all. I would be so happy to come because I promised my mother I wouldn't go to Atlantic City on my own."

I said I could stay at a hotel as long as he would know where I am. But he said, "Oh, no. Come and stay with us." I said, "OK" and away I went to Atlantic City.

Well, when I got to Atlantic City, I was so surprised. His wife was a very attractive woman and they met me at the train. A liveried chauffeur took my bags, and took me over to a Packard car, like a limousine. And here were my aunt and uncle having a chauffeur drive me. So I expected a little cottage like we would see at the Oregon beach, which in those days were pretty primitive. Here was a beautiful two story home, with a maid and a housekeeper.

Aunt Leonore and her sister Ruth just loved me and I got along great with them. So Uncle Alex said, "Well, what do you have to go back for? You better stay here and enjoy yourself." I said I wanted to play at the Sesquicentennial and I had these letters recommending me from the Elks Lodge.

He said, "Oh, those Elks Lodges will never get you in. But I know who could. I've never asked my partner for any favors, but I'm going to ask him if he knows Dr. Herbert Tylie, who has complete charge of the music at the Sesquicentennial. I'll call him and ask him if he will put in a good word for you as a favor to me. You don't need to go. It is hot as hell in Philadelphia, so stay here and enjoy yourself with my wife."

He went back to Philadelphia the next Monday as he always did, and what he did: I was awed. The Sesquicentennial program was already set, but they put me in anyway and it would be published in the paper because I wanted the publicity. I was to play on the following Sunday with Willem Solvane, one of the greatest organists in the country, as my accompanist.

The following Monday, they presented me on the radio. Uncle Alex asked, "About how long do you want to play?" And I said, "Oh, about 15 minutes is all I have ready." So, he said, "Alright, you are going to play on the radio (WCAU). I was just thrilled to death. It was just like magic. I didn't have to go see these people at their offices or anything. I still have that program. I played Meditation from Thaïs because it was a Sunday service and it was just perfect for it. On the broadcast I played Kreisler's Liebesfreud, Liebeslied and Thaïs's Meditation again.

I stayed with Bea Berenson, another sister of Aunt Leonore who had an apartment in Philadelphia in a very nice neighborhood. She went with me so I had company at the Sesquicentennial. I played in the Great Dome in Philadelphia for over 10,000 people.[2]

---

2 Elizabeth played for celebration of the Sesquicentennial of the United States, and I played the Bicentennial celebration.

That was great for my publicity when I came back to Salem. I had no trouble getting the news in the paper because Harry was a very good friend of the editor of the Oregon Journal in Portland. I also had no problem getting it in the Salem papers because my father was a big advertiser. Every Saturday he would take a half page. He had a store for 35 years and was on very good terms with all the newspaper men.

Uncle Alex and Aunt Leonore were so fond of me, they asked me to come back for Christmas vacation. So I did.

I said I couldn't afford to go to Philadelphia from Portland for another trip because I had spent all my money getting my degree. He wrote back to me and said he would pay my train fare, which cost over $300 round trip, because I wouldn't think of anything but going Pullman.

I had a great time when I got there. I didn't know what to bring them for a present because they were so wealthy. I didn't want to give them a check, so I had a florist make a big wreath of Oregon holly. It was so beautiful. I didn't realize it was against Uncle Alex's Jewish beliefs. He said, "Do you know what that holly wreath symbolizes?" I said, "No." And he said that it represented the crown of thorns put on Christ. "I wouldn't have one of those hanging on my door for anything. But I'll tell you who to give it to–give it to my partner who is a Christian and he'll love it." So, I gave it to him in recognition of the nice thing he did for getting me to play at the Sesquicentennial.

Uncle Alex's partner was so charmed that he entertained me for one of my 10 nights there. We went to the Academy of Music for a very high-class classical concert. He said that he was so glad to meet me because he didn't think too much of Uncle Alex's family from a cultural standpoint. In those days they judged you by your spoken English and the way you behaved yourself.

So he was delighted and we got along grand. And that was the end of that. I never heard from or saw him after that.

Uncle Alex had another friend named Ben Buchsbaum, who came to a party at which Uncle Alex had all of his family: his wife, her seven sisters and all their children and grandchildren. There must have been 50 people at the New Year's party.

Ben Buchsbaum had symphony tickets so he gave me a box seat to go hear the Philadelphia Orchestra. He also took me to his home, where he had a player piano that played Kreisler recordings. He wanted me to play the violin with it, but that didn't work out very well because it was not an accompaniment.

In later years Ben told me that all I did was talk music but he was very interested in getting a wife. His first wife had died and he had two boys and he thought I was it. Also, Uncle Alex was his best friend. Ben had just made $1.5 million, his share of having sold the Widener Building in Philadelphia for $15 million, so he was sitting on top of the world.

Mother said she didn't want me to marry a man that had been married before, especially with two children; I would never get along with them. Also, Ben said that I would have to keep a kosher house as long as his father was alive. Mother said, "Oh God, you just don't know how strict they are about those things. You would just go crazy. I don't want you to do that, and I don't want you living in Philadelphia. It would be too far away from me, anyway." So she made me come home right after the big New Year party. She said if Ben was so wealthy and so crazy about me, he would come to Oregon to get me. When I came back so that Diana could attend Curtis, Ben and Kathryn, the girl he did marry, were my closest friends. We still correspond.

Years later, Ben told me, "Why would I leave Philadelphia and go clear out to Oregon to get a girl when I had a city full of Jewish girls at my feet." He was the most eligible, rich bachelor available and all the mamas were after him. I never regretted not marrying him because I don't think I would have been very happy. It would have been difficult for me to adjust. If I had stayed maybe another week we might have been engaged and then he would never have backed down. But it would have upset my mother very much. It wasn't to be.

Kathryn was about five years younger than I. She went out and played tennis with his sons and they all got along so well. She was from the very wealthy Wolf family. The Wolfs later presented Ferenz and Diana in a big musicale at their home. It was to help me get pupils and to introduce Diana to the musical supporters in Philadelphia. This is where we met Mrs. Horace Stern, who became an important patron of Diana.

We became very good friends in our own right, and Ben said he would always be very nice to me. Alex had done him such a very big favor during the Depression — he loaned him $100,000 on the Croyden Apartments. He might have gotten it elsewhere, but this way he got it without any embarrassment.

When Ferenz passed away in New York, it was Ben and Abe Levin, Alex's son-in-law, who came to take care of the funeral arrangements and see that I was in good shape. Just the day before, Uncle Alex and Aunt Leonore had gone to Florida for the winter.

During the two years we were in Philadelphia (fall 1938–spring 1940), Ferenz and I made a foursome, playing pinochle with Kathryn and Ben. One time we had a fresh salmon sent from Oregon. It was very unusual to get a whole salmon. So we baked it.

This was during the Depression. Almost everybody was entertaining at home instead of going out and spending a lot of money. As I say, they were really our closest friends. Even when Diana became engaged to Ed, the Buchsbaums gave a dinner in their honor.

In those two years, Bill and Jean, their children, took violin lessons from me. I think they did it in order to help me along because they knew I had very limited means. That was when Ferenz was so ill with heart trouble.

We went out together on New Year's Eve. I remember quite a party. There were six of us and the fellows put on a show. They took dish towels and draped them around their waists and pretended they were Hawaiian dancers. It was a lot of fun.

This was the main element of our social life. We didn't have many other contacts.

The Depression, Elizabeth's Marriage, Solomon Levy's Death

Elizabeth: After my father died in 1932, things got worse and worse. Then Harry got married to Sylvia Larson, Bobby's mother. He never intended to have any children. They were married nine years before Bobby was born.

My father had his first stroke before my marriage, but he recovered. He wasn't paralyzed in any way. But because of that, he quit working at the market. Until then he used to walk every morning to the market at 7 o'clock in the morning and open it up. Harry wouldn't get down there until about 9 because he had been up all night carousing. Working from 7 til 7 was considered a short workday. My father was running the market and sometimes got there at 6 a.m. and worked until 9 p.m.. Then the boys, my brothers, decided they would quit at 7. Then later they didn't open until 8 after my father died. But he liked to walk from our house and that is really what kept him going so long. He went to work every day and would sleep in the afternoon. He would go up in the office and sit in the chair and sleep for two or three hours. Then he would be up at night.

But he never wanted to go out at night. That is why mother always didn't want me to marry an older man. She said that if it weren't for me, she would be stuck home with her husband. He wanted her to always chaperone me. So she always went with me and got to go everywhere, like to Europe, New York and Georgia.

Marcia: How old was your father when he died?

Elizabeth: He was 87.

Marcia: And what about your mother?

Elizabeth: My mother died in June and I think she was 70 or 71 in January. She was born in 1857.

Marcia: So what about when you moved to Philadelphia? First you lived in Oregon. Did you marry Ferenz there?

Elizabeth: I was married in the studio of Rabbi Henry Berkowitz at Temple Beth Israel, a reformed synagogue in Portland, Oregon on June 3rd, 1931. The only attendees were Harry and Ben, Ben's wife Kate and Lena Belle Tarter, who was my bridesmaid. I was married quite early in the morning, about 10 a.m. We had an early lunch at a very nice place on the outskirts of Portland. Ben hosted and paid for the whole party. I have just two snapshots of the whole affair. Mother had insisted that the family join a synagogue in Portland because if you didn't belong to a synagogue you couldn't get buried in the Jewish cemetery. They were what are called "non-resident members." They paid $60 a year to Temple Beth Israel[3] just to belong so that when either one of them died they would have burial rights. She thought they were getting older and might pass away at any time. And I think she had more heart complaints than she admitted.

My husband Ferenz was a very elegant, striking man, tall and handsome. My friend Tilly's[4] granddaughter once said, "My God, you took a year to decide whether you were going to marry a man like that?!" He was a wonderful dancer. When we went to different dances, if it was crowded and we couldn't swing around, he would always swing me on the corners. He was a good leader and a great lady's man. I was his third wife but I didn't know it. I thought I was his second wife. My mother told me about how my father always bragged so much about his first wife, that she was very jealous of her and she didn't want me to marry someone that had been married before.

After getting married, we immediately left for our honeymoon. I had a big Buick car which I think was an 8 cylinder. It used to eat gas like I don't know what. We took my father as he couldn't be left alone. We drove through Yellowstone, mostly on Route 30. We went to the very northern part of Yellowstone because the altitude was lower than if we had taken 30 straight through. We went through Cody, Wyoming, and from there to a place called Thermopolis. There we began to have some trouble with our car, so we stopped and had it fixed overnight. Then we were very worried. The next best stop was Casper, Wyoming, right near Devil's Half Acre. It was over 100 miles from Thermopolis to Casper. That was a long way to go in our car without a gas refill. There was supposed to be a service station about half way between. But we had left on June 3rd and that was before Yellowstone season was officially open. But we got through there because it was an especially mild winter. Instead of the June 15 opening, we were permitted to go through on June 5 or 6.

On the way to Casper, we were just a block from the Buick place where we were going to have them go over our car again. And then we heard a rattle and the fan dropped out of the car. The fan belt had broken. Fortunately, the Buick agency fixed the car while we stayed overnight in Casper.

Then I wanted to see the Black Hills of South Dakota. I was so disappointed when I got there because I thought they were going to be black stone. The black part was that they had a whole lot of dark green trees. They did look black after

---

3 Elizabeth's ashes are buried in the grave with her mother, Dientje, at Temple Beth Israel Cemetery in Portland.
4 Tilly Mosher was Elizabeth's best friend in Los Angeles.

the prairie that we had gone through. Anyway, that is how they got their name. Of course, now these hills have the faces of the presidents.

We had looked forward to Casper. We stayed in various hotels on the way there and this was one that said they had running water. But they didn't; they hadn't connected it yet because everything was shut off for the winter because it would freeze. They couldn't keep these places warm at night and nobody ever traveled when the weather was severe.

Marcia: Did you have bad weather when you were going through?

Elizabeth: No, it was beautiful. We had a very pleasant trip. Then we went through Iowa and finally landed in Chicago. Again, I was so worried about my father's health that we didn't want to go through the higher mountains, so we went from Cleveland up to Lake Erie.

When we got to Cleveland, the weather was so hot, and we didn't have such a thing as air conditioning in our car, Papa just sort of fainted. I was terribly worried and called the doctor. The doctor only charged $5 to come to the hotel to see him. He said my father was alright, that he could travel, just give him a rest over night, and not make too long a trip. So we went from Cleveland to Erie and from Erie to New York City.

Elizabeth Winkler had arranged for us to stay. She wanted to do something for her uncle Sol. She had written me that a wealthy friend of hers was out of town and had a lovely apartment. They lent her their apartment for us to stay so we wouldn't have to pay hotel expenses. So we stayed there for a couple of nights. We went out and bought the food and I think she spent some of her money, too. She thought she was going to inherit a lot from this wealthy uncle. But she didn't, later to her disappointment.

I didn't feel a bit poor and we stayed at the Taft Hotel right on Broadway because my husband wanted to meet Victor Young,[5] who was an old pal of his. They used to have a trio that played in a big Pasadena hotel.

Then we went on to Philadelphia and rented an apartment near my uncle Alex's home. It was a furnished apartment and quite expensive. But Ferenz thought that he could get work in the east. He didn't really realize how terrible the economic situation was. He thought that surely if he saw some of his old friends, it would work, but at the time you just couldn't get a job for love or money. So we decided we would come back to Oregon and teach.

---

5   A well-known Hollywood conductor and arranger.

ELIZABETH'S STORY
PART 4

Elizabeth and baby Diana, 1933

ELIZABETH'S STORY IN HER OWN WORDS, PART 4

Back to Oregon: Teaching and the Birth of Diana

Elizabeth: After I got married in 1931, it was really the Depression. I had a few pupils left in Salem, including Hortense Taylor and June Director. For a while I went every week and taught them. But I got pregnant in November so they thought it was unsafe for me to drive two and a half hours, and the roads were narrow and frequently slippery.

Ferenz took over in January but he was such a disciplinarian that June Director didn't like him, so she decided to study with another teacher. Ferenz would always go and see my father who still lived in Salem. I went to see him too until it wasn't good for me physically. It was a long bumpy road and they didn't know how it would affect me. I was worried too, as I didn't want to affect the child.

Most everybody liked Ferenz, but if they didn't play in tune or time he was not tactful. Therefore, he couldn't teach beginners. But I could get along with everybody. I never lost my temper. I would explain why they were wrong and never make them feel like two cents.

In fact, I never played with him. Fay [Mort[1]] told me about hearing me play in a trio with him, which was the only time we played together. It was a week before we were going to get married. I felt perfectly capable, but he used to assert himself so much that I just couldn't play with him. So he just played solos.

He had very little money saved. He only made $75 a week as principal cellist in the Portland Symphony and that was considered a big fee in those days. He also taught a cello class at the University of Oregon and was part of the University's string quartet, which gave concerts. I don't know if they even got paid for those concerts. It was part of the job to get pupils. He also belonged to the faculty of Ellison White Conservatory in Portland. But he charged $7.50 a lesson and nobody could pay that, so the pupils quit.

I used to get $5 an hour, $2.50 a half hour, which was more affordable. And then I had as many as five public schools which paid $5 each, so I would make $25 a week that way.

Then Ferenz had his mother come up from California to be with me for a while during the pregnancy. I was shocked that she spoke such poor English. But my brother Ben thought she was the sweetest old lady. He was so nice to her and

---

1 See "Notes and Quotes from Elizabeth's Students and Friends" chapter.

had us over there twice for dinner.

I had the baby [Diana] in Portland and got over 32 bouquets. I didn't have a wedding, so nobody gave me any presents. I didn't send out announcements either. I didn't know what to do to get presents. It never even occurred to me. My mother wasn't alive and my brothers couldn't advise me about those things. So everybody brought me presents for the baby.

Hortense Taylor [Foster], my pupil in Salem who still remembers me, came over and looked at Diana and said, "Oh, she was born with a silver spoon in her mouth. Some babies are just lucky." I have never seen a baby in all my life who had so many things. My uncles from Europe even sent her a gift. One sent her a lottery bond. Uncle Alex sent her not one, but half a dozen little handmade dresses from Japan, where he bought silk thread for his hosiery company. Diana got a dozen different sweaters and booties and several photo albums. We were just loaded with things. I had such good friends.

But anyway, with the Depression we didn't know what was going to happen. I didn't have any pupils to speak of, though I still had the four schools in Portland.

Diana: Was Daddy still playing in the Portland Symphony when I was born?

Elizabeth: Oh, no. He lost his job after the first year. He wanted me to announce my engagement then maybe Willem van Hoogstraaten would have been afraid to fire him. My sorority sister called me up and told me before it hit the public news that she knew from secret sources that van Hoogstraaten was going to fire my fiancé. She knew I was going to announce my engagement and I should think it over. She thought that since I didn't have a mother, she should warn me as a sister. I don't know whether she accidently did it on purpose. I decided I wouldn't announce my engagement on February 14. He also lost his job at the University of Oregon. Those jobs were all run by the symphony. If you had one, you had the other. Ferenz right away said that van Hoogstraaten was a Nazi. To fool people, van Hoogstraaten hired another Jewish man. But that was the end of it. Van Hoogstraaten was such a two-faced person, he had all the Jews backing him in the stadium concerts in New York where he was a guest conductor. But he went back to Germany to conduct for Hitler. There were anti-Semitic people in Portland that were backing him. But no one would believe Ferenz so we were battling against the whole world.

Of course, it didn't affect my teaching and my following. Then around December, a man came to me from the First National Institute and asked, "Do you do class work?" He said he had asked everybody in the state who was the best violin teacher and everybody said, "Elizabeth Levy, she's the top." He told us that he would guarantee us 50% of what we made, but we would have to start easy until it built up. The classes had been hit hard too. It was a dollar a lesson and we could take 10 pupils to a class. So that was $10 and I was getting $5 an hour. So that was pretty good. But it took some time to get built up. We lived on 42nd Street in lower Laurelhurst and were paying rent. I had the money that mother and I had saved, around $4,000 or $5,000. Because I had spent my money going to Europe and getting my degree, I never thought much about it. I knew I was secure.

But of course I wasn't, because everything we would get into would fall apart. The crash was in 1929, but I was unaware of it because my pupils didn't start to quit in Salem. They didn't depend on the stock market. They were ministers' and businessmen's daughters. But someone would lose a position here and there.

I know that the prices had dropped when we bought the house at 39th and Haslow. We bought it for $4,500. I think the guy who sold it to us took the first mortgage on it. The top floor was just ideal for a big class like First National's. We had all the pupils go upstairs and used the upright piano that my mother bought me when I was 16 years old. Ferenz was a perfectionist. He just dolled up that house as much as he could. And he kept spending more money than we were making.

But we finally made $50 a week off the classes. We got up to a hundred pupils and I taught them all. And we saved money. I taught until you were almost six years old, so it grew and stayed solid. First National's first-term students got a free violin, which wasn't very good, but students who stayed for a second term could buy a beautiful violin, bow, and case for $2.00 a week. So they got a beautiful violin for a very reasonable rate.

Diana: You had some students in addition to the First National, didn't you?

Elizabeth: Some of the best ones we would take out of the class and tell them, you know, "He's so good." I think I taught those students for $3.00 a lesson, two half-hours per week.

Diana: Did you still have your school orchestras?

Elizabeth: Oh, yes. I still had public school orchestras because that came early in the day before the kids could come to our house.

Teaching Philosophy

Diana: On the occasion of your 90th birthday I thought it would be interesting to discuss your teaching philosophy, in terms of preparation for beginning private lessons on any instrument, but particularly, of course, the violin.

I know that you have always believed that the very earliest influence on children was extremely important as to how they are going to react to music in general and also to the possibility of their beginning formal instruction. I wonder if you would first talk to me about what your feelings are as far as early influence is concerned.

Elizabeth: Well, I think it is very important because a child, even at three or four years old, can be helped at home before they take formal lessons. You shouldn't just take a child at six or seven and say they should start lessons because a half hour per day or week is not enough music for them. They also must have supervised work at home.

Diana: What specifically would you suggest that a mother or a father do for the young ones?

Elizabeth: Well, I would say that they should sing with them and, if possible, have the child go to the piano and get accustomed to C so that they know it is "do." Then they can sing up to Do-Re-Do, Do-Re-Mi-Re-Do.

Diana: Basically, you are talking about an early form of ear training. Suppose there is no piano in the house? What do you do then?

Elizabeth: Well, get records like Brahms's Lullaby or any good music that would appeal to the child.

Diana: OK, let's take it one step further. You now have this three or four year old child who has been singing and listening to records, let's say for about a year. The child is now about five and the parent has to make some sort of decision: do they continue with this pre-school kind of training or begin to think of taking the child to a professional teacher. What do you think some of the criteria should be?

Elizabeth: One is the child's motor coordination.

Diana: Don't you think that a child's ability to concentrate and take direction is extremely important? I would sum it up that they would need a combination of motor coordination, concentration ability, and a certain amount of maturity in their approach to taking direction. Otherwise, you can't really teach them.

Elizabeth: I can agree with this.

Diana: Let's say a parent tells you, "I want my child (aged 5 to 8) to take violin lessons," and the child seems to be looking forward to it. What are some of the things that you look for when you first interview that child? Do you have some ear tests, or intelligence tests?

Elizabeth: First, right away, I play middle C. Then I'll go quite a distance, and ask them which sound is higher and which is lower. Then I make the intervals smaller and smaller to see how keen their ear is, how they follow it and how attentively they respond to questions.

Diana: Do you find that this is a pretty accurate kind of test for hearing?

Elizabeth: Yes, I think it is about as good as you can get without any previous training.

Diana: You use what is called the "C Major Approach." There is a lot of talk today about not using C Major as an approach to violin playing. If you have some strong reasons, why do you think C is good to start with?

Elizabeth: That is just for ear training. But for actually playing on the violin you should really start in G Major. That is the easiest. Starting with the G string you don't have to use the fourth finger for some time.

Diana: So when you first start a child on scales, you don't make them use their fourth finger.

Elizabeth: No...

Diana: OK, now we have taken this child one step further. Is there any test in that early interview that you can use to tell whether the child has a since of rhythm or do you have to wait until you start working with them?

Elizabeth: I often have them just sit and go one, two, one, two.

Diana: You do this as part of the interview? Do you have them beat time on their legs to see if they can imitate a pattern?

Elizabeth: I usually do that during a lesson. In an interview you scare them to death if you go too far.

Diana: What about motor coordination? After a few weeks with a child working with a violin and bow in their hands, approximately how long do you keep them on open strings?

Elizabeth: About a month, though it depends.

Diana: Do you try to start a child using fingers right away?

Elizabeth: No. You don't do that because it is all they can do to hold the violin up.

Diana: You mention an interesting point. Some of these children have difficulty just getting the strength to hold the violin. Are there any special exercises or training suggestions for a parent to develop strength?

Elizabeth: Don't use the bow immediately. Get them to hold the violin up with their elbow under. Then clamp all the fingers down, regardless of where they go, just for exercise

Diana: How long do you recommend that a five-year-old child try to hold the violin up before they rest?

Elizabeth: Oh, a minute.

Diana: So it really is a very difficult position.

Elizabeth: Yes, very.

Diana: Probably one of the hardest things to do is to learn to hold the bow.

Elizabeth: I put it on a table and have them try to pick it up with their thumb and middle finger.

Diana: Now, we've gone about four weeks. The child is beginning to use first finger and can reasonably use the bow. What do we do then?

Elizabeth: I find that most books say "Take a whole bow." I find that if they just bow the lower half it is easier to hold the bow correctly.

Diana: This is probably a difficult question, but when do you think you can begin to detect a very talented student from the average student?

Elizabeth: Very difficult to say, because it depends so completely on whether the parent makes them practice or not.

Diana: What do you think are good minimum and maximum practice times for the average child?

Elizabeth: At five through seven years of age, 15 minutes twice a day.

Diana: What about school orchestras? How advanced do you think a student should be before they are put into that kind of a group?

Elizabeth: I think the average child needs the discipline of the orchestra.

Diana: We have been talking mostly about the average child. What if you find one who is very gifted? Is there something different you would do with that kind of a student to develop his or her skills? Obviously a child who is very talented is going to progress faster. But, what would you do differently, for instance, if you found you have another Diana or Elizabeth?

Elizabeth: I would immediately ask the parent to have the child take lessons twice a week so they could cover more ground.

Diana: Basically what you are saying is that supervision is extremely important no matter whether the student is average or exceptional.

NOTES AND QUOTES FROM ELIZABETH'S STUDENTS, COLLEAGUES AND FRIENDS

NOTES AND QUOTES FROM ELIZABETH'S STUDENTS, COLLEAGUES AND FRIENDS

Letter from Lena Belle Tarter, a Friend of Elizabeth

A letter dated Friday, September 7, 1942 regarding Diana's playing on the "Message of Israel" radio program from NYC. The program was broadcast nationwide from Central Synagogue, led by Rabbi Jonah B. Wise. Lena Belle sent the letter to the station as well. She was a bright lady and knew I needed fan mail.

"It was your heart I heard last Sunday on the air, dear Elizabeth, the first beautiful low tone so thrilled me I sat with tears swelling. Through the experience I received such joy and inspiration that I thank you and Diana and all who have made so much beauty possible. I am so grateful and feel such ambition for the future that you have molded so beautifully thus far. The culminating years of preparation will soon pass and a great goal will have been reached. Life then will not necessarily be easier, but more recompensed. I lived with Ferenz in spirit last Sunday. How proud he is for we know life does not cease with the release from our physical bodies. How happy your friendship has always made me. Thanks over, and over, and over."

Lena Belle Tarter was an unbelievable lady who lived until she was 99 years old. Never married, she was a Christian Scientist, but she always said she was a practical one. Her brother was a doctor, and if she got very sick she would let him treat her or be treated by another physician. As a general attitude, though, she believed in mind over matter.

In another letter, she wrote:
"This is a short letter to give you (Elizabeth) a welcome home again. But it was wonderful beyond words to see you and Diana, and hear Diana play so wonderfully, etc., and have you here with me. My home is always your home, too, and you may come any time and stay as long as you wish. Now that you have been here you will realize that I make it home for you. Not as a guest. I mean this to both the girls, too. Diligence must be the watchword for them."

Interviews

Note: There may be some discrepancies in the dates cited by various interviewees as all of them were in their 80s or 90s at interview time.

Interview with Nathan Steinbock, a Former Student

August 10, 1997

I was born July 8, 1914. At the age of five, I started taking violin lessons from Elizabeth Levy. When I was ten years old, I decided that I wanted to change violin teachers. I took lessons for about four months when I realized I was getting nowhere and my violin playing was getting worse. I asked Miss Levy if she would take me back. She said she would if I promised to practice and follow her instructions. In fact, she insisted that I come to her home after school to practice.

Elizabeth Levy took a personal interest in me while I was her student. She was very helpful, not only with me, but with all of her students. She was kind yet strict, thorough and encouraging with her students. All of her students liked her. My parents loved her.

One thing I will never forget about Elizabeth Levy is what she taught me about always being prompt. She made it a rule to be prompt and drummed it into me. She taught me well, and I will always cherish this part of my memory of her. Being prompt became part of my life.

Interview with Hortense Taylor Foster, a Former Student

Elizabeth Levy was young with beautiful long red hair, which fascinated me. She was a demanding teacher, yet kind and understanding of her students and their practice time. She was not always patient if half steps were not marked and the fingernails were too long. She kept fingernail scissors for the occasion. Her lessons were 30 or 40 minutes, something my dad reluctantly paid if I did not practice.

My ardor for Elizabeth was one of admiration and worship, for my life seemed to revolve around her and the activities she presented to her students, especially in the Saturday ensembles. Also, three of us seemed to become more involved with extra experiences which she insisted were a vital part of our musical knowledge—that of hearing famous violinists in concert in Portland.

My lessons were concentrated on Leopold Auer books—each book a new experience—especially in vibrato and shifting. It was so easy for Elizabeth as she often played her violin with me to demonstrate bowing straight (looking in a mirror), using full bow, quarter bow, upper half and lower half with a wrist movement almost shaped like an egg. She emphasized the style of bowing to be the German hold for a much stronger tone.

My parents moved to Portland in 1930-31 and so it was then that I could continue my lessons with Elizabeth.

Elizabeth was pregnant with her first child and Ferenz decided to take over her students, and between the two I continued lessons. The first baby (Diana) was a challenge for two people who had never had any experience around babies. I had nieces and nephews so I was a bit more knowledgeable and could offer assistance. One day I was there for the baby's bath and discovered they had put a hot water bottle on the baby's feet to keep her warm and the water was too hot. Luckily her feet were not blistered.

Ferenz was a bit foreign to me in his treatment of students, unlike the kindness of Elizabeth. He was obviously a fine musician in many ways, a cellist of superb rank and a good director. His piano ensemble for the Monday Musical Club performed in excellent style and with uniqueness.

I treasure my time with Elizabeth in many ways. She started me on the instrument, encouraged me to become a music teacher, even if I was not concert artist caliber and provided me with experiences I'll never forget.

A marriage, a musical family of four children, and a happy life are all probably due somewhat to her encouragement.

Interview with Fay Mort, a Former Student

Diana: How old were you when you began lessons with Mother?

Fay: 10.

Diana: Were you a beginner at the time or had you had lessons?

Fay: I'd had some public school lessons.

Diana: Did she have a pianist at any of your lessons?

Fay: She had a piano in her home studio and Margaret Hogg[1] would often be there.

Diana: What kind of teaching personality did she have? Did she coax her students? Was she very complimentary?

Fay: She coaxed them.

---

1   Hogg was Elizabeth's studio accompanist in Salem for a number of years.

Diana: You mentioned you went to the concert with Mother to hear Fritz Kreisler.

Fay: It was through Elizabeth that I heard a number of artists. Our bank had failed so without her I would never have gone.

Diana: Did Mother demonstrate for you at the lesson?

Fay: Yes.

Diana: She had her students play in ensembles. What were those experiences like?

Fay: We rehearsed and she gave us a good deal of help in knowing how to get onto the stage. We had to carry our music stands along with our violins.

Diana: Did you feel like you were advancing constantly or did you get discouraged at times?

Fay: At one time I felt like I shouldn't be doing violin, when I was at Willamette University. That was when she helped to keep me going and have a place to practice because that was a problem at Willamette.

Diana: Why did she want you to continue when you were there, even though you weren't going to pursue it as a profession?

Fay: She just didn't want me to give up. I went with the Willamette Girls Glee Club on their spring tour as their soloist and stayed in the home of the school principal in one little town. And that was how I got my first teaching job.

Diana: I think her general philosophy was that you never gave up because you never knew when you could use it. Did you teach or ever use your violin?

Fay: Yes. I had a class at Sisters, Oregon and taught in Independence.

Diana: So it was supplemental income and also probably a nice change of pace for you. So Mother was right. How did you remain friends?

Fay: We corresponded occasionally. I knew where Elizabeth and Ferenz lived in Portland, and I came to see them when you were born.

Diana: I wanted to talk a little bit about your time in Philadelphia. What were your memories of Elizabeth at that time?

Fay: I saw your picture in the paper when you were going to play with the Philadelphia Orchestra at the Children's Concerts.

Diana: I was already 13 years old. Did you know Mother was in Philadelphia?

Fay: No, I had lost track. But I saw that picture and I told Loren, "I'm going to go, because I know that I will see Elizabeth." I got myself an aisle seat. I kept my eyes open and pretty soon your mother came right up the aisle, so I spoke to her.

After we made that contact, I saw your mother frequently and came to your house.[2]

Diana: What was your impression of my mother then? By that time she was a widow and was teaching a lot.

Fay: I knew she was working hard and considered the cost of everything. I have heard you in these last few years say, "Oh Mother, it doesn't matter how much it costs." She came to me one day at Gimbels, where I was working, because I got a 10% discount. She came to the store downtown and asked me to buy her a girdle with my discount.

Interview with Margaret Hogg, Studio Accompanist for Elizabeth

Recorded in Salem, Oregon when she was 90 years old.

— On Meeting Elizabeth

Margaret: Elizabeth was young, vivacious, and very beautiful.

Diana: How did you meet my mother?

Margaret: My very first teacher, Mr. Harr, knew her. He wanted me to have the experience of accompanying. So he made the arrangements.

Diana: When would this have been, approximately?

Margaret: About 1923 or 1924.

Diana: How much time did you actually spend at that?

---

2 See more about Fay Mort in Philadelphia in "1943-1949" Chapter.

Margaret: She had me play with practically all her students except maybe a few of the very advanced. I wasn't too advanced myself at that time. Elizabeth took me to Ruth Bradley and that is where serious music began.

Diana: What was she like—her personality—when she worked with students? In her older years I found that she was very much loved by her students and that she did amazing things with rather untalented people. She had infinite patience. But when she was such a young person, I wonder?

Margaret: I think she was very enthusiastic. She was very personal. It was not a commercial thing. You were her friend. She entered into your life. I know she did that when she was teaching in Independence and she had quite a few advanced students. Everybody thought a great deal of her.

Diana: Did she mostly work on pieces or would she spend half a lesson on technique?

Margaret: Oh no. You had etudes and some scales. And then you had pieces. She used the Auer[3] technique.

— On Elizabeth's Professionalism

Diana: One focus of this book that I am trying to bring out is that what Mother did was career pioneering from the point of view of a woman. To become successful when women were still supposed to be stay at home. From your own experience, how discriminated against were women as far as being professionals? Were music teachers just considered the little ol' lady down the street? Or were they respected as teachers?

Margaret: That was one of the goals of the first Music Teachers Assocation in Salem, to bring recognition and respect to the profession. You were looked down upon if you were a music teacher.

Diana: Why? In comparison to a school teacher? Or just in general?

Margaret: Yes, in general. Music was not held in high regard.

— On Ferenz

---

3   Leopold Auer, the famous violin teacher in St. Petersburg, Russia, who taught Heifetz, Zimbalist, et al.

Margaret: I think Elizabeth was the Program Chair[4] because Joseph Borisoff came from California as soloist at the convention. Elizabeth engaged him. And that was the day she met your father. Because the woman who was the manager[5] introduced them.

Diana: Did you actually see my father give any lessons?

Margaret: He was very strict with the kids. In fact, he put the fear of God in them. He taught me something in accompanying.

— On Dientje

Diana: Did you know her [Elizabeth's] mother?

Margaret: She was a very lovely woman, a refined, aristocratic type. Her father wasn't so much that way, but she was Dutch. She had had a good education. She was, socially, very lovely. Very gracious.

Diana: Did she speak with a foreign accent?

Margaret: A little. Not too much. It is too bad you didn't know your grandmother. She was very lovely.

Diana: I feel like I do because Mother told me about her so much. And her father was what? Rough and ready, kind of like his sons?

Margaret: No, he was a business man. He didn't want your mother to marry Franz[6] because he said she would be all her life in music. And he, personally, didn't think too much of music.

Diana: He must have made the boys [Elizabeth's brothers] feel that way. Especially Ben, he didn't care for it. Harry liked music and evidently had musical talent. You must remember them. What were they like?

Margaret: Harry stayed with his family and took care of his father and ran the meat market.

Diana: He was very well liked, wasn't he? He stayed in Salem all his life.

Margaret: Yes.

---

4 Actually, Elizabeth was President of the OMTA.
5 Delta Spencer, manager Portland Symphony.
6 Nickname for Ferenz Steiner.

Interview with June Director Nagel, a Former Student

Recorded on June 1, 1992, in Portland, Oregon.

— On the Levy Family

Diana: June, I want to ask you to speak of your memories of my mother. What were your impressions of my parents and my grandparents?

June: My first memory was in the living room of our house. I was 7 years old. Your grandmother Dientje came with your mother, Elizabeth, because she was looking for students for her daughter. I had never given any thought to music at all. Your grandmother was beautiful, grey-haired, dressed lovely with jewelry. Your mother was so gorgeous. Redheaded. Her hair, she wore it with two curls that came around to the side of her head. I walked over and stuck my finger through one of them. I can remember doing that. And my mother stopped me. My mother gave me no choice. All she said to me was, "would you like to take violin or piano?" And I haven't the faintest idea why I said violin. Then I started. Your mother and I just took to each other. I became like her little sister almost. Then all of the sudden I sort of became her protégé. I guess I advanced quite fast, because when I was 10 she gave me a recital all of my own.

Diana: Approximately what year is this?

June: 1927 and 1928.

Diana: What abour her brother?

June: Harry (Levy) I really knew. He had a great sense of humor. And your grandfather Solomon was adorable. I remember him.

Diana: Do you ever remember going into the Midget Market?

June: All the time. My father's store was around the corner. That is where we bought our meat.

— On Being Jewish in Salem

Diana: If you were in Salem, that means there must have been a fairly good-sized Jewish community.

June: Not at all.

Diana: What was it like to be a Jewish girl growing up?

June: I was the only Jewish girl in the high school.

Diana: Was there a synagogue of any kind?

June: No. We went to Portland for everything with my grandparents. And you didn't drive in 45 minutes. You came through Oregon City and it took you an hour and a half. I didn't have any Jewish friends in Salem. The only time I had Jewish friends was when I came to Portland.

Diana: Did you feel Jewish?

June: Very. My parents were never religious. My grandparents were. I knew I was going to marry Jewish.

Diana: And there were no Jewish boys. . .

June: No.

Diana: Were you aware that my mother was Jewish?

June: Oh, absolutely. So did everybody else. The name Levy...

Diana: Did you ever have any sense of anti-Semitism?

June: Never. Never did.

—On Elizabeth the Teacher

Diana: You must have had a real talent on the violin.

June: I played a tremendous amount. The first time I did it, your mother had to shove me out on the stage. And then when I stopped playing, they had to pull me off. I loved being out there on stage.

Diana: Can you describe a little bit what lessons were like with her.

June: Oh, yes. My God, I'll never forget. I had to mark half steps like on every piece.

Diana: Yes, she was big on marking half steps.

June: I remember sitting with her, after we had heard Zimbalist play. Outside the window was a tree and it had just rained and the sun came out. All the drops were full of color and clear. And your mother said to me, "That's the way Zimbalist plays. Crystal clear, with lots of color."

Diana: Little did she know that a few years later she would be sitting in the studio with him.

June: Right. She used to take us all in to Portland. That is how I heard Menuhin at 10 years old. I fell in love with him in his little knickers. I worshiped your mother to the point where it broke me up when I left her.

Diana: Was she strict as a teacher? Did she ever get upset with students, or was she very patient?

June: She was patient. But she was a little bit demanding.

Diana: She obviously was inspiring to you.

June: Oh yes.

— On Being a Professional

Diana: You said something before that my grandmother had brought her over to meet you . . .

June: Because your grandmother was looking for students for your mother and we were new to Salem.

Diana: Do you think a young woman didn't go out and solicit business?

June: I just don't think it was the thing to do. She [Dientje] came to meet my mother and said my daughter teaches violin and piano and maybe you would like your little daughter to start.

— On Ferenz as a Teacher

Diana: Did you ever hear my father play the cello?

June: I heard him with the symphony. When he gave me a lesson he sat and played.

Diana: What did he sound like?

June: I thought a fine musician who scared the hell out of me.

Diana: He was strict.

June: Not even strict. He was just such a Hungarian.

June: After I didn't take anymore it was like we were separated. So that when you called me to say please come to my mother's [75th] birthday, it was like a big reunion to me. Back to my childhood.

— On June's Sister

Diana: What kind of business were the Schnitzers[7] in?

June: They started out with scrap and they are probably one of the wealthiest families in the world today. Arlene and Harold are okay too. Harold didn't stay with the family in the scrap iron business. But now they are into shipping, and you name it. They were in Forbes until they didn't want to give any more information.

Interview with Anne Berenson, a Friend
Conducted when Anne was in her late eighties.

Anne: My husband Milton Berenson met your mother and father when they lived in an apartment house right next door to us in Portland, OR. I didn't have any children yet, and your mother was pregnant at the time with you.

Diana: So that would have been 1932.

Anne: We started having little dinners back and forth. Your father, of course, as you know, was the cellist with the Portland Symphony, and I used to go to the concerts. Then we formed a group of 14 pianos. We went to rehearsals and he had us in a concert. But then after your folks moved to that home [Haslow Street], your mother told me about her family, where she came from, Salem, and that she had never been in contact socially with too many Jewish people. Oh yes, your father used to call her his yiddisha shiksa. So I remember that, because she was red-haired and fair-skinned.

Diana: What was the general level of the pianists in the piano ensemble?

Anne: They all must have been fairly good. I know we played the L'Arlésienne

---

7 Arlene Schnitzer, née Director, June's sister. The Schnitzers donated the funds to build the major concert hall in Portland.

Suite by Bizet.

Diana: Going back to those early days…did you ever hear my mother play the violin?

Anne: I heard your father play, of course, he played in the Portland Symphony, so I used to hear him there.

Diana: Did you ever hear him play as a soloist by himself?

Anne: When he was at the Normal School that time I did, yes.

Diana: What did he sound like?

Anne: He was good. I wouldn't say he was like the top people, but I think he was good.

Diana: Do you remember anything about my father's cooking?

Anne: I remember the first dinner we had. It was a nice veal dish.

Diana: Veal paprika. That was one of his favorites.

Diana: Do you remember how my mother dressed? What was her personality like?

Anne: You know how she wore her hair. I think your mother stayed more or less conservative … I don't remember ever seeing her really in a blouse and skirt.

Diana: Dientje had brought her [Elizabeth] up to be a lady. She always told Elizabeth she could make more money sitting down teaching violin. Then you could hire somebody to do the housework. She always taught me that women in art, music, and teaching were more independent. Her thinking was sort of a precursor of the feminist movement.

OREGON MEMORIES
OF MOTHER

OREGON MEMORIES OF MOTHER
January 1, 1990, Lincoln Beach, Oregon

As I walk through this house, Mother's presence is here so strongly that it is almost disturbing. I keep seeing her in various attitudes. Unfortunately, some of them were the latest ones, which were watching her sit that last summer in a wheelchair, looking at the ocean. Somehow or another she knew something was wrong. She indicated several times that she didn't think she would ever be back. And I didn't really think about her dying. I just thought that maybe she wouldn't be strong enough. But we really didn't have any idea. Which is good, I suppose.

I was just about to start this reminiscence when I got a call from one of her former pupils, Randy Wells, who lives over in Eugene. I am thinking of the variety of students that she worked with over the years that were literally from three year olds to 60-plus. She had this great ability to communicate about what is basically a very difficult technique: playing the violin.

She was very strict. She insisted on a good bow and left hand position. The way students loved her and wanted to please her made them do the best they could, even when some of them were quite limited in their abilities. I think a lot of it was that she was judgmental in that they should do the best they could, but she was never judgmental in terms of their ability level. If they wanted to learn, she was willing to teach.

Mother was very thorough. When I was teaching a lot, I always told her that anytime I got a student from her I always felt very lucky, because they didn't have the holes in their education that so many students do. Maybe other teachers are lazy or impatient, or maybe they just don't know how to organize the material that is necessary to know both note reading, ear training, position, rhythm, all the basics. Even if the student is just playing Twinkle, Twinkle Little Star, it requires all this training. Mother would make sure that they knew every little nook and cranny of that knowledge. How well they reproduced it would really depend upon their own ability, but any problems they had certainly did not come from lack of knowledge as imparted by her.

Also, she had the great ability to go at the speed that was appropriate for each student. She seemed to be able to adjust her method of teaching to fit each individual. I think that was a major part of her success. I know when I teach beginners I seem to have more patience on the piano, because it is definitely easier. You just don't have position and intonation problems, etc. People can know a lot less and begin to play something on the piano.

One is so tempted to push forward and assume that students are just never going to get certain things anyway so you might as well just skip it. I don't think Mother ever did that. However, she was practical. She knew that you had to keep the interest of the youngster.

For instance, when she was a child she was taught in the really old-fashioned way by intuition only. She told me once she literally had a teacher who would cut the music up by lines and hand her a line a week, and make her practice it over and over again until she had it perfect. No child today would accept that. We are talking probably 80 years ago, when children did what the teacher told them and never questioned it. If that meant you had to do the same line 100 times for a week, that is what you did. Today, kids are much more questioning of authority. They are used to doing things quickly and, unfortunately, sort of in a cursory manner.

Mother seemed to be able to strike a happy balance. She realized how boring and unacceptable that kind of approach would be for today's student. As she herself got older she was constantly in touch with the latest pedagogical developments. Her body got older, but her mind, attitudes and approaches kept pace with the current thought. Nonetheless, she always demanded quality and thoroughness in the learning process. That is why she was so outstanding.

I go back to the fact that she had a personality that people just warmed to; they loved her.[1] The kids wanted to please her, even when sometimes they wouldn't want to please their own parents.

For example, she had one little boy who was terribly spoiled, a doctor's son. The father told Mother, "Frankly, I know he doesn't practice between lessons, but the association he has with you I think is important." She said that sometimes they would play the music and sometimes they would just sit and talk. His father realized that sometimes the boy would come in very angry and upset. (I think the parents were divorced.) His association with Mother helped him. When he graduated from high school, she was invited.

There was a sense of caring and true interest in each individual student and how they progressed emotionally and technically. She always said, "I don't get involved in their personal lives unless they talk to me about it." But she was the kind of person to whom people liked to talk.

For example, I was giving a pedagogic lesson the other day on working with beginning violin students. The first thing I did was to chide one of my students, a teacher, for overwhelming her own students with too much abstract information instead of getting into the nitty gritty of feeling the music. Mother was the one who taught me that.

---

1 See comments from June Nagel in "Notes and Quotes from Elizabeth's Students and Friends" chapter.

When I was a little kid and watched her with other young ones she always worked with rhythm immediately. It is part of the innate sense of music that music has discipline. Students get so involved in the technical and physical aspects of playing a violin it is tempting to ignore the rhythmic impulse. Right away she would have students marching to time. On the piano, for instance, she would have them play on middle C and the hands would march back and forth: left, right, left, right. She would have them do the same thing with the violin bow, either with pizzicato or the bow. Without rhythm, she would say, it was just noise.

She shared what she had learned about handling publicity, promoting yourself and making friends, what she called putting eggs under the hen. I don't think I would be successful at all in managing my own career or The Debussy Trio[2] if it hadn't been for what I learned from her. And she said she had learned it from her mother.

That her mother, Dientje, knew anything about PR is absolutely amazing. With her, it was just brightness and innate good sense. After all, Dientje came from a European background where she would have been sheltered. She certainly had no practical experience with things like newspaper publicity or clubs or anything like that. When she came to Oregon she had to learn all of that–how to stay friends with people so it would help her husband's business and later her daughter's musical career.

Of course, the Levys were frequently the only Jews in the small towns in Oregon in which they lived. So they had to walk that old chalk line: "You were a good Jew," "You weren't like all the other Jews," or "I didn't know what a Jew was like." Dientje imparted this sense of making friends, keeping friends and trying to avoid making enemies while at the same time watching her back. And she taught Mother.

Mother shared all these various experiences with me. There was the back-biting, the meddling, all the stuff that you read in novels about women's clubs, church clubs, all the way to secret societies. In a small town there was just no place to escape. Everyone knew what you did.

Of course, Mother always told me about watching "your reputation." Girls in those days had to be so protected. She told me how in Europe it was so bad that when she wanted to continue studying in Belgium and let my grandmother Dientje go home, her uncles wouldn't let her stay alone.

This was true in Oregon small towns, too. It was very, very difficult for women who were trying to push ahead or become professionals in any fashion; they would be looked upon as either masculine or aggressive. If someone got mad at you, townspeople would start rumors.

Mother told me the story of another local woman violin teacher who was jealous. When Mother went to Europe to study violin, this woman spread the story around that Mother had really gone for an abortion!

They managed to scotch that story–Dientje had friends in high places in the

---

2 Marcia's group, see "The Third Generation" section.

clubs and private societies. They made this woman correct the error and say she didn't mean it the way it sounded.

As I sat in Mother's bedroom at the Oregon beach house, I started to think about the relationship that both Sallie and Marcia had with "Gracoo,"[3] which is very revealing about her character, an extension of her ability to teach and empathize with people. Her relationship with the girls was very, very close.

Gracoo was a lady with a strong point of view. She first came to take care of Sallie when I was just out of the hospital. She was the kind of mother who dropped everything if her daughter and new grandchild needed her, and she came instantly. She took care of Sallie the first week and a half of her life. She got up at 2 and 6 in the morning to bring her to me so I could nurse.[4] She was just wonderful, never a whimper.

It was less than two months later that she was mugged in Philadelphia and left with a broken ankle to die in the snow. By some lucky coincidence a good samaritan driving by saw her, picked her up out of the snow, and took her to the hospital. After a week in the hospital with a cast up to her hip she was totally unable to take care of herself. She never really learned to use crutches. She didn't have the strength in her shoulders.

As she had definitely broken her ankle, it was going to be a minimum of six weeks before the cast could be removed. So we had the hospital put her into a cab and one of her friends took her down to the airport and we met her at LAX with a wheelchair.

Over the years, whether it was his mother or mine, Ed would say, "Just stick 'em in an airplane, bring 'em out, and we'll take care of them." And sure enough we did.

When Mother came, we made a bed for her on the living room sofa. I would put her by the telephone with the baby's crib and in a comfortable chair. She'd have a bottle of water with a little Karo syrup in it. Then I'd run off and do my errands. I'd call every once in a while to make sure everything was okay.

She built a very close relationship even at that very young age with Sallie. They just adored each other.

Then, we made a family decision that Mother should move out to L.A. At first she lived in our back room. After about six months, she got herself situated with a teaching job and was able to make a living.

Her lessons were too reasonable, which was unfortunate, but she was so frugal.

We had given her our old Ford, and when that fell apart she bought herself a little Plymouth Valiant. That was in 1962. She kept it until six months before she died in 1987, when we convinced her to stop driving.

But it took guts. In the rain, in the cold, in the snows in Philadelphia, she would take the subways and the buses. Then when she got to Los Angeles, she drove her little car. Sometimes it would be cold, dark and rainy when she came

---

3 The girls' nickname for Elizabeth, their grandma.
4 I was very weak from a serious kidney infection.

home at night. She used to tell me, "I just take myself in hand. You can't be scared. You gotta get out there and do it. No one is going to do it for you." She was very independent, though I am sure that lots of times she was lonely and scared.

She was never idle. She sewed clothes for Frances and me when we were growing up and made baby clothes for my kids and Frances' daughter, Sarah. It wasn't so much to keep busy, it was that she said you had to have a purpose in your life.

One summer, Mother got up at 8 a.m. to pick up Sallie and take her down to the Singer Sewing Center in Santa Monica and wait while she took her sewing lesson for about two hours. She thought it was useful for Sallie to learn how to sew.

Mother said that her mother had always said that playing cards sharpened your wits. So she taught the girls how to play Kaluki, Double Solitaire and Gin Rummy, and she would make them keep the scores. She said that was good arithmetic training.

On many of the trips we made, even when Sallie was a teenager, we took Mother. The last big trip we made together was the Princess Cruise to Alaska. By that time the girls really didn't need a chaperone, but Gracoo and the girls were buddies and we wanted Mother to make the trip. They shared a stateroom and they got along quite well. She and the girls loved each other.

The first time we went to Yosemite, we stayed at the Ahwahnee Hotel with Mother. Later on we started coming up to Oregon, staying at the Salishan Lodge. (By 1971 we decided to buy the beach home.) In 1976 when we took the girls on a bicentennial trip it was the first time we didn't take Mother with us, nor did we on trips to Asia and to Europe. The trips were too hard for her by that time, and too expensive. But we took her back east, to Hawaii several times, and always to Oregon, of course.

We took Ed's folks to Oregon one time only. It was really too hard a trip for his mother, and his father was already starting to have fainting spells. It wasn't too much later that he developed Alzheimer's and couldn't travel.

But Gracoo came. She would walk on the beach, sit and play with the girls. She was always gung-ho. She would picnic with them, or anything they wanted her to join in. Marcia started cooking under her direction. The only thing Mother worried about was that Marcia, being short, would burn herself on the stove or her hair would catch fire.[5]

When Mother came to Los Angeles, it was a big adjustment for her. I had a new baby to care for and though we saw each other every day or so, it meant she had to build a means of living and a social base. Mother started to make friends. She was a joiner partly because of her upbringing in a small community where it was good if you belonged to a group.

---

5 Her mother's hair did catch on fire from a stove. Dientje was only saved by her son's quick action of rolling her in a carpet. This memory lingered forever.

In Los Angeles, Mother joined Hadassah (a Jewish women's organization) and the Music Teachers Association of California (MTAC), reconnected with her music sorority Sigma Alpha Iota, and before long, she had friends. She even started a bridge club. She thought playing cards was good for her mind and kept her alert.

I know she used to complain when she was in her 80s that she was a little slower because most of the women she played with were at least 10 years younger. She felt that even though she could think clearly, keep her card count and was very good at keeping score, she was a little slower in moving the cards and shuffling. It annoyed her.

Probably it was because her eyesight got so bad. She had cataract surgery a few years before she died but she was losing the central field of sight in one eye to macular degeneration.

Ending Note:

Mother's presence stayed with me at the time of these memories in 1990, when the loss was fresh. Writing now in 2009, she is with me still, as I review her section of this book and appreciate her very being. She aged well. I could only hope to do as well.

– DSD

Courtesy Family Archives

Dientje Levy with Elizabeth's brothers, Harry and Ben, 1897

Courtesy Family Archives

Dienjte van Straaten Levy, about 60 years old, as Elizabeth's students remembered her.

Courtesy Family Archives

Solomon Levy, Elizabeth's father in his early 80's

Courtesy Family Archives

Dientje and Elizabeth in high fashion visiting Balboa Park, San Diego, 1919

Levy homestead in North Carolina, about 1897.

Courtesy Family Archives

Below: Elizabeth's professional flyer on return to Oregon from Ithaca Conservatory.

Courtesy Family Archives

Courtesy Family Archives

Autographed photo from Adolfo Betti (one of Elizabeth's teachers) and the Flonzaly Quartet.

Right: Photo autographed to Elizabeth from her teacher, violin pedagogue, Cesar Thompson.

Courtesy Family Archives

Left: Leanore and (Uncle) Alex van Straaten meet Elizabeth for the first time, and visit in Atlantic City, NJ.

Right: Elizabeth with one of her many large classes of violin students.

Elizabeth could sit on her beautiful red hair. She usually wore it in a thick braid, early 1920's.

CENTRAL SYNAGOGUE
55TH STREET AND LEXINGTON AVENUE

RABBI JONAH B. WISE
34 EAST 62nd STREET
NEW YORK

October 2, 1944

Mrs. Elizabeth Stelzer
1900 Barrington Avenue
Philadelphia 49, Pa.

Dear Friend:

I was delighted to hear that Diana
won out in the audition to play with the Philadelphia
Orchestra for the Children's Concerts.

All of us are tremendously concerned
with Diana's attainments, and I am especially so.

Please give my most loving greetings
to the girls and to yourself.

Yours sincerely,

Jonah B. Wise
Rabbi

Rabbi Jonah B.
Wise letter continues
interest and
friendship in 1944

Courtesy Family Archives

Programs attended by Elizabeth and her students, Zimbalist (1915)
and Heifetz (1920). Never in her dreams did she expect to know
them, up close and personal, as she did through Diana.

Lena and Abe Dickstein (Ed's parents) visit from Philadelphia around 1964, pictured with Elizabeth in front of Bundy Drive house, Los Angeles.

Elizabeth's former student Fay (Irvin) Mort and husband Loren in front of their beach house in Lincoln Beach, OR.

Lena Belle Tartar, Elizabeth's dearest friend, at age about 95.

THE SECOND GENERATION: DIANA AND FRANCES

2

MY BEGINNING
1932-1940

"Before such gifts, one must be humble." Nadia Boulanger

"A really exceptional talent... possesses the material from which great artists are made." Alfred Hertz

"No doubt she is one among the elite." Marcel Dupré

Diana dressed for Curtis Audition, April 1938

MY BEGINNING, 1932-1940

I was just up in Oregon, and it always brings back a lot of memories of my early childhood. I was born in Portland, Oregon and lived there until my sixth birthday. In April 1938, I won a scholarship to The Curtis Institute of Music. At that point my parents decided to pull up stakes in Portland, give up their home, teaching, friends and relatives to move to Philadelphia.

What follows are my recollections, beginning with my earliest memories in Oregon. I have made every effort to include the most accurate dates and facts possible, but where dates and facts have been impossible for me to verify, I have included information that is accurate to the best of my knowledge.

Our House

I have mental images of those first few years. We had a little white house on the corner of 39th and Haslo Streets. When we visit Portland, we still can pass by that house. It had wooden shingles and a lovely garden with a trellis type of fence covered with climbing roses. Mother used to tell me that our roses were so beautiful that people would drive by just to look at them. Of course, Portland is called the Rose City, so it was natural to grow roses there. But it seemed that ours were particularly beautiful. It is still a nice little house today even though in the 1990s someone painted it a garish deep pink. In 1949, when I was still a teenager, I was a subject of psychological testing for a college student who was doing her master's thesis. She had me draw my dream house. Without realizing it, I drew that first house with the big picture window and me sitting at the piano in front of the window picking out melodies.

The Depression

The Depression hit in the East in 1929 but really began to affect the West a couple years later. In 1933 and 1934 it was very difficult for people to make a living, but they still wanted to be educated, even if they didn't have much money, so my folks did what they could.

Mother told me that they could hire a maid for $15 a month who would get Thursday afternoons and every other Sunday off. They were mostly young women who came in from the rural areas who needed the money—any kind of money—that they could send home. People were starving. At least maids got room and board.

These were mostly poorly educated girls straight off the farm, but occasionally there were some that were very educated–school teachers who were taking jobs in homes just for a place to live and have food in their mouths. They did everything: cleaned, cooked, baby-sat, whatever was necessary.

At least at my house the food was always good. My parents home-canned everything. They would buy hundred pound sacks of apples and potatoes. They canned cherries, peaches, pears, cucumber pickles, etc. Our basement was cool and lined from floor to ceiling with shelves with hundreds of filled Mason jars. Mother also made jams and jellies. She would heat hot paraffin to seal the jars. It was all very good, and much cheaper.

Steiner's Music School

My folks had a contract with First National, a commercial musical instrument company. I guess it was an early version of a franchise. They rented or sold violins and may have had a percentage arrangement on the teaching. Students paid 25¢ a class, so with 10 students in a half hour, a teacher could make $5.00 an hour.

Mother gave lessons in the sun room behind French doors off the living room. My bedroom and my parents' were on the first floor. Though the second floor had a small maid's room, the rest was not partitioned, so it was used for music classes and recitals.

My father taught violin classes upstairs. At about two and half years old, I remember proudly carrying an apple and a paring knife up to my father so that he could cut it in halves and quarters to illustrate for the students the relationship between a half note and quarter note.

Between the ages of two and three I was watching probably 100 students a week come through our house. All of them came to study violin or cello, and my father occasionally coached piano. He was trained in Europe and New York, and had come to Oregon from California to be first cellist of the Portland Symphony. He, like mother, was a leading musician in town.

Before he came to Portland, Mother was President of the Music Teachers Association, and had a very big class of violin pupils. Even when she was pregnant with me she was still conducting school orchestras. In those days women didn't teach in schools after they "showed," so she wore a very clever coat to hide her pregnancy. One of her stable jobs was conducting in five different public schools around the city.

Naturally, some of those kids came and studied privately with her as well. My whole life revolved around my home, my parents and what they did, and all those music students that came to the house regularly. I was either listening to them learn or watching my parents teach.

My Imagination

I had my own little room with a table and chair, modeling clay and my dolls. I lived very much in my imagination, as I guess children do. I remember being very fearful of the dark. My parents used to have to leave a night light on for me. Nobody realized that I was terribly astigmatic. So I would see double. I would see faces and was terrified of my ceiling light fixture because it had bunches of flowers that looked like eyes, a nose, and mouth. My folks finally had to change it because I had such nightmares. I would get so paralyzed with fear that I couldn't speak.

As soon as my parents recognized the problem, they exchanged the fixture for something that was absolutely plain and white that had no "face."

I was an overly sensitive, empathetic youngster. Mother told me that one time a child came to visit who had hurt his leg and was walking around with a crutch. They didn't think anything of it, but a day later I started limping around the house. It took them a while to realize that I was imitating this child.

When I stop to think of the instinctive kind of psychology that my parents had to practice, I don't know if I was unusual or not. Every parent has to deal with children's fears and their own. I know parents were terribly afraid of illness; families lost children. For example, my godparents lost their first two children before age 10 to measles and leukemia. Children would die in two or three days with strep throat.

When I was in Philadelphia at the age of six I got strep throat. I made the medical journals because I was one of the first people saved with sulfanilamide. Mother was so terrified because the Oregon governor's son, a teenage boy, died within three days of strep throat. We just don't know how lucky we are today. You go to the doctor, they prescribe an antibiotic and your kids are fine.

Early Talent

It was so natural for me to play music. I seemed to have a real talent for melody and composition.

From the age of two, in the mornings, especially when my folks would sleep late, I would go to the piano and improvise by the hour. By three, I was making up tunes with a left hand rhythmic bass.

Absolute Pitch

When I was about two, Mother discovered that I had absolute pitch. My father was always very strict in making sure that anything I heard was only of the best quality and correct intonation. He wouldn't let me listen to popular music. Even our maids were not allowed to play popular music in the house when I was around.

All I heard was the Sunday Evening Hour with the Detroit Symphony, the New York Philharmonic on Sunday afternoons and sometimes the Metropolitan Opera on Saturday. We would sit and listen to the radio broadcasts and I just loved it.

Mother reminded me about her discovery of my absolute pitch, but I also remember the incident quite clearly myself.

Though I didn't have my own violin yet, I had learned to identify the letter names of the notes on the keyboard. Mother used to teach me a little bit at a nursery level.

One hot summer day, the electric fan was running in the living room and I came to her and said, "Mommy, that fan is singing F." And I started humming the F. She had a good ear, but she didn't have absolute pitch. When I finally got her attention, she started listening and went over and played the note on the piano, and sure enough, it was the same F.

She told my father, who also had absolute pitch, and he tested my ear, confirming that I had this natural gift. Since that time, scientific tests have proven on CT scans that people with absolute pitch show an increase in the size of a portion of the dominant hemisphere.

My First Violin

At this early age, I would go upstairs to the closet where my folks stored violins for sale. The smallest ones, which were probably half-sized, were so big that I couldn't really play them, though I was always trying. So my folks decided for my third birthday that they would get me a little eighth-sized violin of my own and it wasn't a cheap factory-made one either.

My father went to the violin dealer in town, Rudolph Schmoll, and chose a beautiful eighth-size violin handmade in Germany with a lovely sweet sound, along with an eighth-size bow. I still have this rare little violin.

At that point Mother started giving me formal lessons in a class with another youngster about age six. She taught me in a very solid, basic manner. We used to put our bows on our shoulders like soldiers and march around to feel rhythm. And then we would play little duets together. I was also allowed to take my violin to my room. While they were busy teaching, I was busy practicing. I would play concerts for my dolls, imitating everything I heard.

Within a few weeks, Mother began teaching me in the Maia Bang books. Ms. Bang was a student of Leopold Auer, the teacher of Heifetz and Zimbalist and many other famous Russian violinists. As one of Auer's few female students, she had gone into pedagogy and had written the finest set of beginner violin books at the time.

I began to make very rapid progress. When I was three and a half, my father showed me off at a Christmas concert playing a Bach Minuet and Silent Night, Holy Night. I was a surprise soloist at a special holiday concert of the Portland Piano Ensemble which he conducted on regular radio broadcasts and in concerts.

There were 20 pianos with 40 pianists, two women at each piano, quite an unusual organization. I was so little that my father stood me on top of the piano so that everybody could see me.

A short while later, an 11-year-old boy, one of Mother's pupils, was studying a 1st position student concerto by Seitz. The first movement is about four pages long and he had been practicing and rehearsing it for weeks with both my parents coaching him to prepare for a big Music Teachers Association competition.

The student was having problems memorizing the piece. One evening, my folks were sitting at the dining room table (I always ate with them), discussing this problem. They didn't know what they were going to do with the student because he always forgot in the same place. Mother said that I piped up and said, "I don't know why he forgets, because I never do." They looked at me amazed, "You don't even know the piece." Mother was under the impression I was only working on the elementary books she gave me.

I told them I could play it. Being good parents, they said, "Show us." I got my violin and promptly played the Seitz concerto for them. I went into the living room as usual to stand by the piano. My mental image of this incident is distinct. My father lay on the maroon mohair sofa as I played the concerto perfectly. He rolled off the sofa in amazement, which I will never forget.

At that point I guess my parents decided they had really better start taking me seriously. Mother started practicing with me every day. When I was four, I also started taking formal piano lessons with Edna Burton, a very sweet lady who was my father's piano accompanist and played in his Piano Ensemble. She came two or three times a week to give me piano lessons.

By the time I was five and a half years old, when I auditioned for Curtis on the piano, I was able to play the Mozart Fantasie in D Minor and two Czerny Etudes Opus 299.

In that same period, on violin, I progressed to the level of Kreutzer Etudes and the Vivaldi Concerto in A Minor, which I played for my Curtis violin audition. Now that has become the piece that every kid can play. Suzuki has watered down the first movement, but I could play the whole concerto.

My folks continued to be leading musicians in Portland, so they frequently invited visiting artists to our house.

One of them was Mishel Piastro, a well known Russian violinist who also conducted the famous Longine Symphonette, which broadcast over national radio networks for years. He came as a guest conductor with the Portland Symphony.

He was invited to hear me when he visited our house. He could play the piano, and asked if he could accompany me. Mother says that I said, "Alright, but don't worry, if you get lost I'll just keep on playing."

Maia Bang, the woman who wrote the violin books I studied, also heard me.

My folks were beginning to realize they had a tiger by the tail. They had never seen a student like me. Neither one of them had been prodigies. They knew about them, but they had never encountered one themselves.

They were concerned they would be thought of as just fond parents. So they kept having me play for various visiting famous musicians to get their opinion. After all, these artists heard talents all over the world and had no personal interest in me, so they could give an honest opinion. These musicians were all favorably impressed.

Finally my father took me down to San Francisco on the train and I played for the conductor of the San Francisco Symphony, Dr. Alfred Hertz. He recommended that I leave Portland to go to San Francisco or New York. He said that I needed to go to a major teacher.

Yehudi Menuhin had recently come on the scene as a prodigy and then there was Shirley Temple. I was such a cute little girl, my father thought I might be a violinist Shirley Temple, but I could not dance. Though we tried it, I was a klutz. But they really thought I could become another Mozart. I could improvise like he did. They could give me four or five notes and I would make up a tune on the spot, which came out very classical, of course, because of my training.

The Curtis Institute of Music

It was recommended that my parents write to Juilliard and to Curtis Institute. I guess my father probably knew about Juilliard because he lived in New York as a teenager, but I'm not sure he knew anything about Curtis. My parents did know that Louis Persinger at Juilliard was the teacher of Yehudi Menuhin, so they wrote to Persinger, but they also wrote to Curtis.

Many of the Curtis teachers were great touring concert artists, and while they were on tour, if some outstanding student was recommended to them, they would consider giving the prospective student an audition.

Josef Hofmann, a pianist and the Director of Curtis at the time, was coming to Seattle to play a concert, and he agreed to hear me there. So my father took me to Seattle and I auditioned for Hofmann. He immediately accepted me on the piano, but said that if I wanted to study violin, I would have to go to Philadelphia to let Zimbalist hear me, because Curtis had never accepted a five year old before. Zimbalist had never taught one, either, so Hofmann couldn't accept me for him. Still, Hofmann guaranteed that if they went to the expense and I wanted to become a piano major, I would have a scholarship with him at Curtis.

My folks had to travel all the way from Portland to Philadelphia. The trip took a month: five days to get there, a week to get acclimated, a week for the auditions, and another five days to return. They had to take off a month from their lives just to let me go to my audition at Curtis.

So there they were with this child prodigy. And then by that time, my sister had been born. She was an infant when we went to Philadelphia.

That was an exciting trip for us! On the trains, people were so wonderful. The porters and everyone were so accommodating. They let Mother go into the dining car galley and sterilize baby bottles for my sister. She was born in February and we went in April. It could be very dangerous for babies. The train had refrigeration to keep the milk cold. But Mother had to sterilize the bottles by boiling them and the nipples.

When I got accepted to Curtis, they went back to Portland and sold their home.

Starting at Curtis

The Curtis Institute of Music is located at 18th and Locust Streets in Philadelphia, across from Rittenhouse Square, a European-style square surrounded by high-end apartment houses. The building was originally built for the Drexel family, after whom the Drexel Institute is named. You enter the building through two very heavy glass doors adorned with wrought iron. The lounge or "Common Room" is two stories tall with a balcony on the second floor. The wooden arches and stained-glass windows were all imported from castles in Europe. It was common for wealthy people, like the Astors, Rockefellers and Drexels, to import parts of old castles or else have them duplicated for the homes that they built in the United States.

My poor eyesight was discovered when I couldn't read the clock on top of the fireplace mantel in the Common Room. They thought I was stupid until they learned that I couldn't see the hands.

The old library, which is now the board room, has murals painted on its high ceiling. The walls are beautiful, hand-rubbed wood paneling. The flooring is covered with magnificent Oriental rugs and the window seats have velvet padding. It's not your usual conservatory building. The auditorium has a magnificent pipe organ and the stage floors are parquet.

Across the alley next door there was a four-story limestone building owned by Curtis. From the founding of the school in 1924, Mrs. Bok (later Mrs. Zimbalist)[1] granted stipends for students to live near the school. She also wanted to make sure that everyone was well-fed, so the upper floor of that building was a magnificent cafeteria where you could get a hot meal for 15 or 20 cents. She hired a live-in housekeeper who planned the meals and acted as a majordomo to make sure the buildings were properly maintained, almost as if it were still a private mansion.

A truly genteel tradition established by Mrs. Bok, which continues to this day, is the Wednesday afternoon tea. At four o'clock, educational activities would come to a halt. Faculty, administrators and students were invited to partake in a traditional

---

1 Curtis founder.

English tea. Mrs. Zimbalist would sit in the corner of the Common Room behind a fancy brass samovar. She served tea in real cups–no plastic or paper–with silver spoons, "one lump or two?," a slice of lemon or cream if you wished, and some dainty little cakes. We could stand around, cup of tea and cookie in hand, and socialize. It was a mandatory ritual in Mrs. Bok's day. Sometimes her friend Edith Evans Braun joined her.

During my earliest years at Curtis, when Mrs. Bok entered the Common Room, we girls would immediately curtsy and the young men would stand at attention with respect. Mrs. Bok was a lovely lady with an aristocratic demeanor. Her hair was very white and always beautifully coiffed. She always wore the same style of suit. They were hand-tailored suits, made to order for her in many neutral colors with lovely silk blouses that were also neutral (mauve, grey etc.). Except for when she was dressed in evening gowns for the parties, I never saw her in anything but those suits as long as she lived.

The Zimbalist studio, which is where I studied with him all those years, is now dedicated to him. It has very high ceilings, beautiful paneling, built-in bookcases, Oriental rugs, and big curved, arched windows that look out onto Rittenhouse Square. The adjacent studio was Josef Hofmann's at the time, and was later dedicated to Mieczyslaw Horszowski, with its two Steinway grands. That is the studio where I was auditioned. I vividly remember being scrutinized by the judging panel,[2] which literally got down on the floor so that they could observe my way of holding the bow.

During my first two years at Curtis, I learned ten concertos, including Viotti and Spohr. Besides my lessons with Zimbalist, I had two one-hour lessons with his assistant, Frederick "Freddie" Vogelgesang, a talented student of Zimbalist. Curtis ended in May and started in October, so there was a five month hiatus in the summer. I was assigned quite a bit of work during the first summer, including the Paganini Concerto in D Major. I had no conception of how difficult it was, and Mother almost dropped her eye-teeth when she realized that she had to teach it to me. But I learned it.

I was invited to perform at a music festival at the Greenbriar Resort in West Virginia on August 27, 1939. Like Chautauqua and other major music festivals, this one had instrumentalists attending from various major orchestras in the area, including the Richmond Symphony. This was my first solo appearance with orchestra. I had just turned seven and played the Vivaldi Concerto in A Minor, which I had performed at my audition for Curtis. Father was guest conductor

The second school year, one of the first things that Zimbalist assigned me was the Prelude from Bach's Partita No. 3 in E Major. Its four pages of constant

---

2   The judges were Efrem Zimbalist, Lea Luboshutz, Josef Hofmannn, and Jascha Heifetz's father.

sixteenth notes is quite a tour de force, even for professionals. At the time I didn't have the physical strength to get through it. It took me about three months to get to the point where I didn't feel like my bow arm was about to fall off. In the spring of 1940, Zimbalist had me play the Bach as the opening "act" on his student recital. Curtis would have one teacher present his or her complete class of students in a single recital. Nowadays, things are a bit more user-friendly. Several students who played in that recital also went on to major careers, including Rafael Druian and Veda Reynolds. By the time I reached the end of that year, I had already learned the first movement of the Mendelssohn Concerto and the Scherzo-Tarantelle by Wieniawski. The summer of 1940, I went back to Portland and played a full recital which included the Bach, Mendelssohn, Wieniawski and some other short pieces.

The focus at Curtis was on your major instrument in chamber music, orchestra and especially solo. We were to be virtuosos. There was no question about that: the singers were to make the Met, the pianists were to be Rubinsteins and the violinists were all to be a Zimbalist or Heifetz. We all thought that we would do exactly that. And a few of us did.

Composition classes were pretty small, but Curtis did produce Samuel Barber, Gian Carlo Menotti, Leonard Bernstein, George Rochberg, George Antheil, and more recently Daron Hagen and Jennifer Higdon.

I took piano lessons with Freda Pastor Berkowitz. She was very sweet and we remained friends over the years. She taught me during my first two years. She told me that I came to her lesson once, just sighed and sat down. She asked me what the matter was and I said, "Oh, Miss Pastor, I've never worked so hard in my whole life!"

I would only get a half-hour lesson so I became a self-taught pianist. Zimbalist gave me two extra years of lessons so I studied with Billy Sokoloff's wife, Eleanor. She didn't really like working with secondary students. Though we got along alright, I never wanted to practice. I wanted to do accompanying. I could sight-read anything, so I wouldn't practice solo assignments.

Earlier I mentioned listening to broadcasts of the Longine Symphonette. The theme song for the broadcast was the opening movement of Beethoven's Moonlight Sonata and because it was played by strings, the piece had been transposed from the original key of C# minor to C minor. For one of my lessons for Eleanor, I had done my usual trick of quick memory and not bothered to look at the piano music after the first reading. When I played it for my lesson neither one of us opened the music and I played the sonata in C minor because that was what I had freshest in my ear from the radio. When Eleanor opened the music to assign something else we were both surprised as she had never even noticed that I had transposed and played the whole piece without a hitch in the wrong key!

In the spring of 1940, my parents were informed that I couldn't continue at Curtis because Zimbalist wasn't well and had to drop all students except for those about to graduate. When they found out, my parents began looking for other opportunities.

I was accepted at the Mannes School in Manhattan to study on full scholarship with Paul Stassevitch. So we moved to New York City after my return from my Portland debut recital in September 1940. My father became ill with heart disease, but he found us a nice apartment in Queens where we settled for the moment—with big changes to come.

LIFE CHANGES
1941-1942

Diana and Frances at playground across from small apartment.

Queens, NY, Winter, 1943

LIFE CHANGES, 1941-1942

Father's Death, 1941

My father had such big dreams for me. He wanted me to beat Yehudi Menuhin and make my New York debut before I was ten. He got that wish.

He had gone with me when I auditioned to perform as soloist with the New York Philarmonic, playing the Mendelssohn Concerto, when I was nine. My father knew I had won the audition and he was very excited. That night he had a heart attack and died.

He had been very sick. It was really the first day he had gone out after his most recent attack; he'd had three major heart attacks since we went east in 1938. He died on October 23, 1941. It was a terrible thing.

That was October and Pearl Harbor was less than two months later. Mother was stuck in New York with two little kids–a nine year old and a four year old–with no money, and an impending war. It was really something. She was an unbelievable lady.

So we stayed in New York, and then went back to Philadelphia a couple of years later to continue on at Curtis.

I don't think Mother was ever sorry about staying in the East. There were a couple of times during my teenage years when she could have married again, but it just never really worked out. The guys were nice, but they each had children, and I didn't fit very well with other children. I needed a lot of attention, and Mother was so determined that nothing would get in the way of fulfilling my potential. So she really gave up those two or three chances. I don't know that I could have been that self-sacrificing.

When Mother was widowed, she was left literally without a penny. My Father had a $7,000 insurance policy, which in those days would have been a huge amount of money, but he had not paid the insurance premium. Somehow, in his illness, he just let it lapse. So when he died, there was absolutely no money. Her uncle Alex van Straaten generously stepped forward to help. He gave her $50 a month for the first few months, and he probably paid for the funeral. Jonah B. Wise, the wonderful rabbi at Central Synagogue in New York, did the service and he may very well have arranged for the burial without expense, though I have no way of knowing now.

When Uncle Alex started giving us a monthly allowance, he very practically told Mother, "When I die, you are going to inherit several thousand dollars. Instead I'll give it to you now when you need it." Though she was giving music lessons, if it hadn't been for him we would never have been able to stay in the East. She would have had to go back to Oregon and beg off her brothers.

She taught a number of students, making a decent amount. But it wasn't enough to keep us. Without that extra help it would have been very, very difficult. Even then, we really scrimped and saved.

Early Jewish Connection

I mention above that Rabbi Jonah Wise presided over Father's funeral. Rabbi Wise was from Portland, so he knew Mother there. We had a continuing relationship with him and later on I was confirmed at Central Synagogue. Rabbi Wise was quite famous and an important part of the reformed Jewish movement. He was married to the daughter of one of the founders of Portland's major department store, Meier and Franck. He was friendly with my parents in Oregon; when Mother and Father moved to New York they rekindled the friendship. He was very supportive of Mother after Father's death as both a rabbi and a friend.

In those days, there was a half-hour Sunday morning radio program, "Message of Israel," broadcast on a nationwide network. The program had a wonderful organist and cantor, and Rabbi Wise would give a short sermon. On Yom Kippur, the cantor would always sing Kol Nidrei. When I was nine years old, Rabbi Wise had me play Kol Nidrei on the air, which was a nice boost for me.[1]

While we were in New York, Frances and I attended the Sunday school. I used to accompany the chorus and take classes, a nice experience. After all, I was not attending public school, so it was the only time I was in a classroom with other children. It also gave me some musical sight reading experience.

Later, when I was 15 and wanted to be confirmed, Rabbi Wise arranged it for me. Though I had not attended much Sunday school, I knew Biblical history. I was confirmed at Central Synagogue, wearing a white gown and carrying red roses, with a large group of boys and girls. I also played the Nigun by Bloch on violin. One of the girls in that class was Joan Friendly, whose grandmother was Mrs. Horace Stern, one of my mentors in Philadelphia. Mrs. Stern's husband was the Chief Justice of the State Supreme Court of Pennsylvania. We were close friends for many years. Joan's father was Henry J. Friendly who was a judge on the District Court of Appeals, one of the nine federal district courts.

---

1 See "Notes and Quotes from Elizabeth's Students and Friends" chapter.

New York, 1941-42

When our family first got to New York City, we had a rather nice two-bedroom apartment in a newer building in Queens. After Father died, Mother couldn't afford it, so she moved us about four blocks away to a smaller apartment. Fortunately, it was across the street from a playground, so Frances and I could play on the monkey bars, slides and swings. Also, Mother had begun to establish a class of pupils in that little neighborhood which was an interesting area, sort of a mini-United Nations. The elevated train ran on Queens Boulevard, which was lined with "mom and pop" stores, including a bakery, a delicatessen and a hardware store. You did not go to the supermarket; rather, you shopped in small specialty stores. New York is still much that way today. If you live in a big apartment house, there are frequently a grocer, a deli or a fruit stand downstairs.

Mother made friends among these businesspeople and began to get students. For example, Mrs. Lederman, whose husband was a dentist, had a nice little bakery and she would promote Mother's talents. It was the kind of gathering place where everybody knew everybody and she'd say, "My kids are taking piano lessons with Mrs. Steiner, and she's just wonderful! You ought to try her." And the next thing Mother knew, she had a dozen students. We lived on the $50 a month that Uncle Alex sent, plus what Mother made as a music teacher.

Mrs. Lederman was wonderful. At ten years old, I had a tremendous appetite and was growing so fast. Once, she sat me down in the back of the store with a pie and a quart of milk and I ate the whole thing.

Childhood in New York

During the Second World War, Frances and I, as little kids, loved exploring the city with Mother. The subway was only a nickel and the cheapest way to get around New York. If we wanted to stay above ground and really splurge, we would spend a dime and take the 5th Avenue bus, which was a double-decker like they have in London. It was great fun to be able to ride these buses. You could ride to Greenwich Village on a rubberneck ride or you could go up Riverside Drive to Fort Tryon Park and the Cloisters, looking across the Hudson River to the Palisades of New Jersey. It would be quite breezy on the open upper level of the double-decker, which felt wonderful on hot days. You could sit up there and watch the passing view. Sometimes we took the nickel ride on the Staten Island Ferry to cool off in the summer.

People talked about the New York Irish cops, but the guys who ran the buses were also mostly Irish. They came around just like they do on the trolleys in San Francisco and held out a little hand machine. You would put your dime in and it would ring a bell. If kids were below a certain height, according to a little marker at the door, they got to ride free. Frances got to be a little bit taller than the marker, but she was a cute little redheaded girl and looked Irish, so the fare collectors would say, "Oh, let the little one go," and they would sit her up in the front of the bus and let her have the best view. Half the time they let me ride free too. I don't know whether we looked shabby or not. In any case, we were obviously just going for an outing. They were always very nice to Mother, too. (She was also redheaded!)

As Frances and I had never gone to public school, we hadn't picked up the slang of the average child, and we spoke a fine King's English. Though we certainly didn't have British accents, we didn't have New York accents either. Mother's speech pattern was definitely Oregon in those days, and she had quite a western drawl. I pronounce some words like she did to this day, like "tin" for the number ten. Once, while on the bus, a lady heard us speak and came up to Mother to ask if we were English refugee children. Relief agencies had been bringing boatloads of children over from England and local families opened their homes during the war to save the children from the bombings and possibly from Germans who might overrun the British Isles.

Musical and General Studies in New York

During 1942 and the spring of 1943, I continued my studies in violin, piano and theory at the Mannes School of Music. Our family was struggling, but at the same time, I made my debut with the New York Philharmonic. Otto Herz was my coach and Paul Stassevitch my violin teacher.

When I played with the Philharmonic, it brought me to the attention of the truancy officers. They came to our apartment to verify that I wasn't being abused. I was supposed to be in school, but they didn't force children to do so as long as they were being educated.

I had a tutor, Sadie Blank, who was a public school teacher. She was a very nice lady who lived about three blocks from our apartment. I used to go to her home on Monday afternoons for a two-hour tutoring session. She would check up on what Mother was teaching me in workbooks by Lennes in arithmetic, spelling, grammar and geography.[2]

I loved history books and biographies. There was a public library a few blocks away where I could borrow three or four books at a time. I would read my way through all the works of individual authors like Louisa May Alcott. I just adored her books and read every one of her works in the library. I also read books like The Little Princess, Little Lord Fauntleroy and The Five Little Peppers and How They Grew. I was a big fan of the book series for girls: Nancy Drew and Sue Barton,

---

2   Mother received her teaching certificate in Oregon.

Red Cross Nurse. Before the Lassie Come Home movie came out, I read all the Lassie books.

Mother worked very hard. During our last year in New York, the War was making things very difficult. Our one-bedroom apartment had just two rooms in which we fit two beds in the bedroom and a grand piano in the living room which doubled as our piano studio. Space was very tight.

Otto Herz

Otto Herz first came into my life when he accompanied my encore at my debut with the New York Philharmonic on February 23, 1942. I was soloist with the Orchestra under the direction of Rudolph Ganz in the Mendelssohn Concerto, and then played Schubert's The Bee with Dr. Herz at the piano. I had made history as a prodigy but that day was the first time that air raid sirens sounded in NYC. No one was particularly interested in a nine year-old violinist. I did have a manager and Herz and I played a few concerts but all focus centered on the war effort.

Herz was Hungarian and had known my father. He was a fabulous coach to both instrumentalists and singers. He originally came to the United States as accompanist for the French violinist Zino Francescatti. He decided to branch out after touring with Francescatti for several years.

After Father died, I needed a lot of encouragement and extra coaching. "Herzy" provided just that, not only during the time I was in New York; even after we moved to Philadelphia, I made the trip to see him many times.

Years later, when I was 17 and preparing for the Naumburg audition and solo performances with the Philadelphia Orchestra and the National Symphony, Herz helped me a lot. He had the kind of personality that would inject a player with both confidence and enthusiasm. He became the primary accompanist for African American singer William Warfield, who toured all over the world singing everything from German Lieder to French chansons d'art. Warfield became a household name, however, when he sang Old Man River in the movie Showboat.

Friends in New York: Ruth Bradley Jones and Franklin Jones

Among our closest friends in New York were Ruth Bradley Jones and her husband Franklin Jones. Ruth had studied with Leschetizky and was a reasonably good pianist and an excellent teacher. She was a fairly aggressive, strong minded woman and was certainly a good friend to us over the years. She admired Father very much from the days she coached with him in Portland and she loved Mother. Franklin, a really lovely man, was a retired editor of The Mechanic's Handbook and seemed financially comfortable.

The Joneses had an apartment overlooking Washington Square and a country home in Lumberton, New Jersey, on the little Rancocas River. It was a great boon to Mother, Frances and I when we got invited down there for a weekend. We were city children who loved getting out into the country.

Ruth and Frank's home was on a couple of acres with a "victory garden" that included corn. Ruth used to say that corn was only good if you had the water boiling in the pot before you cut it. Then you cut the corn and ran like hell to drop it in the pot.

Franklin was a fine amateur oil painter. He would never sell his work, but he occasionally gave one away. When Ed and I got engaged, we drove to New Jersey at Frank's invitation. He displayed about a dozen of his paintings from which we could choose as a wedding gift. A beautiful country snow scene on the Rancocas was our first real work of art, which we enjoy still. All of the scenes Franklin painted were of the New Jersey countryside. People talk about Renoir blue, but Franklin developed a blue that I call Franklin Blue. It made the shadows on the snow and hills look amazing. That was one of his hallmarks.

After Father died, Ruth immediately started giving Frances and me free piano lessons. She would be very strict with Frances because she had to be pushed. I was also floundering. Father had been so strict but Mother didn't have the time. Ruth would really give us a verbal slap.

Meanwhile, Frances took cello lessons with Dad's first cello teacher, Mr. Ebann, who had a studio in the famous Flatiron building, which has since been declared a historical site and restored. It is an oddly-shaped triangular building, 23 stories high which was considered tall in those days. Mr. Ebann's studio was on the top floor right in the point of the triangle.

He gave Frances lessons on her little quarter-sized cello, which mother would have to drag through the subway from Queens. We would cross the Queensborough Bridge into Manhattan, then change subways at Grand Central Station, take the Lexington Avenue subway down to 23rd Street, get off there, then get back on again and go down to Washington Square to take piano lessons with Ruth. It was a day's excursion. It was hard, but Mother was a brave lady. It didn't seem hard to us at the time, but she wasn't young. She was already 45 and struggling to make ends meet. Despite it all, though, we were always happy. If she was worried, she didn't tell us. She used to talk to me a lot, and I knew things were tight. But it never seemed like we were going to go hungry.

Later when I was married, Ruth and Ed hit it off. She was very big in the National Federation of Music Clubs and was also a member of Mu Phi Epsilon Sorority. She pushed me into affiliating with these organizations. It was very good advice because they really have been wonderful groups for me to be part of throughout my life. I would never be running the Debussy Trio Music Foundation today if it weren't for my experience with Federation. It is something women miss today. They do not have the time to gain organizational skills like they did.

In 1959, when I won the NFMC Young Artist Award in San Diego, Ruth was at the convention. She knew I was a finalist and she was there rooting for me. Rosalie Speciale was the Mu Phi national president and she was there too. Ruth said, "Mu Phi is going to ask you to be a member, and I want you to join because you can be a really active member of this organization. I know your mother is a Sigma Alpha Iota member, but the SAIs will only give you an honorary status and we will give you full membership."

Sure enough, as I came down the steps of the auditorium after I had won, Rosalie came up to me and asked me to join Mu Phi. Fifteen minutes later I was stopped by the national president of SAI and she also asked me to join, but I told her that I had decided to go with Mu Phi.

Mu Phi has been a lovely association for me. I've made many good friends.

When Franklin died, Ruth was on her own. She traveled and went to the music conventions. She would always tell it like it was and we always liked her. She was a one-of-a-kind lady.

DIANA
1943-1949

Mrs. Zimbalist greets Diana after graduation ceremony
at The Curtis Institute of Music. May, 1949

DIANA, 1943-1949

Back to Philadelphia and Curtis

In the spring of 1943, Mother decided we were not getting sufficient general education and Frances would have to start going to school. She talked to our cousin Roslyn, who told her that if we came to Philadelphia, she could help us find an apartment and help Mother establish a neighborhood studio. Mother went to Curtis to see Zimbalist, who had become director, and told him about Father's death. He invited me to play for him, after which he said that if we came back to Philadelphia he would reinstate my Curtis scholarship. Mother knew this was the best thing to do. In addition to a complete music curriculum, they offered daily academic tutoring.

Philadelphia was a much more family-friendly city than New York. It was the best move for us. Mother first tried to find an apartment in the center of town within walking distance of Curtis, but nobody wanted to rent to her with a piano, a violin and two young girls. There were no laws against discriminating against families with children. Apartments were in old, dreary converted brownstones and we were in the middle of the War so there were few vacancies. People had come to work in the Navy Yard and other industries, and there was much disruption in family living.

We were lucky, though, because Roslyn's husband, Abe, was the Republican committeeman for their neighborhood on Warrington Avenue in West Philadelphia. Now, it is terribly run-down, but at the time it was a very nice, mostly middle-class Jewish neighborhood. Abe learned of an apartment that was going to become available. It was in a three-story end row house which the owner had converted into three apartments. The middle one was the largest, including a small deck, and it was on the opposite end of the block from where Roslyn lived. There were 65 houses in a row, a Jewish synagogue up the street and a good public school a few blocks away. They used to call that school the Jewish private school because all the Jewish kids from the neighborhood attended, while the Catholic kids all attended Most Blessed Sacrament Parochial School a few blocks in the other direction. The public school was small, with about 300 students, and it was a great place for Frances to attend.

Across the street from us there was a delicatessen. Down at the corner was an ice cream and sundries store which was the hang-out for all the kids. A half block away was the beauty parlor where Mother used to get her hair done. A block past that was a cleaning establishment. Usually the families who bought the end houses would run stores in their basements. Ed's Uncle Morris made his living in a store like that. Sometimes they lived in the back and rented the upper floors. It was really quite the day for family-owned neighborhood businesses.

Our Philadelphia Apartment

When we got that apartment, we thought we were in heaven. It had a living room with a fake fireplace and French doors opening onto a small deck, a bedroom, a kitchen and a full dining room, in which Mother had her beautiful Berkey & Gay Italian Renaissance-style dining room set. We blocked off the door from the kitchen and turned the dinette into a bedroom for me, but it didn't have a closet, which worked as I didn't have many clothes anyway.

The bathroom had a bathtub and palatial shower with four showerheads. You could get sprayed in four different directions. There was also a basement in which Mother could put her washing machine, which was an old-fashioned one with a hand roller, no spin dry here. The furnace made it nice for hanging clothes to dry inside in the winter time.

We didn't own a hair dryer, so Frances and I used to sit in front of the gas oven with the door slightly ajar to dry our long hair. We washed our hair every other week if we didn't have a cold, because that was considered too dangerous. Mother was getting a little bit grey in front, which she touched up with a Clairol coloring pencil. She hated it because the color rubbed off on the pillow and she would have to retouch it every day or two. But that's the way it was.

Puberty was difficult. We had oil heat which was rationed, so we were only allowed to take a hot shower once a week. I'm sure that's one of the reasons I had major problems with acne.

These were also the days before penicillin, so we were terrified of getting sick. Mother had already gone through strep throat with me, when I was saved by Sulfa. We had colds frequently. Indoors, we lived in over-heated rooms wearing our wool clothing, and then we would go out into the winter cold. Even when I was 11 or 12, I wore leggings. All the neighborhood kids seemed so tough that they wore what were called Navy pea coats and went bare-legged and bare-headed. I wore hoods, scarves, heavy gloves and sweaters under my coat. I also wore snuggies, which were stretchy, elasticized cotton underwear that went from the waist to the knees. Sometimes I even wore two or three pairs at a time. Of course, in the summer it was too hot, just the opposite problem.

Our frequent colds were a big worry to Mother. There was a nice Jewish doctor in the neighborhood who ran an office in somebody else's basement. He had a dispensary with all kinds of free pills. You paid five dollars, then he sprayed your nose, checked your ears and gave you aspirin and something to settle your stomach. He also made house calls to patients who were too sick to venture out into the cold.

We didn't have much soap either. Detergents were not yet available, so we had to use bar soap. Mother used to save all the little pieces which got all mushy. That was what we used to wash dishes. For laundry, we used either Fels-Naptha bar soap, which was very harsh, or Ivory Flakes. After the war when we got products like Duz detergent, it seemed like a miracle.

Once, Mother cooked a ham dinner for one of her gentlemen friends, Mr. Valois, who was an absolute doll. He was a big Irishman who worked for the PR firm that handled the Borden Company account, a very good job. He used to bring us things like powdered milk, because even milk was scarce. The night of the ham dinner, Mr. Valois washed the dishes and got up to his elbows in grease. The saved soap bits didn't cut grease. We had a single sink and couldn't run the hot water, so we had to wash the dishes, then let the soapy water drain and rinse them again with clean water.

Because our apartment was on the end of the row, we had three-way ventilation. I'm amazed to think of how small those rooms must have been even though we used to have recitals up there. Mother had 15 or so students on that one block alone. Mother, Frances and I would play trios as a big finale, or Frances and I would play Tchaikovsky or Bizet four-hand pieces on the piano. All of the students played the piano and we would squeeze chairs out into the hallway for the audience. People were accustomed to small homes, so ours seemed relatively large. When I met Ed, his family lived in a little row house which was even smaller.

Life in Philadelphia

I was growing taller very rapidly and you just couldn't feed me enough. I grew from 5' to 5'6" in about a year and a half, growing from a little girl into a fully developed woman.

You could get vegetables, but flour and sugar were rationed. Things were delivered by horse and cart, which would come down the back alley. Our milk man came every day, bringing glass bottles to our second floor apartment. Milk wasn't homogenized, so in cold winter weather the cream rose to the top, becoming like an ice cream stick, which we loved.

Mother went to the kosher chicken butcher with Roslyn once in a while to get a fresh chicken. The rest of the time, we went to the A&P or Penn Fruit Market, which were the precursors of today's supermarket. The knife sharpener came along with his pack on his back. He had a round wheel that he turned by hand to sharpen knives and scissors. The garbage was picked up by horse-drawn wagons.

Also, there were electric trucks like those used by the Curtis Publishing Company, which published the magazines Ladies' Home Journal and Saturday Evening Post. The company had big trucks that traveled about 15 or 20 miles per hour and were almost silent.

We were quite poor. Cousin Roslyn eventually started giving me a five dollar monthly allowance so that I wouldn't feel so bad around the other girls in the neighborhood. Five dollars went quite far as things were relatively cheap. A movie, for example, cost 15 cents. Girls who worked in dime stores on Saturdays earned 55 cents an hour. William Padlasky and his wife Grace lived above us and were going to have their first baby. He made $100 a week as a civil engineer, so he was considered well-off. They were delightful neighbors; in fact, he tutored me in math for a couple of years when I got into algebra and geometry.

Mother earned about $3 an hour when she started teaching, but a lot of students only took half-hour lessons. The minute kids came home from school they would come to our house. Mother taught from about 3:00 to 6:00 and would run to the kitchen between lessons to make dinner. I had to practice, do my homework and supervise Frances. At best, Mother could have taught only 20 hours a week, so she was making about $350 a month, including the allowance from Uncle Alex. Our rent started at $65 and gradually rose to $85 a month. And then she had to pay all other expenses (including utilities, food, clothing, trolley fare, music, and health costs) with the balance.

Student Days at Curtis

I was so into music and The Curtis Institute was my whole life. First of all, my scholarship was on the line constantly like all the other students there. School started in the beginning of October and if you weren't doing well, by December you got a pink slip and you were out by Christmas. If you managed to survive the first semester and your grades in February weren't too bad, you stayed through the following May. I kept surviving, but I had some rough times. I used to be so nervous during my lessons with Zimbalist, but when I think back on it now, he wasn't very intimidating.

Fortunately, Zimbalist liked Mother. He had great respect and sympathy for her as a widow struggling through World War II with two children. Mother told Zimbalist that she didn't know what to do with Frances because she couldn't afford to keep giving her cello lessons. But Frances was also very talented on the piano and Mother contemplated having her audition for Curtis on the piano. Zimbalist told her that Frances didn't have a chance on the piano since there were so many applicants, but suggested that she audition on the cello.

So at age eight, Frances auditioned for Gregor Piatigorsky, Efrem Zimbalist and William Primrose. Her cello teacher at the time was a Curtis graduate, Orlando Cole. They primed her for the audition and I accompanied her. She played a concerto by Goltermann. She had gorgeous red hair that she wore in a pompadour with long, large ringlets. She had a dimple in her chin, those big, snappy brown eyes, and a little Dutch face. She played a half-sized cello so small that Piatigorsky, who was tall and big, just picked it up and put it under his chin. She played very well for an eight-year-old. I have seen many talented kids since, and they can't touch her. Practice or no practice, even at eight, she was phenomenal.

Frances was accepted to Curtis where she continued her musical studies and began receiving tutoring like I had, which went on for four years. A short time later, she had to go to public school in our neighborhood.

I continued my studies at Curtis until 1949, when I received my diploma. During that period, I also studied chamber music with William Primrose and Karen Tuttle, one of Primrose's graduates and a phenomenal violist. Karen hit the glass ceiling for soloists. For some reason she never joined an orchestra, but she stayed on as a faculty member at Curtis for the rest of her career. I vividly remember her stunning performance of the Walton Viola Concerto at Curtis Hall.[1]

Primrose was very precise and exacting. Once in a while he would grab a violin and play it with quite a heavy hand because he was used to drawing a tone on the viola. It was certainly an eye-opener to start coaching chamber music with him. This was before my Marlboro days.

Among other faculty members influential in my Curtis training was Marcel Tabuteau, who conducted the string orchestra class. During my first year in the orchestra, we performed the Prokofiev Classical symphony and the Mozart Haffner symphony under his direction. Also, Rudolf Serkin was soloist in the Beethoven 4th Concerto with us. Tabuteau was a fabulous oboist and taught us phrasing in a way that all Curtis students who ever worked with him remember to this day.

I also studied theory and harmony with Constant Vauclain. At one point, he told me, "Your tunes are the best yet brought into class."

1945 Philadelphia Children's Concerts

Until 1944, the Philadelphia Orchestra had never held open auditions for young soloists to play at its Children's Concert series.

Two years before I tried out to play solo with the Orchestra, it held an open competition for children to submit an original composition that the Orchestra would play. I always went to the children's concerts, and when I heard the announcement, I thought it was a great idea and decided to try. I wrote a theme and variation, which was quite sophisticated. I was eleven. The piece was rejected because they thought "a child could not have written it."

After hearing the simplicity of the winning piece, I was so furious that the following year, Frances wrote a 32-bar Country Dance. She composed a hoe-down

---

1   Now Field Concert Hall.

and I put it together for her. She entered and won, so her piece was played by the Philadelphia Orchestra. She and the two other children who won were pictured with Eugene Ormandy in the Philadelphia Inquirer. As luck would have it, those two children were the granddaughters of the founder of Curtis, the Bok girls: Rachel and Enid.

When I went to hear Frances's piece, the conductor announced that since the children's composition competition was so successful, the Orchestra had decided to hold open auditions for young soloists. My ears perked up immediately and I decided to compete. This time, I won. The Orchestra held the competition in September 1944 and on January 4, 1945, I was soloist in the Saint-Saëns Rondo Capriccioso. After the concert, I was greeted by over 100 autograph seekers. Roslyn sent flowers and after the performance I had my first lobster thermidor for lunch at the famous seafood restaurant, Bookbinders.

The regular conductor, Eugene Ormandy, along with Saul Caston, the associate conductor, had chosen me. But they engaged a young, talented conducting prodigy to lead the orchestra at my concert: Lorin Maazel. He is retiring now (2009) as conductor of the New York Philharmonic and has had a major career as a conductor all these years.

One interesting aside is that Saul Caston, later conductor of the Denver Symphony, crossed our paths again. In 1958, Ed was doing his residency at the Philadelphia General Hospital with a grant from the American Heart Association for research on the effects of smoking, cholesterol and lipids on heart disease. One of the patients who came to him was Saul Caston, who was a heavy smoker and having some problems. Ed came home and said he'd just begged Caston to stop smoking. Saul was a good-looking and relatively young man, but he refused to quit. I think he died two or three years later of a heart attack.

Stage Door Canteen, 1945

I had been brought to the attention of Mrs. Meyer Davis, the wife of the most important commercial bandmaster in Philadelphia.[2] Mrs. Davis was a pop pianist and her job at the time was to supply musical talent for the USO Stage Door Canteen, the entertainment organization for soldiers and sailors on leave. I had turned 13, so it was pretty exciting for me to be included in a group of teenage and young adult performers. Bach or Mozart would not have worked in this venue, so I played my own arrangement of Don't Fence Me In and Mrs. Davis accompanied me at the Philadephia Stage Door Canteen on February 27, 1945.

---

2 Meyer Davis's orchestras played live music for every major wedding, bar mitzvah and college dance at the time. If anybody was having a party with a dance band, they would want to hire Meyer Davis's orchestra.

Miami Beach, 1945 (and 1951)

I went with Mother and Frances to Miami Beach in April 1945 to perform as one of the "stars" for a major fundraising dinner to benefit Zionist causes. This was when American Jewish people were strongly in favor of the establishment of a homeland in what was then Palestine. My Uncle Alex was the co-chairman for this big dinner. There were some big Hollywood headliners who came to Miami for the banquet at the Victor Hotel on April 11.

The next night, Franklin Delano Roosevelt died. In my diary, I wrote that I cried all night. He was the only president I had known, as he had entered office the same year I was born. He was the father figure for the country and certainly for me, especially since my father died when I was so young.

I returned to Miami twice more to perform in programs related to Uncle Alex's activities as local president of the Zionist Organization of America, first for the American Jewish Congress in July 1945 and then in April 1951 at the Casablanca Hotel.

More Student Days at Curtis

From 1943 through 1947, I only played in the Curtis string orchestra because rehearsals were over by 6 p.m. Full orchestra rehearsals ran from 7 to about 10 p.m., and Mother wouldn't let me come home that late on the trolley, so I was excused.

The 1948-49 year was the 25th Anniversary of Curtis and Alexander Hilsberg was conducting the orchestra and I became a member. He was also quite influential in my training and a true friend. The Anniversary was celebrated in a two-night festival. The first was a symphony concert, for which we played the American premiere of Samuel Barber's Second Symphony and the Brahms Double Concerto with Zimbalist and Piatigorsky as soloists. The second night was an evening of opera conducted by Zimbalist, which included Menotti's early opera, Amelia Goes to the Ball. Zimbalist also coached the two African American student singers, Louise Parker and Theresa Green, in phonetic Russian. They sang the "Letter" scene from Eugene Onegin. Theresa and I crossed paths again when we both performed on the first Community Concert Series for African Americans in Beaufort, South Carolina in 1953, where I was the first white artist to perform on such a series.[3]

---

3 Both had been winners of the Marian Anderson Award. See the full story in "1952-1955" chapter.

Marcel Tabuteau

As a teacher in string class, Marcel Tabuteau was musically strict and expected the best from everyone. When he wasn't pleased, there could be some fiery outbursts of temper, but it was never long before a bright and mischievous twinkle came to his eye and soon we would be hearing a tale of what a real devil he was in his student days, or an amusing incident from his long list of experiences in orchestras and concert halls.

One of his favorite illustrations for the rise and fall of a phrase was a skyrocket and a fireworks display. He said that so many musicians let phrases behave like the smoke of a cheap cigar, which he said just fell from the cigar instead of rising.

I will never forget the time he told us about an incident that occurred when he was playing in an opera house pit orchestra. A rather overweight tenor was singing the role of Siegfried under a tree on stage and when he was finished, he was unable to get up. Three strong stage hands had to come on stage to give him a hand. Tabuteau, in his exuberance of telling the story, hopped onto the platform at Curtis Hall and sat on the floor while describing the tale. We were all laughing as the story ended when he attempted to rise from the floor and found that he could not, whereupon two husky lads from the orchestra had to help him. Of course the students roared even louder. For a minute, Tabuteau seemed a bit angry, but then joined in our laughter. I swear he laughed the loudest!

Alexander Hilsberg

Hilsberg was concertmaster and assistant conductor of the Philadelphia Orchestra and conductor of the Curtis Orchestra during my student and post-grad days. He had piercing blue eyes that could look daggers at errant players when necessary. He was a Russian Jew who had escaped anti-Semitism by going to Asia and always seemed to have a bit of that culture's demeanor. His rehearsal dress was usually a dark blue mandarin jacket.

He was very strict and really tried to impart all of his knowledge and experience. We were always ready to be called stand by stand, or even individually, to play a particularly difficult passage in the piece of the day.

I enjoyed the years I played in the orchestra, but more importantly I enjoyed the personal friendship with Hilsberg. To so many he was a distant, rather stiff man. But, I know that he had a real father instinct that was only fulfilled by his work with children. He had none of his own. Maybe he reminded me of my own father who also had a certain European strictness with a loving underside.

It was my habit to walk up Locust Street with either Veda Reynolds or Hilsberg on Friday afternoon after the Philadelphia Orchestra concerts. I would wait at the backstage door and meet one of them and either walk Veda to Curtis when I was her studio accompanist that day, or I would walk along with Hilsberg to his apartment house further up the street. My walks with him were infrequent but I fondly remember several.

One time when he had chosen Frances to play as soloist with the Philadelphia Orchestra Children's Concerts (she was the first cellist ever chosen as soloist), Hilsberg wanted to be sure the performance was solid. He told me to arrange for her to come up to his apartment for a couple extra coaching rehearsals, with me accompanying on the piano. We did that and the performance went off well.

I am convinced that Hilsberg would not have had the rapport and success he had leading the Children's Concerts if he didn't have that underlying love for children. You can't fool kids.

I remember, too, how excited he was when he was appointed as conductor of the New Orleans Symphony. He was in his sixties and commented to me that he was so young for such an appointment. In those days, one had to be very grey and distinguished to get principal conductorships; the situation is so different now. These last fifty years have seen such amazing changes for women and youthful conductors.

Good Times at Curtis

Despite the rigor of our work, all was not serious study at Curtis. The fun times are frequently the ones I remember best. For instance, Curtis subscribed to a proscenium box so that students could attend the Philadelphia Orchestra concerts. The Academy of Music boxes resembled European royal boxes, with upholstered, high-backed chairs with wide seats. There were eight chairs per box, but of course there were many more of us who wanted to go to the concerts. The young guys, usually the brass players, would take the stubs of those of us who had tickets. They would then climb down the fire exit stairs to the ground floor and hand the stubs to the Curtis students who didn't have tickets. So we'd end up with a dozen people in the box. We'd put the seats together and three of us would sit on two chairs. So we frequently heard a lot more concerts than our allotted four per season.

One of our "inside jokes" was that Marcel Tabuteau, the principal oboist, would play in an almost vaudevillian way to the Curtis box. I particularly remember the Tchaikovsky 4th Symphony second movement, which has little answering phrases between the woodwinds. Tabuteau would play his little five-note figure, and then look up at us and smile to let us know that he knew he'd just played it beautifully. He would frequently tell us in our classes, "I have so few notes, I have to make each one of them a jewel."

Then there was Mrs. Zimbalist's magnificent annual formal Christmas ball. The first portion of the evening was devoted to some sort of entertainment. One year, Menotti had just composed Amahl and the Night Visitors, a Christmas opera of about 45 minutes, which was the first and possibly only opera ever commissioned by a television network (NBC).[4] Mrs. Zimbalist engaged the whole production as the entertainment for the 1952 ball. After the entertainment there was dancing and food.

Another time, the faculty put on a set of skits making absolute fools of themselves. One skit that sticks with me was a spoof on an auditioning Curtis piano prodigy. Rudolf Serkin was wheeled on stage in an old-fashioned wicker perambulator, dressed in a pink-and-white baby bonnet, puffed sleeves, and baby shoes. He crawled under the piano, onto the bench, then played magnificently. He then popped off the bench, crawled back into the carriage and was wheeled off stage. Then Martha Massena[5] played the Minute Waltz by Chopin, wearing gloves. The program finale was an orchestra made up of faculty members who traded instruments. It was pretty dissonant. There were cellists playing violin and violinists playing oboe or clarinet. The solfège teacher, Madame Sofray, played tambourine. The farce was very much in-house. For those of us who were stressed from lesson to lesson, seeing these people out there on stage being so human and silly was absolutely hysterical. Years later, something very similar took place at Marlboro, where everybody switched instruments–Serkin, Busch, et al.– that was equally funny.

Mother's Suitors

Mother's re-marriage opportunities were fairly slim. She was a very attractive woman and only about 43 years old when Father died, so while we were in Philadelphia, she was still in her late 40's. She had only been married a little over 10 years. I guess if "Mr. Right" had come along, she would have remarried. It wasn't that her suitors weren't nice, it was just that she was particularly concerned about taking on step-children.

Mr. Valois did make overtures. He was a devout Catholic and a very nice, tall and handsome man. He had been introduced to Mother by Johnnie Vincent, a friend of hers from Oregon who was quite successful as a food editor for one of the New York newspapers. Johnnie was a tall, good-looking woman with red hair, also a widow, who may have dated him too. Mr. Valois evidently liked red-heads.

As a salesman, Mr. Valois had to travel a lot. His daughter lived at Ravenhill, a Catholic boarding school in the suburbs of Philadelphia. It turned out to be a nice connection for me as I played concerts at Ravenhill even long after Mother and Valois stopped dating. I also took school achievement tests there.

---

4   The TV premiere was in 1951.
5   She was a faculty secondary piano teacher.

My General Studies

Mother was concerned about my academic standing. I was about 12 when I started taking the Pennsylvania state exams, which were mainly for adults to earn their high school equivalency certificates. I didn't have to take these, but Mother always wanted me to have the piece of paper that could prove my academic achievement. She thought it was very important for me to get a real high school diploma, which I finally got from West Philadelphia High School. There were hundreds of adults at the exam held at the Pennsylvania College of Pharmacy; I was the only child. Exams were two or three hours long. English and foreign language exams earned 1 to 4 credits, depending on how well you did on the test.

The first time, I took a four-year, four credit English exam and didn't pass. Mother said that if I passed two years, that was fine, but I should just do really well. Nobody coached me. My Curtis tutor didn't know about the exam and Mother had never taken one. The sections were timed and if you didn't get through at least part of every section of the exam, you didn't pass. I didn't understand that timing was crucial and that I should stop a section when time was up. I worked my way through the first workbook but never got to the second. The desk monitors were kind; they sent back comments saying that I had done very well, except that I obviously didn't know how to take the exam, and they explained the problem to Mother. The next time, Frances took the exams along with me so she could learn the routine. She passed five units at age 11 which set her up for high school graduation at 15 and two bachelor's degrees by 18.

I look back on what was such a self-motivated education. It is living proof that a person with good little grey cells will become educated given the opportunity. I was so excited about learning.

An extra tutor became available when Mother's former violin student, Fay Mort, came to Philadelphia for a year or two while her husband was stationed at the Naval Base. She was a biology teacher from Salem, Oregon. Mother asked Fay to teach me. She lived only two blocks from Curtis, so I would go to her apartment where she would give me lunch and teach me some basic science, including biology and physiology. Fay would send me to the public library with a science reading list. The tutor at Curtis would not touch any topic that had to do with science.

I did elementary lab work in Fay's kitchen. My fondest memory was drawing the digestive system. She piqued my curiosity, so I read more and more books on my own.

The library at Curtis seemed to be filled with anything that someone decided to buy. There was a limited number of children's books; I read them all. With the Curtis tutor, Miss Wesner, we read Shakespeare as well as Beowulf and Chaucer in old English. She was a Bryn Mawr alumna and very much into the classics.

I was very good in history. Later when I went to college, I was able to take an advanced course in U.S. government, as I knew the history so well.

Since we traveled a lot, I adored geography and knew it well, especially U.S. geography, which I frequently learned first-hand.

During this time we were at war with Japan and no one was interested in Asian geography. The propaganda against the Japanese was very complicated—at least for children. There were frightening posters that presented caricatures of Japanese soldiers. At the time I had no idea of the Holocaust or what was happening to Jews. I knew that Hitler was a bad guy. We were extremely patriotic. Our country was being threatened and we were acutely aware of shortages and blackouts.

World War II Memories

Pictures seem to flood to mind when I look back on my experiences during World War II. One is the enjoyment we used to have with train travel. Trains were so comfortable. We were poor and had to sit up in coach, but even then, on trains like the Super Chief from Chicago to Los Angeles, the ride was great. There were dome-liner cars from which we could see everything, a great living geography lesson.

Years later when I flew over areas like the Grand Canyon, Arizona and New Mexico, I had a vivid memory of what I had learned traveling by train. I was able to point out specific spots in the terrain to the stewardess, even better than some of the announcements from the pilot.

If you could afford to have a roomette on the train, it was very private, with a berth and bathroom. It was a bit of a problem if you had a small roomette; once you put the berth down you couldn't use the toilet because it was underneath the bed. There was a bathroom at the end of the train car for urgent situations.

People were so polite. The porters, waiters and conductors were very accommodating; it was like being on a cruise ship today. Between Chicago and New York, the porters were still very nice but the trains weren't as clean or new. The eastern trains didn't have the lounge chairs like the western trains.

The trains were constantly filled with soldiers; it was really very exciting. When I was ten, we traveled west for the first time after Father died. The train was full of young guys. I was just entering pre-adolescence and the kids that were soldiers did not seem much older than me. They looked so glamorous in their uniforms. During my teenage years, servicemen were it! Maybe that is why I fell in love with a sailor.

We traveled through such beautiful scenery, places like the Green River in Colorado. In Arizona and New Mexico, a Native American came on board as a tour guide. He pointed out interesting sights all day long; it was an educational experience for the children. We saw Indian villages near the tracks. It looked romantic to me then because it was like I saw in books, but they must have been quite poor.

I vividly remember the young soldiers. We all felt like those boys were family. We felt so close as a country. We felt a swell of pride. I kept scrapbooks with newspaper clippings that explained how the war was going.

We read the newspapers and watched the newsreels at the movies to follow the progress of the war. Five-minute newsreels called "The Eyes and Ears of the World" were shown in theaters before the featured movie. They used to turn a camera towards the audience, as if the lens was looking directly at us.

Everybody was involved in patriotic acts, including children. At first we were told to save aluminum foil because in those days each stick of gum was wrapped in wax paper covered with aluminum foil. We made balls of it and when they reached about the size of a baseball, we would turn them in for scrap metal.

Many basic necessities were rationed. For instance, you could not buy a new tube of toothpaste unless you turned in your old tube, and it had to be pretty well squeezed out if you wanted to get a new one. There were no plastics.

You couldn't buy tires. A lot of people just put their cars up on blocks for the duration of the war. Gasoline was rationed anyway, so unless you were a doctor or contributing to the war effort in some way, it was difficult to obtain.

Nylon did not yet exist for hose; it came in after the parachutes. Mother had 2 or 3 pairs of silk hosiery and she darned them if they got a run so she could wear them again. Those hose lasted her through the whole war.

When the war first broke out, when we were still in New York, part of my patriotic effort included knitting woolen squares for the Red Cross to make into afghans for the soldiers. They had to be a certain number of inches square. I often dropped stitches, so I always had a hole someplace or else pulled it out of alignment because I split the yarn. Still, I would sit on the subways and buses and knit those squares. Some poor soldier must have thought there were moths in his blanket.

People helped each other without much fanfare; there was no other way for everyone to get along. My uncle Harry used to empty out his cash register of ration coins. These were cardboard coins that came in various denominations and were used as change for food stamps. Uncle Harry would send packets to Mother so that she could use them for extra food. Also, he would send us slabs of bacon and cans of ham to keep us going.

There was such excitement on V-E Day, May 8, 1945. Everybody was downtown celebrating the victory. Frances and I went there with Mother and Nina, a friend from Portland. There was such a crowd, it was unbelievable. A young sailor ran up, grabbed and kissed me because they were kissing every girl in the area.

We were by the Academy of Music at Locust and Broad Streets. It was packed with screaming people. There were horns, whistles, cars honking and church bells peeling. We stayed for a couple of hours, walking and just watching the crowd. Harvey's, where we usually bought ice cream sodas, was so jammed and everybody was so thirsty that the soda fountains ran out of fizz.

As Frances, Mother and I had been going to Oregon in the summers, we were more aware than some of our Philadelphia friends of the Japanese war front. In Philadelphia, there was more interest in the European front so I have no remembrance of any shock over dropping a bomb over Hiroshima. All I knew was that the Japanese had surrendered. My friends really knew little of what was going on in Europe, but Mother worried about her first cousin Gertrude and her daughter Jacqueline in Belgium. Gradually, we learned that Gertrude's husband and mother had been killed in the camps, and that Gertrude and Jacqueline had escaped to the south in so-called free France. Gertrude got in touch with Cousin Herbert van Straaten after the war to ask for help. We sent food. Gertrude and Mother had met when Mother was studying in Belgium and they had remained friends. We became aware that there had been a tragedy but all my thoughts were on Curtis and graduating.

Kennebunkport, Maine–Summer 1948

Mother, Frances and I spent the summer of 1948 at Kennebunkport, Maine. Our dear friend, Ruth Bradley, was music director for an arts and music camp called Music Meadows. Ruth was playing a series of concerts there and she invited Frances and me to join her. The camp arranged for us to live very inexpensively. We could spend the summer in Maine and get away from the heat of Philadelphia.

We rented a room in the house of the Congregational minister, Reverend Neal, for about $60 for the summer. The rent included kitchen privileges but we usually ate dinner at the camp. It was a good experience in terms of our musical studies. I learned a lot of new repertoire and Frances did, too.

In return for the Neals' hospitality, I played during offertories every Sunday at his church. Reverend Neal used to say that when I played they got more money in the silver plate. They partly lived on that money.

Kennebunkport was a picturesque, typical New England town with its white clapboard church. There was a semi-professional summer stock playhouse which featured some big-name Broadway actors as headliners. I remember meeting Libby Holman who is probably unknown today but had a fairly big career on Broadway. I was so excited because I got to be an usher for a whole week, wearing a black skirt and white blouse. Then we got to go backstage, meet the actors and get a little smell of grease paint. It was so much fun.

Then the camp hosted a big sixteenth birthday party for me.

Second Performance with the New York Philharmonic, December 18, 1948

When I was fifteen years old, I won a competition to be soloist with the New York Philharmonic for the second time. The final audition was an hour-long broadcast playing the Tchaikovsky and Mendelssohn concertos on WQXR. That was when I first met Abram Chasins, who later became quite influential in my broadcasting activities. Leonid Hambro and Jascha Zayde accompanied me on the piano. The following fall, when I was sixteen, I played Mendelssohn with Igor Buketoff as the conductor of the concert at Carnegie Hall.

From Student to Staff at Curtis

My last year before graduation, Zimbalist decided to give master classes on Sunday, from noon until 7:00 p.m. Each student got an individual lesson while the rest of us listened. He did that for about two years. Amongst the other students were Aaron Rosand, Toshiya Ito, Joseph Silverstein, Joe Pepper, Marie Shefeluk and Vivian Bertolami. Billy Sokoloff[6] would usually accompany the classes.

I had always been an excellent piano sight reader. As the other violin students couldn't play the piano very well, when they saw me walking by the practice studios, they'd ask me to come play the piano part for them so they'd know how it sounded. I got quite good at playing just about any accompaniment to concertos, sonatas, etc.

Billy knew about this. One Sunday, he was to play in a chamber music concert at the Academy of Music. It was a 3 p.m. concert, so he had to leave class by 2. Zimbalist excused him and Billy asked me to sit in for him, which I did. I don't know if Zimbalist realized how good I was on the piano, but I did a good job. About a week later, I got called into the school business office and was told Zimbalist requested that I take over the studio accompanying for Ivan Galamian, Veda Reynolds and others as needed. Zimbalist had decided to put me on the staff and pay me the royal sum of $1.50 per hour. I accompanied eight to ten hours for Galamian, and about six hours for Veda. I got to be very busy. Fortunately, I had finished all of my academic work, so all I had to do was the accompanying, my violin lessons, the many orchestral rehearsals leading up to the 25th Anniversary concerts, chamber music, and prepare for my graduation recital.

Zimbalist took me out to lunch one day and told me that he wanted to give me my diploma, but would continue to teach me as a post-graduate. He said that I could also stay in the orchestra. This arrangement would allow me to play in competitions and concerts without the written permission required of all students. So he freed me to do what I wanted, while still allowing me to complete post-graduate studies at Curtis and stay on the staff. Zimbalist always treated me with kindness and his extension of my education was generous and supportive. At heart, he was a "father" who loved his musical "children" as his own.

Felix Sitjar was my orchestra stand partner in the 1948 and 1949 years. He was of Filipino descent and a good violinist. I only found out recently that prior to attending Curtis, Felix was in the only movie that Jascha Heifetz ever made, They

---

6   Vladimir ("Billy") Sokoloff was Zimbalist's accompanist and a member of Curtis faculty

Shall Have Music. It was sort of the precursor to the film Fame that came out some years later. While re-watching that film, I suddenly realized that I was seeing this young Filipino boy, my buddy Felix, in the youth orchestra accompanying Heifetz. I'd seen the movie many times before and yet I'd never noticed him. In 2007, I finally found out that he had been in the Los Angeles Youth Orchestra, Felix's hometown orchestra. Of course, the film was made in Hollywood, so they used the local youth orchestra.

I continued with my work as Curtis staff accompaniment for almost seven years. Meanwhile, I had access to all the activities and privileges of Curtis without the student restrictions. Zimbalist didn't really let me go as his student until I won the Naumburg in 1952 and played my New York debut. When I started touring for Columbia Artists, I didn't have much time for accompanying either.

Curtis Graduation, 1949

During my graduating year,[7] I formed an all-girl Curtis string quartet with Nancy Heaton, second violin, Marilyn Woodruff, viola, and Jackie Epinoff, cello. We played several concerts around town, including some contemporary music programs. It was the beginning of what has been a wonderful career addition for me: playing chamber music.

---

7 In 1957 I graduated again, receiving a Mus.B. degree.

VEDA REYNOLDS

Autographed portrait, 1947

VEDA REYNOLDS

Veda and I would have known each other as students from 1938 through 1940. I have no conscious memory of her, though she said she remembered me. We both entered Curtis at the same time, but she was seventeen and I was five. We both played on the same concert of Zimbalist students when I was seven.

When I returned to Curtis at the age of eleven, she had already graduated and was Zimbalist's assistant. Shortly thereafter she joined the Philadelphia Orchestra as a young woman of about 22 years old.

All the young men had been drafted for World War II. So, miracles of miracles, the Philadelphia Orchestra hired a woman, which in those days was very unusual— there were only a couple of other women.

Veda was in the first violin section, and certainly the first very young woman to hold that position in the Philadelphia Orchestra. She was taken on a provisional contract, which was supposed to be for the war time only, on a year-to-year basis. It was assumed that when the men came back, her contract would not be renewed.

However, Ormandy appreciated quality. When the men came back from the war he had to take back those who had been drafted, but there was always some attrition. Instead of having auditions and hiring someone else, he kept Veda. That's how she ended up playing in the Orchestra for 23 years.

As Zimbalist's assistant, she taught me in so many ways and was an important influence. I was a very stubborn student and had very definite ideas of how I was going to handle the instrument. Veda had training other than from Zimbalist as she had studied previously with Carl Flesch and Ivan Galamian in Paris and Belgium. As a result, she had some different ways of approaching the instrument: especially the bow arm. We used to have some royal fights. She would show me and I would try her way, but I really couldn't change my bow arm. I didn't want to and Zimbalist said I didn't have to. In spite of that friction, I learned a number of bow techniques from her, along with so many other valuable things including Veda's analytical approach to learning.

As a teacher, Zimbalist wouldn't work on basic technique. That was to be done by the assistant. It was always the major technical material that I had to improve, which I worked on with Veda. Zimbalist would tell me what he wanted and then I would have Veda explain what he really meant. He and I always tussled over fingerings and bowings as our hands were so different. He had his way of playing suitable for a man's hand and I frequently didn't find it comfortable. He would get very upset with me because he wanted me to play it exactly the way he told me.

Veda would commiserate with me and sort of ameliorate things by acting as a go-between. If something was really uncomfortable she would allow me to say, "I talked this over with Miss Reynolds, and she suggested maybe you could let me try it this way." That didn't happen very often though.

She had a darling elderly mother, Naomi, who was an amazing Scotch lady. Naomi had beautiful blue eyes and was thin as a rail. She could really save a penny, but I think they always had to until Veda got hired by the Orchestra. Before that, I don't think they had two pennies to pinch. So Veda's mother cooked for her, kept the apartment, shopped and made all of her clothes.

Veda never got married, though she had several opportunities. I know that there were a couple of fellows from her church who courted her.

She was the truest and most honest friend. She was one of the few people in the whole world that I could trust; if I said something to her I knew it would go no further. I was a jabberer and she was a listener: a perfect pair.

As I became a young adult, our roles began to change. She was always my teacher, but as I matured we became really close friends.

It seemed as though she had never really had a childhood, so I let her share mine to a certain extent. One time I decided we should go to the Barnum and Bailey Circus because I had never seen one and I discovered she never had either. So we went to the circus and sat right in front. (Even in those days I always liked the best.) All of a sudden, a huge gorilla got loose and jumped into the stands. The next thing I knew, the gorilla had pounced behind my chair, put his arms around me, and they took my picture. Everybody was just laughing like fools. It happened so fast I didn't know what was going on. I was so near-sighted that I didn't realize until he had left and everybody was laughing that it wasn't a real gorilla, just a man in a gorilla suit.

When I was about 17, I started going to New York by myself to prepare for big competitions. I would go for coaching by Otto Herz. Though Zimbalist heard me occasionally and I was taking a few lessons with Veda, I needed an inspirational coach with a piano.

I went into New York on the train, often on Tuesday because the Philadelphia Orchestra played at Carnegie Hall on Tuesdays.

Jesse Tatton, the Philadelphia Orchestra librarian, would take me into the Hall with him from backstage to hear the wonderful concerts for free. That was how I happened to hear Emil Gilels, the Russian pianist who was one of the first Russian artists to come to the United States after World War II. This was during Stalin's rule and there was great difficulty in getting anything or anyone out of Russia. David Oistrakh, Gilels and the Moiseyev Ballet were the first to come that I heard.

The concerts at Carnegie Hall started at 8:30 and ended by about 10:00. This made it impossible to catch the last late express train. Frequently some other orchestra members, Veda and I would go out and get a bite to eat. Then we would get on the slow train from New York to Philadelphia, called "the milk run" because of all the stops. An express from New York to Philadelphia took an hour and a half while the milk run took 2¼ hours. Then I would have to take a cab home.

I think now how frightened I would be to have a young girl come home at 2 o'clock in the morning from the railroad station, frequently with a borrowed Strad. But then nobody ever thought anything of it. When I got into a taxi in Philadelphia or New York or wherever I traveled, I felt totally safe. With those taxi drivers it was like having a dad drive me. They would talk to me and walk me up to my door and make sure that my key was in the lock. Nowadays they sit in the front seat cage and hope they don't get killed. How things change.

Veda was a wonderful violinist. I think the only reason she didn't become one of the world's great violin soloists was because she just didn't have that extroverted spark. Even though she obviously was self-confident, she had no sense of trying to push herself forward.

She had to support herself and her mother, so when she got into the Philadelphia Orchestra and the money was so good, there was just no other choice. I don't remember what they paid in those days, but whatever it was it was certainly better than you could get on tour as a soloist.

She did get some wonderful orchestral opportunities, including assistant con-certmaster at the Robin Hood Dell several times. One summer she was concert-master of the National Symphony in Washington, D.C. at the summer concerts at Watergate. She made history there as the first woman concertmaster of any major U.S. symphony orchestra during either the summer or winter seasons.

Veda received wonderful reviews for her New York debut at Town Hall. She played the Brahms G Major Sonata, which I loved. It is still one of my favorites.

At Curtis, I accompanied Veda's student lessons. She was always so kind, thorough, and gave constructive criticism. Sometimes her students would come in and things just wouldn't be good at all. I would think to myself, "Oh my, she is really going to tear them apart." But I learned very rapidly that she always started with an encouraging remark. Whether their playing was good, bad or somewhere in-between, she would always find something nice to say. As a teacher I have followed her example with all my students, even when the lesson is poor. I always first say, "This was really quite good" or "You made real progress," even if I have to stretch a bit to say it.

After she left Curtis, several of her students—like David Harrington of the Kronos Quartet, and Gilles Apap—became quite successful.

When Veda started the Philadelphia String Quartet (originally the Stringart Quartet), it was composed of musicians from the Philadelphia Orchestra. The Quartet began by playing "Coffee Concerts" at the Benjamin Franklin Hotel, which served coffee and pastries while the audience listened to chamber music concerts.

As the quartet gained a bigger repertoire, the four musicians decided they didn't want to spend the rest of their lives playing in the Orchestra. So they got a position at the University of Washington as "quartet-in-residence." This was still a fairly unusual kind of situation in 1966, when they moved to Seattle.

After Veda moved to the Pacific Northwest, we saw each other infrequently. She visited us in Los Angeles a few times, including a couple of times when the Quartet was performing in town. Also, she visited our second home in Lincoln Beach, Oregon. She was always wonderful with our girls. Although she never had children of her own, she had worked with kids all her life, so she had good instincts with them and they liked her very much.

When the Philadelphia String Quartet, came to Los Angeles to play a John Vincent work, the Los Angeles Times ran an article on January 15, 1969 announcing the reception that Ed and I were hosting after the concert on January 24. At the time John was Chair of the Music Department at UCLA and a good friend. The Quartet played the West Coast premiere of his String Quartet No. 2 on the program at Schoenberg Hall, UCLA. As I was so involved with Los Angeles composers, hosting a reception was just a natural thing to do for him and the quartet.

After a number of years, Veda decided to move on from the Quartet. First she went to the North Carolina School of the Arts in Winston-Salem, where she was on the faculty and played in the school's chamber orchestra. I think she spent two or three years there, during which time she had started going back to France to visit during the summer.

She had lived in France and Belgium from the time she was two years old until she came to Curtis. She spoke fluent French and was very comfortable with the culture and the people. She started doing summer master classes outside of Paris, where a friend acted as a manager for the sessions. This friend had been very close to Ginette Neveu, the great French violinist who was so tragically killed in an airplane crash on her way to her third tour in the U.S., right after the Second World War. I think the success of the master classes clinched Veda's decision to move back to France permanently.

In a way, the French people were more respectful to senior citizens, and she was getting up in age. She also liked a minimalist lifestyle, didn't like to do a lot of cooking and was very comfortable living in a one-room studio apartment. She was appointed to the faculty of the Conservatories in Paris and Lyon. But France had a mandatory retirement age of 65, so at that point she had to relinquish her official position of professor at both schools. She continued to have a very large class of private students, many of whom were preparing for the very strenuous conservatoire entrance exams and auditions. She would travel once every otherweek from Paris to Lyon to continue her teaching there.

When Marcia was a sophomore at USC, we decided to go to France for a few weeks to see if it would be a good place to study during her junior year. We spent a week with

Veda in Paris and then went on to the Academie d'Eté in Nice. Marcia studied harp while I did some violin teaching, assisting my colleague Aaron Rosand.

Another time, when Marcia performed with the Los Angeles Philharmonic at the Salzburg Festival, Ed and I made the first of several trips abroad to hear Marcia and also took advantage of the opportunity to travel in Europe. Ed, Sallie and I took the Transalpine train to Paris. (Marcia had to return to L.A. for the Hollywood Bowl season.) Sallie went on to England, while Ed and I spent five days in Paris visiting Veda. We had dinner together every night and spent the days together. It was very special.

Our last visit was the summer when we were on our way to Prague for the 1999 World Harp Congress. I had started videotaping oral histories of a couple of the seniors from Curtis who I thought were so special, including Eudice Shapiro and David Schwartz. Fortunately, I was able to videotape Veda for about an hour. We covered her early life, opinions on music and experiences in the Philadelphia Orchestra. Considering that it was only a 60-minute tape, the video reveals a rare insight into her way of thinking and her personality. At the time I was concerned because she looked so very thin. She seemed to have a good appetite and was getting around, although she was having some eyesight problems. She remained extremely independent.

Then, all of a sudden, in December, I got a phone call from a former student of hers, Evan Rothstein, who was a violin professor in Paris. He'd been trying to reach her for close to a week. She had not shown up to her class in Lyon and her students called him, so he called Curtis for outside contacts, and Curtis referred him to me. Fortunately, when I was in Paris that last time, I had insisted that she give me a legal contact in case she got sick so that I could fly to Paris and possibly take care of her, because we were that close. I called the woman in Paris who was her executor, and she told me that Veda was ill and had gone to a Christian Science retreat in Germany, and she gave me the phone number.

Meanwhile, I called Professor Rothstein back because he had been calling the police and hospitals. I told the executor that there was going to be a police investigation if she didn't reveal that Veda was alive and okay. Veda was upset because she didn't want to be disturbed. She was a very devout member of the Christian Science religion, which the French government didn't recognize, so she had to go to Germany. Two weeks later, I was informed that she was gone. Nobody ever knew what her illness had been. The Christian Science Center wouldn't tell, and if her executor knew, she wouldn't tell. I knew some of Veda's cousins in Philadelphia and got in touch with them and we did what we could. One of the things that I was concerned about was her violin, which I knew she had willed to Curtis. I wanted

Curtis to know so that the violin didn't get lost or stolen.[1] Because of the French tax system, it took Curtis over five years to get the violin to Philadelphia.

That is basically the end of the story of our long and wonderful friendship.

A few years before her death, around her 70th birthday, with the help of Director Gary Graffman I convinced Curtis to honor Veda. The school brought her to Philadelphia from Paris for the event. We invited all of her students from around the world to a concert in her honor and had a big picture of her hung on the wall at Curtis in her former studio. I was pleased to be able to arrange that because so many of what I call the unsung heroes of Curtis are not sufficiently recognized. Veda was certainly one of them.

In the spring following her death, I was able to arrange a memorial gathering at Curtis for all of her students. We showed the videotape, which is now in the Curtis library archives.

So I've been able to at least ensure her place in the archives at Curtis.

Veda remained a part of my life until her untimely death in January 2000.

---

1 This happened to Erica Morini's Davidoff Stradivarius, which was stolen from her apartment following her death in 1995.

TANGLEWOOD
SUMMER, 1950

"I remember very well your splendid playing of Mendelssohn Concerto."
Vladimir Bakaleinikoff, November 13, 1950

Jacqueline Ibert, harp; Diana; Jacques Ibert, composer; John Shu, cello
After American premiere performance of Ibert's Trio for harp, violin & cello.

TANGLEWOOD, SUMMER 1950

I attended Tanglewood in the summer of 1950. In 1949, right after graduating from Curtis, I had tried to earn enough money to buy a good violin bow. I worked my tail off by literally sitting on my tail playing the piano for 8 to 10 hours a day as a dance accompanist at Tripp Lake girls' camp in Maine. By the next summer I'd had enough of that and was relieved when I won a full scholarship to attend Tanglewood.

My audition was at Carnegie Recital Hall before Isaac Stern and William Kroll.[1] At the last minute, Stern decided to ask that the violinists play scales for which Heifetz was supposedly famous for requesting. Each candidate walked in with umpteen concertos and yet they were uncomfortable with scales. It's an old, famous story: So backstage everyone was furiously practicing scales and I thought I'd show them right off the bat that I was prepared. When I went on stage, the judges said, "Will you play a scale, please?" Most violinists go through all the standard scales in three octaves, but there are a few scales that go four octaves. I knew all of them, so I promptly launched into the hardest one, B major, which is as high as you can go on the E string. I remember Stern saying, "Hmm, that is very interesting...do that one again." I just ran it up and down. Along with the pieces I played, that blew them away. I got the scholarship.

On the way north to Massachusetts, I had obtained a job to play for two weeks before Tanglewood started. Veda had played at a fancy health resort at Lake Mohonk and told me about the job. The hotel hired classical musicians to entertain its guests. I was there about 24 hours, rehearsed and played only one concert when I got the worst ear infection of my life. I was in pain.

I was 17 years old and the only other time I had ever been away from home was the summer before at Tripp Lake. Fortunately there was a doctor at the hotel who looked at my ear and said I had an abscess. So I got on the train for the ten-hour trip to Philadelphia. I called my mother and I think I got home by 7 o'clock that night. I thought for sure I was going to be deaf.

I lost 10 pounds and missed the first week of Tanglewood. But they held my place and I finally came up there feeling very weak. The first week I became assistant concertmaster of the Tanglewood Symphony. Also, I was assigned to the orchestra pit at the opera house which was cement and felt like a refrigerator. I finally went in to talk with Ralph Berkowitz, who was Director. We are now very

---

1 First violinist of the Kroll Quartet.

friendly but he was difficult and rigid in those days. I remember he'd say, "Oh, dahling, it's good for you. It's good for you." Well, the cold pit was not good for me and I finally got out of that.

Tanglewood is located in a beautiful setting, nestled in the Berkshires overlooking a lake. It was always a temptation to play hooky. Friday night was the Tanglewood Orchestra's big concert and Saturday morning we would sight-read. As concertmaster from the second week on, I was supposed to maintain discipline to a certain extent. I remember one very hot Saturday when everyone was exhausted. As players snuck out, the orchestra kept getting smaller and smaller and I think we ended up with a string quartet sight reading Beethoven's 9th Symphony! Then we finally all ended up in the lake.

I played under many amazing conductors that summer, including Serge Koussevitzky, the Boston Symphony Orchestra (BSO) director. During my first week, I saw him for the first time. He was probably 5'2"or 5'3" by my estimation in comparison to myself. He was quite elderly; in fact, he died the following year before Tanglewood started again. I was really very lucky that I got a chance to work under him, because he is an important part of the music history of the 20th century.

Koussevitzky had a number of personal eccentricities. In July, he would come dressed in a full suit, a wool tweed cape that went down to his knees, a cap with a visor and white gloves. He would shake your hand but wouldn't touch you. All he would do was just roll the part by the palm back so that you'd feel the sense of his touch, but his skin was very sensitive and he didn't want to touch anybody or come into contact with germs.

During our rehearsal, he walked up and down the stage at the Tanglewood Shed, listening stand by stand to the first violin section as we played. He had never heard me before. I was very competitive in those days and when he came by, I played my best. I got called into his office the next day and was offered the opportunity to play solo the next Friday with the Symphony at the Shed. He wanted to know what concertos I knew and I listed them. He chose the Mendelssohn Concerto and coached me with the selected apprentice conductor. He agreed to excuse me from the orchestra that week and after that I would be concertmaster.

I traded the concertmaster post on alternating weeks with Robert Gerle, with whom I remained friends until his death in 2005. He ended up at USC before me and married Marilyn Neeley, a Los Angeles pianist. He later became a conductor and violin professor at the University of Maryland, Baltimore County. I remember he was a refugee from the Nazis, just a teenager at the time. He had saved his life by playing the violin. He wasn't sent to a concentration camp, but evidently was hidden by his violin teacher. The story I heard was that he had been stopped in the street with his violin case by some Nazi soldiers or Gestapo, and they made him identify himself. They wanted him to prove that he was a violinist, demanding that he play immediately. He played the Tchaikovsky Concerto on the street. The soldiers were educated enough to realize Bob was really playing Tchaikovsky and let him go.

Bob played the Brahms Concerto with the Tanglewood Orchestra when I was concertmaster, then he was concertmaster the week I played the Mendelssohn Concerto. After that, I continued on as concertmaster for the rest of the festival.

I was also placed in a string quartet coached by Jean Bedetti, a wonderful cellist who had been principal cello of the BSO. Though retired, he still came back in summertime to coach. He was one of those vociferous Frenchmen who were marvelous musicians. He took me outside in the hallway after the first rehearsal with the second-rate group in which I'd been randomly placed and said, "You know, this is not for you. You leave it up to me. I'll get you in a good group." So I was put in a super group. The cellist was another Curtis graduate: Robert Sayre. The violist, Bob Oppelt, was a fellow whose name I've seen many times since in the American String Teachers Association Magazine.

Bedetti assigned us the Ravel String Quartet and worked with us for two weeks. Then he put us in the Festival Chamber Music Recital and we were recognized for the best chamber music performance of the summer.

Then one day I received a letter in my mail slot explaining that I had been awarded the Sigma Alpha Iota prize by the faculty, which was awarded to "Most Outstanding Woman Student" for the summer. It came with a full scholarship, which I already had anyway, so it was just another honor.

That summer I also played de Falla's El amor brujo under the Brazilian conductor Eleazar de Carvalho. It was a funny coincidence that a couple of years later, when I auditioned for the Philadelphia Orchestra and I lost, Ormandy offered to make me concertmaster, on his recommendation, in São Paulo under de Carvalho. However, I didn't want to go live in Brazil.

De Carvalho was a real character. He would dress in absolutely spotless white trousers with a dark blue blazer and a Mexican peasant straw hat. People would find him sitting alongside the road with his feet in the ditch studying scores. And when he would conduct our orchestra, he would beat time on his chest, saying, "di ga, di ga, boom, di ga, di ga..."

We also played El Salon Mexico by Copland. Copland was a formidable contemporary American composer, certainly the granddaddy of them all. He was a relatively friendly man, quite tall and kind of rangy. He held composition classes every year at Tanglewood and had a close relationship with the BSO.

I saw Copland again on his eightieth birthday when he went around the United States attending several music festivals held in his honor. David Berfield, the pianist with whom I worked at the time, was on the faculty at California State University, Fullerton, which hosted one of these festivals. David and I had recorded Copland's Ukulele Serenade, which was one of two violin pieces that Copland composed in the jazz idiom. It is short, rhythmically very tricky, extremely syncopated and just a devil of a little piece to put together.

David decided that we should surprise Copland and put it on one of the festival programs. At the end of a concert of Copland's chamber music, David asked Mr. Copland to come out on the stage and sit down. We then came out and played the Ukulele Serenade. The audience absolutely loved it. Copland turned to me afterwards and, right in front of the audience he said, "Did I write that?" We gave him a copy of our recording as a present and assured him, "Yes, Mr. Copland, you really did." He had written it so long ago he had forgotten. I guess nobody had played it for him in a while and probably over 50 years had passed since he had written it. That was such a wonderful experience for me. I remember we went to the reception following the performance, and Copland was walking around clutching his little record, so happy that he had rediscovered his piece.

Leonard Bernstein

I also worked with Leonard Bernstein at Tanglewood. I've known a lot of famous musicians in my life, but without a question this man was one of the true geniuses of the 20th century. There just wasn't anything he couldn't do and do it better than anybody else. If there is really such a thing as a musical genius, he was the living, breathing epitome of what one should be.

I could read score from the piano, transpose all the instruments in the orchestra, play violin and piano, and improvise. I knew an awful lot about music. And I didn't just think I knew it. I knew I knew it. I was very confident, even egotistical. Despite all of that, I was totally in awe of Bernstein. His genius made mine seem piddling by comparison.

He was a formidable pianist and such a natural. I vividly remember him playing one of the major Ravel orchestral scores in Koussevitzky's dressing room at the Shed. The BSO used a Baldwin piano at the time and the company supplied a little Acrosonic spinet in the room. Bernstein could sit down at that little Baldwin, play a full symphonic score, and make it sound like the horns or winds and he'd sing other parts and never miss a note.

Bernstein was born in 1918, so he was only in his early thirties at the time. He had studied at Harvard and Curtis. He was a brilliant man and could be a "bad boy," but everybody liked him. Some people would make fun of him for his flamboyance, but it was always with admiration. I don't know if it was just before or right after that he took dance lessons from Martha Graham. I had been an accompanist for a dance teacher who was a graduate of Martha Graham and I had watched classes in modern dance, so I was very familiar with the moves. There was no question in my mind that he did a lot of the so-called contraction and release movements. He incorporated those dance movements naturally into his conducting.

Friends of mine in the Philadelphia Orchestra, who were frequently nonchalant about everything because they played with everybody, said that when it comes to contemporary music, Bernstein's movements always seemed to fit. Some called it an act but it was very natural and I don't think he could have conducted otherwise.

The week that Bernstein conducted the Tanglewood Orchestra, we also did an all Bach concert with him, with concertos for two, three and four pianos. I was concertmaster and all of the other girls were so jealous. They said, "Oh my God, you get to be so close!" During the concert, instead of walking off the stage between pieces, he came over and stood by me and just sort of draped his arm over my shoulder. I wasn't going to wash that shoulder for a week! Everybody thought he was being so friendly and treating me like a real colleague.

I remember one Bach analysis class during which a group of violinists, myself included, were asked to play movements from the Solo Sonatas. BSO concertmaster Richard Burgin was holding the class when Bernstein just popped in. He analyzed the sonatas and made us begin to recognize the structure and form of the Fugue movements. He had us separate the parts, each following a part through. The voices are so intertwined that it was difficult for one of us to stay on a single voice. This was an example of the kind of thought processes the man had.

I was 18 that summer and got married when I was 23. So it must have been not too long after that summer that Bernstein got the idea to write Candide, because Ed and I saw it on our honeymoon in 1956. Then a couple of years later he wrote West Side Story. At the same time, he was playing Mozart concertos with the orchestra and conducting. He seemed to have an infinite store of energy.

He would kid around at orchestra rehearsals so there were a lot of discipline problems. Koussevitzky was extremely strict and Bernstein wasn't at all. He'd kibbitz around and make jokes, and the kids took advantage.

Koussevitzky had a strong sense of leadership, much like Sir Thomas Beecham, who was well known for his discipline. If ever the audience would titter or talk, Beecham would turn around and hold up his hand and make them stop. Koussevitzky worked similarly. He wouldn't talk, but he would turn around and hold up his hand. He wanted absolute silence before he began a performance. He would just stand there and nothing would happen. We had to sit, bows at the ready, not knowing when he was going to start. One time when we performed the Tchaikovsky 4th Symphony with him, the trumpets also had to be on their toes. Koussevitzky would stand with his head sort of bowed, and his arms down in a totally relaxed fashion. Then, all of a sudden, hardly even looking up and certainly with no pre-signal, the right arm would shoot out and he would just point, like a gun. It was amazing how the musicians responded.

Koussevitzky would stop us when there were discipline problems, which was often since the kids (the Tanglewood Orchestra) would fool around as kids do. The adult members of the BSO were often worse than the kids. I remember him stopping one time and saying, "You know, democracy is a wunderful ting, but not in zee orchèstra." He really meant that.

Probably because of this discipline, when the orchestra played under him, we played extremely well. In fact, a lot of people found the student orchestra more exciting than the professionals. As I was in the orchestra, it was very difficult for me to judge. But if I go to Philadelphia and hear the Curtis Institute Orchestra, I can believe it. I have tape recordings of the Curtis Orchestra from some time ago when Sergiu Celibidache conducted; the orchestra was so outstanding that every note sounded like it was part of a Carnegie Hall solo debut. In fact, they did play at Carnegie on a weekend the Philadelphia Orchestra played and everyone said Curtis was better because the kids were so capable and had endless energy. However, Celibidache had demanded 18 rehearsals!

After Tanglewood, the next time that I saw Koussevitzky was when he came to Philadelphia on tour with the Israel Philharmonic in the spring of 1951. Israel had only been founded in 1948 and they already had a major orchestra. Koussevitzky helped bring the orchestra to the United States. He didn't conduct the whole program, as he had become so frail. I was able to visit him briefly backstage at the Academy of Music. He was really sweet and seemed glad to see me. I was one of a hundred kids from the summer before and though I was one of the leaders, I was honored that he remembered me. He agreed to have the Orchestra's professional photographer take our picture together. He died a few weeks later, in June 1951.

There were so many wonderful conductors at the Tanglewood festival. We played under Richard Burgin who was then the concertmaster of the BSO. Lukas Foss did Schumann's Spring Symphony with us. When we performed Schelomo by Ernest Bloch, there was a big thunderstorm that made it feel almost as if God were present! Margaret Hillis also conducted that summer. She did primarily choral conducting. Women orchestral conductors were still quite unusual in those days.

Tanglewood's Shed stage curves out and there would be thousands of people sitting under the roof and so many more on the lawn that you couldn't see all of them, nor could they see you. There was such a cold breeze there at night, I used to sneak a short-sleeved sweater under my white concert dress because as concertmaster I would sit out in the farthest part of the curve and got the worst breeze. I was so afraid I'd get another cold, especially having just recovered from the ear infection.

We played eight to eleven hours a day: three hours of orchestra, three hours of chamber music and then there was contemporary music. All the student composers were begging the best players to come play their works. So we would sight-read chamber music for fun at night. We had regular symphony and a chamber music concerts each week. After I did the Ravel Quartet, I was put into a trio with Jacques Ibert's daughter, Jacqueline. Ibert was the composer-in-residence that year. We did the American premiere of the harp, cello and violin trio that he wrote specifically for Jacqueline. In fact, one of the reasons there are so many harp parts in Ibert's pieces is because of his daughter. She was a fine harpist and an absolutely charming woman, so petite and so French. She was a mother of three children at the time.

We were coached by Bernard Zighera, principal harpist of the BSO. Then Ibert came in and gave his blessing. Jacqueline had performed the world premiere in France, so she knew the piece well and knew what he wanted. Because the pedals changes are quite difficult, she would swear in French at her father for having written them. I kept in touch with her for about a year; soon after that, she was killed in France in a tragic automobile accident.

That summer I heard Alexander ("Sascha") Schneider as a soloist for the first time. He was the second violinist of the Budapest String Quartet. In one afternoon, before and after dinner, he played all six Bach Solo Sonatas in one shot! Little did I know that when I went to Marlboro, Sascha and I would become close friends. In fact, when he came out to conduct the Los Angeles Chamber Orchestra at the Ambassador Auditorium in Pasadena in the early 90s, I went to see him backstage and helped him prepare to go on stage.

Another conductor under whom I played that summer was Hugh Ross, the choral conductor. Hugh Ross was very English: tall and quite gaunt. His conducting style was rather stiff. We did the Brahms Alto Rhapsody as part of a whole program under his direction which was new for me because I had not been exposed to very much choral music since we didn't have a chorus at Curtis.

Each summer Tanglewood recruited a massive chorus that included anybody who didn't play in the orchestra and most of the singers from the opera department. Many came just to be around Tanglewood. One of the young women who came to sing was my roommate Barbara Blaustein, now Hirschhorn, the daughter of Jacob Blaustein, one of the founding supporters of Israel. He was the president of the American Oil Company (AMOCO) at the time.

Marni Nixon was there, too. She later became quite famous in Hollywood as the singing voice for such movie roles as Audrey Hepburn's Eliza Doolittle in My Fair Lady. The opera group put on Hansel and Gretel and Marni was Hansel. That was one of her first major breaks and I was very impressed. Later, when I came to California, she also became very well known in the contemporary music scene. She made one of the most beautiful recordings of the Vocalise from Bachianas Brasileiros. She has absolute pitch and a pure voice, and is an intelligent singer and very fine musician.

At Tanglewood there were also apprentice conductors. The lead apprentice at the time was Irwin Hoffman. Later, he went to Seattle and then settled in Florida for many years. He ended up marrying a gal named Esther Glazer, who was one of the violinists who was ahead of me in several competitions. It seemed like I had to wait until she would win or quit trying a competition before I could win. Another of life's queer turns happened in 1979 when I was asked to be the only non-harp judge for the American Harp Society's major award at its annual convention in Portland, Oregon. The girl who won that competition was the daughter of Irwin and Esther: Debbie Hoffman. At the time she was in the Pittsburgh Symphony and then went on to be the principal harpist of the Metropolitan Opera Orchestra in New York.

The Korean War broke out during that summer of 1950. Several male students were drafted in the middle of the session. We were in a war again. So all the young men were facing the same thing they had faced a few years before during World War II: conscription. It took the cream of the crop again.

I went back to visit Tanglewood, but I never went back to play. During that one summer in 1950 I had done everything, so there was nothing left to accomplish there. I had won all of the awards, was soloist and concertmaster. I had worked with Koussevitzky, Copland, Bernstein and Ibert. I had done an American premiere. Repetition is frequently a disappointment and with Koussevitzky gone, the Festival was in a state of flux the following year.

The summer of the Tanglewood Reunion in 1990, fortunately or unfortunately, was our farewell visit to some wonderful people, both there and at Marlboro. The Tanglewood Festival decided to have a reunion with as many former students as they could get to come for the 50th anniversary. Approximately 200 alumni showed up. They pulled out all the stops. We had tickets to the BSO concerts for the weekend, various meetings, and a reunion dinner. We stayed at Wheatleigh which, when I had gone there, was an upscale boys' boarding school during the winter and was taken over by male Tanglewood students as a dorm in the summer (the girls were housed in The Lenox School for Boys). By 1990, Wheatleigh had been turned into a very high-class B&B. There were large stairwells and a magnificent gourmet restaurant. When Ed and I traveled, we went five-star whenever possible.

The most important concert that we heard was the Boston Symphony Orchestra, playing Beethoven's 7th Symphony, conducted by Leonard Bernstein. Ed and I were sitting in one of the box seats in the Shed, the big concert hall at Tanglewood, and Joe de Pasquale, the former BSO principal violin, was sitting next to me. We'd known each other since the 1950s and at the time he was on the faculty at Curtis and Principal with the Philadelphia Orchestra. The de Pasquale family was famous in the music world. The older brother, Francis, had been a cellist in the Philadelphia Orchestra; I had known him, but not as well. Billy, Joe's youngest brother, was one of Veda Reynolds's pupils at Curtis, whose lessons I accompanied. We've been friends ever since. Billy retired in 2007 as associate concertmaster of the Philadelphia Orchestra. Another brother, Robert, played in both the Philadelphia Orchestra and the New York Philharmonic.

As we watched Bernstein, Joe and I noticed that something was not right. He seemed to be having difficulty even standing there. By the time he got to the third movement, he just dropped his hands and stopped conducting. The orchestra continued playing and he gave them a head nod now and then. The Orchestra knew the piece so well that they could play it in their sleep. Bernstein sort of lifted his hands a little bit. I remember he wore a white tuxedo jacket with a red handkerchief in his lapel. When he left the stage, he didn't return. People were cheering, but he couldn't even come back for a bow. He died in October, shortly after that performance.

The reunion took place during the first week of August, but it was very cold. There had been a huge rainstorm and I remember we had to walk through mud to reach the Shed. It was so cold that we wrapped ourselves in plastic bags. The first thing I did the next morning was to go buy a wool suit. After that one cold concert, Ed and I walked back to Wheatleigh. The bar was about to close, but I wanted a cognac to warm me up. We were the only people at the bar. There were wonderful choices of aged cognacs. The bartender lined up six or eight little glasses, pouring several to see which one we liked. We discovered Moyet, which we still enjoy. That was one of my fondest memories of the Tanglewood Reunion!

Then there was the moment when one of the other alums came up to me. He remembered sitting in one of the back rows of the violin section when I played the Mendelssohn Concerto. He told me he knew I'd be a famous violinist and admired me. The whole trip was worth it just for that.

PERFORMANCES & COMPETITIONS
1950-1951

"The greater the fireworks the better she played...Yesterday, my admiration grew for the variety of gifts this highly attractive artist possesses."

Paul Hume, *Washington Post*, January 20, 1951

Serge Koussevitsky greets Diana backstage at Academy of Music in Philadelphia after concert of Israel Philharmonic on tour, 1951.

PERFORMANCES AND COMPETITIONS, 1950-1951

Friday Morning Music Club Competition and Awards

Soon after returning from Tanglewood, in the early fall of 1950, I competed for the first Friday Morning Music Club of Washington, D.C. Patrick Hayes Award. I won.

The required repertoire was fairly substantial. I had to play a couple of concertos and a full recital program. This club was affiliated with the National Federation of Music Clubs. The FMMC decided to hold its own national competition and invited young musicians under the age of 25 to compete. It was open to strings, piano and voice.

The preliminaries were judged by a panel of the club members. This preliminary panel listened to individual categories (violinists, pianists and vocalists). Finalists from each category competed against each other and in the end I was the only winner.

One of the preliminary judges, Elma Bergman, with whom I later became friends, came up to me after the first round. She wished me luck, telling me that she was the only violinist on the panel and had voted for me. She was very supportive. When I won she was ecstatic.

The award included a solo recital in Washington, D.C., a cash prize of $1,000, and an appearance as soloist with the National Symphony under the direction of Howard Mitchell at Constitution Hall.

Paul Hume[1] reviewed my solo recital. He became famous shortly after when he wrote a mediocre review of the vocal debut of President Harry Truman's daughter, Margaret. Truman was famous for doing things off the cuff and wrote Hume an irate letter. Newspapers all over the country reported that Truman had gone after his daughter's reviewer. Later, at a luncheon held by the FMMC, during which Paul Hume was presented with an award, my mother said, "He's such a nice young man." Hume had given me a gorgeous review.[2]

When I soloed with the symphony, playing the Tchaikovsky Concerto, the audience included a crowd of adolescents. I wore a sea-foam green chiffon evening gown and when I walked onto the stage, some of the audience members gave me wolf whistles which made the Washington Post headline the next day in addition to the review of my performance.

---

1 The prime music critic of the Washington Post.
2 See quote on chapter page plate.

A nun in the audience, Sister Lillian, sent a personal note backstage for me. She was chaperoning a group of girls from the convent school where she was Mother Superior (Dumbarton College). She said, "I think you are the daughter of Ferenz Steiner who was my cello teacher when I was a novice back in Ogden, Utah." This was true as he had taught in Utah before he moved to Portland and married my mother.

Sister Lillian wanted to meet me. Mother and I were of course happy to meet her. That friendship lasted many years. Sister Lillian had a high-level position in the Catholic hierarchy. Over the next few years she hired me for concerts at the schools where she was in charge. It was particularly helpful to have venues to try out new programs.

Philadelphia Orchestra, 1950

That same fall, I also played the same Tchaikovsky concerto with the Philadelphia Orchestra as a result of having won the Youth Competition for 13-25 year old performers.

The Musicians' Union was so strong that the two and a half hour rehearsal was timed with a stopwatch. If a rehearsal went over by even five minutes, the musicians were paid for an extra half hour. In order to maintain the budget, the conductor—Ormandy in this case—was extremely careful. I remember him looking at his watch, ready to start my rehearsal, and then putting his hands down and saying, "No, we've got 30 seconds to go."

Fortunately, I had already done the concerto in Washington. The first movement is about 17 minutes and Ormandy didn't want to spend the whole time since the Orchestra knew all the tuttis. So he said we would just play my solo sections. This saved about four or five minutes. I also skipped the cadenza, which saved another couple minutes. That was the only rehearsal I got, just one run-through. It was amazing that Ormandy had such faith that I knew exactly what I was doing, because otherwise that would have been a pretty inadequate rehearsal.

Benny Goodman, the famous jazz clarinetist, played the Hindemith Concerto on the same program.

Eugene Ormandy

My path crossed several interesting times with Eugene Ormandy. The first time of course was at the Children's Concerts competition. The next time was when I auditioned for the Philadelphia Orchestra solo competition at the youth level.

Our next meeting came a few months later when I auditioned to become a member of the Philadelphia Orchestra. I prepared for the audition by learning 65 first violin parts, including all of the major Strauss tone poems. In fact I could play all the Strauss by memory, like concertos. Ein Heldenleben was being performed early in the orchestra season so I was prepared with that one in particular.

The other works I auditioned on were Stravinsky's Firebird, Beethoven's 7th Symphony and my own solo concertos. The Stravinsky was in manuscript, a special version used by the Philadelphia Orchestra. There were over 30 candidates, a large number for those days–unlike today when there can be double that. It came down to two of us, me and an older man from NYC. I lost, partly because I was young. At that time I was still a minor. The Orchestra used to travel a lot by train, weeks at a time with two people sharing a stateroom. There were only four other women in the orchestra and it became clear that they didn't want to become my chaperones.

Ormandy sent word that I was probably the better violinist but the age was a problem. Nowadays, the union would have said that they had to say this up front. Also, I believe that Ormandy knew that I wouldn't plan to stay as I was more interested in being a soloist. As it is he did me a favor because I shortly won the Naumburg for my New York Town Hall debut and went under Columbia Artists Management.

A few months later when he saw me on the train traveling back from a Philadelphia Orchestra concert in New York, Ormandy offered to recommend me for concertmaster of the São Paolo Orchestra in Brazil. I was pleased to say thanks but no thanks because I had just signed with Columbia. I honestly don't think I could have stood the grind of a major orchestra. I would have either broken down or given in and become a grinder.

After that we didn't meet until years later when the Philadelphia Orchestra was on tour in Los Angeles in the early 60's. I bumped into him at UCLA. I introduced him to Sallie at about age three.

We met only once more when I was president of the Curtis Alumni Association West and we decided to honor him with an award at a Philadelphia Orchestra concert at the Ambassador Auditorium in Pasadena.

A few years ago, I was interviewed for the Ormandy archives at the University of Pennsylvania. So a partial oral history of mine is there.

Baltimore Symphony Performance, 1950

The performance with the Baltimore Symphony took place at the Lyric Theater with conductor Reginald Stewart. I only got one rehearsal for that performance as well. It was in the rehearsal hall with the associate conductor, as Stewart was out sick. The conductor assured me that Stewart would be there for the performance. I met with him about a half hour before the performance and quickly went through the various tempi changes. We did this quick run-through in his dressing room backstage and then went out to play the concert.

GREGOR PIATIGORSKY

L to R: Diana, composer John Vincent, Gregor Piatigorsky and Frances.
Reception hosted by Ed and Diana after concert of Philadelphia
String Quartet at UCLA, January 24, 1969

GREGOR PIATIGORSKY

Piatigorsky is probably one of the most fascinating characters I have ever known in my years in music. Though it might seem odd to describe a man who is over six feet tall as a friendly puppy, that is how I would describe him. He was a magnificent personality on stage and a superb cellist. Before Rostoprovich, he was the most famous concert cellist along with Emanuel Feuermann. In the late 20th century and early 21st century, Yo Yo Ma has gained the greatest fame. Earlier at Curtis, there was Felix Salmond and after Piatigorsky there was Leonard Rose.

Piatigorsky's Performances

Piatigorsky ("Grisha" to his friends) had the unique style of walking out on the stage with his cello held high in front, pointing the pin forward like a lance. He seemed almost to be in a trance-like state when he played. His body would sway and his eyes closed. He had an aquiline face and was a very handsome man. His sound was magnificent and he pulled tones out of his cello that could make an audience cry. His technique was marvelous.

Among Piatigorsky's performances which left the greatest impression on me include a trio concert at Curtis Hall with Zimbalist and Isabelle Vengerova, the Brahms's Double Concerto with Zimbalist and the Curtis Orchestra under Hilsberg at the 25th anniversary of Curtis,[1] and Bach's C Major Solo Sonata at the Bach-Mozart Festival Series at Tanglewood in 1950 when I was a student there.

Piatigorsky's Teaching Method

Frances studied with both Piatigorsky and Rose at Curtis. She started with Piatigorsky and then graduated with Leonard Rose, who became the cellist in the famous Stern-Istomin-Rose Trio. Sometimes I sat in on Frances's cello lessons and listened to Piatigorsky philosophize on art and the sweat and tears needed for achievement. He loved all the students and just adored telling stories. In later years, Piatigorsky did not always want to practice, but he was always charismatic.

Piatigorsky taught by example. He picked up the cello and the student had to be quick enough to learn from the way he played. At the time, most of the great

---

[1] I was in 1st violin section for that concert.

performing artists who taught at Curtis were not analytic teachers. At Curtis, there was usually a graduate or senior student who worked extra hours with the younger students, like my sister and me. This process was supposed to work out all of the little performance bumps and techniques before students went in and played for the great masters who could then give artistic advice. Generally, the master teachers were not interested in doing the "dirty work."

Piatigorsky was always fun. Any time there were two people around with an adoring eye, he was ready to sit down and tell stories for hours. All the students would just hang on his every charming, Russian-accented word. He frequently walked around with a cigarette in his mouth which was often unlit. We used to laugh about it and call it his "blankie." Unfortunately, I guess he lit it more than we realized because he died of lung cancer.

Hollywood Bowl, 1955

Frances and I heard Piatigorsky at the Hollywood Bowl with the Los Angeles Philharmonic in 1955, the summer we went to UCLA. He played the Dvorak Concerto with Edward van Beinum conducting. Right after intermission, Piatigorsky walked on stage in his characteristic way, cello held high. The reflections of soloist and orchestra were fascinating in the pool at the edge of the stage. He played with more fire and vigor than ever. The tone sang out shimmering through the live acoustics at the Bowl.

We had wonderful seats just behind the box section. Mom, Frances and I went backstage as Piatigorsky had told us to meet him there. He greeted us warmly and gave Fran a hug and kiss and told us to call him the next morning at his home.

We called him from a booth at UCLA and were invited to spend Friday afternoon at his home in Brentwood. (Little did I dream that in 1961 we would be neighbors for the rest of his life!)

We arrived at 3:00 in the afternoon and walked up the block-long drive to his house. The house and lawn were surrounded by a whitewashed brick fence. As we entered the gate we were greeted by the sight of many tall eucalyptus trees, assorted fruit trees and a lovely rolling lawn. The house was a white colonial two-story with an open porch and green shutters.

Piatigorsky answered our ring in person and we were both astonished to see his left arm in a sling. Answering our immediate query, he informed us that he had just returned from the doctor who had ordered him to rest the arm for two months which would necessitate canceling all of his engagements, including appearances at Tanglewood, as well as playing and recording with the Boston Symphony Orchestra.

It seems he had fallen in his swimming pool a few days previously and the muscles in his shoulder were severely strained. He said that the pain had been excruciating during his appearance at the Bowl.

Frances played for Piatigorsky as he hadn't heard her since she was a little girl. We then played the Halvorsen Duo which we were soon to play at the Los Angeles County Museum of Art Series. He noticed the poor violin which I had and had an immediate suggestion as to whom I should contact for a violin.

Then, we went for a swim in his large pool. On the way to the pool we were ushered through a large den/bar/dining room combination which had walnut paneled walls and early American furnishings. This room was quite a contrast from the living room which resembled a European music room. A long upholstered sofa faced a large black fireplace with a marble mantelpiece. There were several miniature cellos and other tiny musical figurines on the mantle. Much of the wall space was covered with an impressive variety of original paintings by Chagall, Seurat, Picasso and others.

Immediately outside the house we encountered a brick patio and a view of the flower garden with abundant roses. We crossed the hedge-lined badminton court, went through a wooden gate, and reached the pool which was lined by eucalyptus trees surrounded by a wide apron of grass. The bathhouse was a small cottage with dressing rooms and a large main room containing bamboo furniture, a ping-pong table and a roll-out barbeque.

After our swim, the maid brought us tea and cakes. Grisha, Frances and I talked of many things, from the music and concert field of the day in America, to the type of man one should marry. He revealed an amusing account of his recent experience in learning to drive. His reason for learning was so his teenage children would not feel their father was different. It seems he had great difficulty with left turns, so whenever he was to drive someplace, he had to plan his route carefully. He described a short trip to his dentist in Westwood, where parking was often a problem. Evidently when he arrived the curb was empty so all he had to do was pull up and stop. When he came out of the dentist's office it was a different story. Two cars had sandwiched his car in back and front. But he had planned for this too. He simply got in the car, turned on the radio and picked up one of the books he had brought. Eventually one of the people came and drove away, allowing him to get out of the parking spot easily. He told this story with great relish, laughing at himself all the while.

Grisha's family was away in Europe and he was stuck with a bad arm, so he seemed anxious that we stay as long as possible.

It was after 5:00 p.m. when we went back into the house. Piatigorsky offered to let us hear the master disks of his new recording of all the Beethoven sonatas and the two sets of Variations on Mozart Themes, which he had recently recorded in England with pianist Solomon. The recordings were truly superb, delicately balanced, with every phase perfectly turned, giving an overall sense of harmonious chamber music—as it should be.

Grisha, Our Neighbor

A few years later when we were neighbors, his daughter Jeptha and I were expecting our first children within a couple of weeks of each other. Grisha became more and more nervous, like a good grandpa. Jeptha was on the East Coast, so he could not keep track of her on a daily basis. So he frequently checked in with me as a surrogate. Both of us did fine. Jeptha had Jonathan and I had Sallie. Two weeks after Sallie's birth, in fact the first day that I was alone with the baby, there was a knock at my front door. As luck would have it, I had just started nursing and was a bit deshabille. I quickly buttoned my blouse and answered the door. There was Grisha, looking a bit sheepish, holding a beautifully wrapped package. He said, "Here is something for the 'leetle' one." Of course I invited him in and he wanted to see the baby. He gave his blessing and approval when he saw a little pink face with beautiful red hair.

Grisha had driven himself to Bullocks Westwood department store where he purchased two very practical and pretty outfits for Sallie that we enjoyed for quite some time. Considering his reluctance in driving, and slight embarrassment at being in a baby department, I was particularly touched by his thoughtfulness.

For a number of years it was my Christmas tradition to make spectacular traditional plum puddings from scratch using the recipe from The New York Times Cookbook. It took a couple of days to create the masterpiece which divided into several ample puddings. I decided to bring one over to the Piatigorskys'. Along with the pudding, I also supplied homemade hard sauce made from butter, brandy and nutmeg.

The day after Christmas, Grisha came by to thank us for the pudding. He said that he had wakened in the middle of the night and couldn't resist a trip to the kitchen to sample a bit of the pudding leftovers.

As a good neighbor, he came for visits on a fairly regular basis, especially if Jacqueline was away. One very memorable moment for Ed was when Grisha came for dinner and noticed a cello lying on its side under the piano. I had been "teaching" Ed how to play the cello at a fairly elementary level. This was an alternate instrument because, try as he might, he really didn't do very well on the piano. Besides, he quit piano when he realized he would never play the Brahms Quintet. So we tried the cello in hopes he could learn enough to play a Haydn quartet. He got so he could play a few scales and I taught him the opening few measures of the Dvorak Cello Concerto.

So when Grisha came to dinner and noticed the cello, he turned to Ed and said, "So, I hear you play zee cello." Whereupon Ed, with the chutzpah of a true beginner, took out the cello and sat down to play. He played the only thing he knew, which was the opening measures of the Dvorak. After the sweeping finale of the fourth measure, he put the cello down and said, "That's it. I quit. I've reached the pinnacle of my career, having played the Dvorak Concerto for Gregor Piatigorsky." We had a wonderful few years as neighbors.

MARLBORO
1951-58, and 1990

Rudolph Serkin greets Diana after her performance
while holding Judy, his youngest daughter at the time.

Photo on lawn of Marlboro campus (probably 1952).

Courtesy Family Archives

MARLBORO, 1951-1958 AND 1990

Following my summer at Tanglewood, I went to Marlboro, Vermont in 1951 for the inaugural year of a new music festival. The founders wanted to find really top young people to come and put together a chamber music experience, so a number of Curtis grads were invited.

The setting was Marlboro, a little New England college with white clapboard buildings on top of a mountain. It looked like a movie set. The idea to start the festival came from Rudolf Serkin and the Moyse family, who made their homes in the area. Marcel Moyse was a world famous flutist, a contemporary of Debussy, and later the teacher of James Galway. His son, Louis, was also a fine flutist, pianist and conductor. Louis's wife, Blanche Honegger Moyse, a violinist and conductor, was the niece of the French composer Arthur Honegger. In those days, there weren't as many festivals as there are now when it seems like every farmhouse and mountain top has one.

Serkin lived nearby with his family on a farm that had been built for Lunt and Fontanne, the famous acting couple. It was a 250-acre working dairy farm.

The Moyses had settled in Vermont when they were escaping the Second World War. The Serkins wanted to raise their children there rather than in the pressures of the city of New York. Rudi would tour from Vermont. Adolf Busch[1] and his family came and lived there too. It was an interesting community; there were a number of German, French and Swiss expatriates who were famous movie directors, philosophers and professors. They were all quite different from the natives, yet they all became regular Vermonters.

Marlboro granted me a full scholarship, including room and board, for each of the six summers that I attended. We spent eight weeks playing chamber music under the guidance of Serkin and the others. He also coached the talented pianists individually. Among the amateurs was Rosalie Leventritt Berner, the daughter of Edgar M. Leventritt, of the famous Leventritt Competition. Another was the son of the president of Paraguay. It was quite a varied group of people.

That first summer, the faculty included Adolf Busch, a member of the famous Busch family of musicians. Adolf was the first violinist of the Busch Quartet and Hermann was the cellist. They were leading musicians of their day and Serkin had grown up in their home from the time he was a teenager. I have always

---

1 Rudolf Serkin's father-in-law.

attributed his lyrical sound to this influence; his ear was more attuned to strings than percussion.

Fondue Party

As an opening get-together, the Moyse family threw a party for approximately 50 people. It was a wonderful, traditional Swiss-French fondue party. That was the first time I had eaten fondue. They set up lanterns and red-and-white checkered tablecloths. They served a crisp green salad with a light dressing as a side for the cheese fondue which, as it was made properly with Kirchwasser and the wonderful imported Gruyere and Swiss, was very rich and almost indigestible. The cheese starts off hard and melts in the pan, but then it gets hard again in your stomach. We drank white wine with the fondue and had coffee. They told us not to drink water because fondue makes you very thirsty and drinking water can cause problems.

Adolf Busch

I will always value the honor of coaching with Adolf Busch as a rare opportunity and experience. He had a bad heart and should have taken things easier, but he just could not keep his boundless energy and vitality in check. He always gave himself to the music completely and without restraint.

Musical ideas of everlasting import on the interpretations of Mozart, Beethoven and Brahms are just a few of the things I remember. In terms of the violin, he had very useful ideas on how to make things sound. His approach to bowings, for example, was quite different from the Auer school. I found that after getting accustomed to them, they had serious merits when playing the German classics.

As he could not contain his own energy while playing, he could not tolerate a lackluster spirit in others. He would not stand timid playing and slipshod preparation. If a student so much as once finished a phrase unmusically by landing on the last note, it was a base crime punishable by much extra rehearsing.

Yet at the same time, Busch's heart was always with his children and grandchildren. He also had a wonderful sense of humor. Once, he and the other faculty dressed like an old-fashioned beer garden band with false mustaches and music clips on their instruments as they played for the students, complete with sour harmonies.

Another time, he loaned us the music for Mozart's Sextet, the "musical joke." When we performed it at a party, emphasizing the musical faux pas, I am sure he laughed the loudest.

He led the chamber orchestra from the first chair with exuberance and always played with such rhythmic vitality that, as he said, we really did not need a conductor. With a few rehearsals, we gave very well-integrated performances. As a conducting concertmaster, he mostly sat, standing up at infrequent intervals during the performance to conduct particularly tricky sections, sometimes with his bow, and sometimes continuing to lead with the scroll of the violin.

In May of 1952, before the season started, I got a phone call from Ray Benner and Joe Cohen. Ray was a bass player and a fellow Curtis alum. Joe Cohen was a flutist and an early Marlboroite. They called to tell me that Adolf Busch had died and that there was going to be a special memorial concert in Brattleboro and they wanted me to join them and play. The memorial concert was going to include the chorale from Marlboro College.

Ray and Joe picked me up and we drove all night so that we could play the rehearsal in the morning and the concert that evening. We were being put up in various farmhouses.

One of the pieces which we did, that I love to this day, was the Fauré Requiem. We had only maybe six violins. Berl Senofsky and I sat first stand. This is usually played with a fairly good-sized orchestra, but I think we had about 15 players. We all just played out of love for the whole family and respect for dear Adolf.

Rudolf Serkin

Marlboro was the first time I had been around musicians of this level in a situation that was so egalitarian. Most of us knew Serkin as a musical giant, but he was very informal. For concerts, he always wore white jacket and black pants. On one occasion, though, he forgot to change his shoes. That morning one of the cows had calved and he was still wearing the shoes he had worn in the barn. That day we all sat in the audience watching him pedal with mud-caked shoes.

The first time I played chamber music with Serkin was a surprise. The scheduled pianist did not arrive on time for a lesson on the Brahms D Minor Sonata. He said, "Well, you and I will play it." To my wonderment, he sat down and played the whole sonata by memory with me.

He once told me, "Don't be afraid to do with music what you want, because your innate musicianship will keep you from doing anything wrong." This statement gave me courage in many a trying musical moment.

Serkin recorded two Mozart concertos with our festival orchestra that summer. Columbia Records set up its recording equipment in our "concert hall," an open barn-style room with exposed beam ceilings where the crickets set up camp. The Columbia engineers kept picking up cricket sounds on the recording.

Serkin was a man of dynamic nervous energy and power hidden under a cloak of meekness and extreme humility. He was known for making noises when he played, stomping his feet and singing under his breath. The recording engineers put carpeting on the floor so that his foot stomping wouldn't be louder than the music. The hall was similar to those a lot of stock companies used, a very popular kind of summer festival setting.

In those early years, there were very few practice rooms, so we used to practice and occasionally have classes out under the trees. Sometimes you'd hear some wailing horn player practicing up on the hill. The backdrops for our music-making were quite interesting.

Peter Serkin

My earliest memory of Peter is when he was about nine years old. Quite often, Peter was page turner for his dad in chamber music concerts. He was a thin pale-complexioned youngster with dark circles under his eyes. During that summer I was unaware of his prowess as a pianist until he played the Haydn Piano Concerto with the Marlboro Orchestra.

Peter played beautifully, with grace and amazing phasing. We all sat up and took notice. After that it wasn't until Peter was a teenager and off into contemporary music that I noticed him again. He was obviously going in another direction from his father's German romantic bent.

Many years later Ed and I heard him in a sonata recital of three Brahms violin and piano sonatas with Pamela Frank, daughter of Claude Frank and Lilian Kallir. It was superb chamber music and elegant instrumentalism. It was definitely in their genes, aided of course by the early childhood exposure to the best.

Peter was one of the youngest children of Rudi and Irene Serkin and the only one that made a major career in music. Judy became a fine cellist touring with the Marlboro players and John played French horn but was more involved in the mechanics of the piano. Elizabeth (Betli) was a vivacious person and luckily had a son, David Ludwig, a very talented composer, a Curtis graduate in composition and now on the theory faculty there.

Memorable Performances

The main hall at Marlboro served as both auditorium and dining hall. On Sundays we performed public concerts, frequently with a small chamber orchestra which Louis Moyse conducted. I played the Mozart Concerto No. 5 there that first summer, on July 28, 1951. Frances came that first year as well as later. In 1958 she played a Brahms trio with Eugene Istomin and the Mendelssohn Octet with Alexander Schneider. She also participated in the master classes of Pablo Casals.

In 1951, I also played the Mendelssohn Octet with Busch. He loved to show off his bow arm prowess. In the scherzo movement, Adolf loved doing about 12 to 16 notes in a row of thrown down-bow staccato. Then he would look at me slyly with his eyebrow raised. I was to perform it in concert as first violinist but he would sit next to me at rehearsal and sort of join in every once so often in unison.

I played the Brahms Piano Quintet with Serkin. He knew, of course, that I was very strong in piano. In fact, a couple of years later I coached both piano and violin concertos by Mozart and there was some discussion about my playing both concertos in a concert. But I chickened out. I did do a chamber music performance on piano, though. However, I don't think Serkin realized some of my technical deficiencies. I certainly could not play some of the difficult passages in the Brahms. I didn't have big hands and I'd never really intended to be a great pianist. At this particular coaching session, during the last movement of the Quintet, at the section of contrary motion thirds in both hands, Serkin turned to me and said, "You know I always have great difficulty with this passage. Don't you, too?" I just sort of smiled, "Oh, yes, sir." I couldn't have played that if my life depended on it! I used to fake it by playing the upper note. But that was just the way he was. That was the camaraderie, mutual respect and spirit that we had during my years there.

On August 17, 1952 I played the Ravel Trio. Having won the Naumburg that year, I was also preparing for my New York debut. I had yet to play the program for Zimbalist, so I left Marlboro for a few days to play for him at his summer home in Camden, Maine.

Seymour Lipkin's sister Luboshutz (a Curtis piano graduate) learned my debut recital program and we previewed it in a warm-up at Marlboro.

Another performance which stands out in memory was the Prokofiev D Major Sonata, played with Larry Smith, who became a very well-established conductor as Lawrence Leighton Smith. He was with the Louisville Orchestra for a number of years, and was also on the Yale University faculty.[2]

Then there was a performance with Claude Frank: the Beethoven Sonata in G Major, Opus 30, No. 3 on August 17, 1957.

Alexander "Sascha" Schneider

I first became aware of "Sascha" Schneider at Tanglewood in 1950 when he played a concert of all the Bach solo sonatas. In 1956, he came to Marlboro. Though we became personally acquainted at Marlboro, I had already performed in front of him, as he had been one of the judges at the Leventritt Competition when I was competing for the second time. This was the year after I was runner-up to pianist Van Cliburn.

The next time violinists were allowed to compete, pianist John Browning and I were automatically in the finals because we had been the runners-up to Cliburn.

---

2   As luck would have it, in 1993, Marcia and The Debussy Trio played the world premiere of Triple Concerto, night's midsummer blaze by Augusta Read Thomas, commissioned by the Trio, with Larry conducting the Louisville Orchestra.

At this time, I was touring with Columbia Artists and playing a Paganini Concerto every night. So I marched into the audition and did something that was considered very gutsy–I opened with that concerto. I lost again. They picked John Browning. Only a couple of violinists have won the Leventritt over the years.

So when Sascha came to Marlboro, we had never been introduced. When he was a Leventritt judge, along with Arthur Judson and Joseph and Lillian Fuchs, he only knew the competitors as "Contestant A" and "Contestant B," so he didn't even know my name, but he remembered what I played.

On this occasion, I was walking down one of the pathways toward the practice rooms. Sascha saw me from a distance and pointed at me, screaming, "Paganini Concerto!" From then on, we were close friends. He was a wonderful chamber music coach. He had some wonderful ideas and I found him quite inspiring and helpful.

Sascha always made a point to visit when he toured through L.A. with the Budapest Quartet. He loved home cooking and liked to use our kitchen. His favorite was a thick steak and a cognac.

In fact, when he came to conduct the Los Angeles Chamber Orchestra at the Ambassador Auditorium in Pasadena in the early 90s, I went to see him backstage and helped him prepare to go on stage. Schneider had been a very robust kind of man with tremendous energy. During that last visit he still had the energy but he looked like all of Ed's old uncles: little tiny Jewish men. He still had the sparkling eyes but he'd shrunk. Well, that is what happens to people when they get to be very old. The next day I went down to his hotel in downtown Los Angeles, met him in his room where we sat and talked. I wanted him to see my Strad. We had been buddies over the years.

Marcel Moyse

Of equal musical importance to the roles of Busch and Serkin was coaching the music of the French Impressionistic composers with the Moyses, especially Marcel. His phrasing and approach to the music was so nuanced. I find many of the current performances of Debussy rather disturbing. Sections of a work that look sprightly and fast, such as the Violin Sonata's 2nd movement, are played like a perpetual motion. Marcel, who was a colleague of Debussy, emphasized that these should be a little bit under tempo, much more graceful and controlled. It is difficult for me to listen to current performances of that piece because it's just so inappropriate for what Debussy really had in mind. Now there's no memory. It makes one wonder whether we're just as far off about other music written hundreds of years ago. We think we're following tradition and yet we probably are not.

Then there was a Vermont dairy farmhouse, where a farmer made homemade ice cream with an old-fashioned ice cream maker that you cranked by hand, using just salt and ice. They made an absolutely fabulous ice cream, with little bits of chocolate chips in it. The cream was so heavy and thick, I don't ever expect to taste ice cream like that again. It was also great in what we now call root beer floats, though they called them black cows.

A gourmet treat awaited us at the restaurant at the Newfane Inn, about 25 miles from Marlboro. It was an interesting historic building from the early colonial days, during which half the building was used as the town jail. In the 50s, the jail was kept as a museum. People came from all over and you had to get advance reservations even back then.

1990 Return to Marlboro

In 1990, Ed and I had a poignant return visit, our last with Rudi Serkin. We were on our way to Tanglewood for its 50th anniversary, my 40th there. It was almost the 40th anniversary of Marlboro too. We decided to stop by, as Rudi was not well. He was very weak and no longer able to perform. Ed and I hadn't been to Marlboro since my days of performing in the old barn. Now, they had built a separate auditorium which seated approximately 700 people and had a real stage for the orchestra. To me, it wasn't as much fun, but things do have to grow.

It was, sadly, the first time that Serkin was unable to perform his traditional finishing piece for the final concert every summer. He had always played Beethoven's Choral Fantasy. In its place, they played the Mozart Symphony No. 40, and Felix Galimir was there as concertmaster.

The festival was over and everybody was going home. Rudi asked Ed and me to stay and have family dinner with him. It was just Rudi, his wife, Irene, and very few others. Rudi was doing his usual kidding around and trying to be as cheerful as possible. I was so touched, as was Ed, that he considered us family. It was just an example of the kindness with which he treated us. Less than a year later, he was gone.[3]

---

3 Rudolf Serkin died on May 8, 1991.

Other Fellow Marlboro Musicians

Many of the people I worked with up there had major careers, including Gary Graffman and Eugene Istomin. Berl Senofsky and Shirley Trepel, who were married at the time, were there too. Shirley became the first cellist of the Houston Symphony. Berl toured and became a professor at Peabody.

Amongst the successful young pianists was Richard Goode. He was 12 or 13 years old at the time. Anton Kuerti was another wunderkind. Susan Starr was there too; I had known her since Curtis, when she was 5. We played the Schumann Piano Quartet together. She was so musical.

The list would be incomplete without the image of Irene Serkin and Blanche Moyse playing viola in the 6th Brandenburg Concerto of Bach.

Claude Frank

I knew Claude for a few summers at Marlboro and loved working with him. He is a musician's musician. His thinking and performance are elegant, artistic and well thought out. His music brings pleasure to the listener with subtle nuance and unexpected bursts of technical display. I coached a number of works with him, including the solo piano part of the Mozart Concerto in D Minor (#20). We gave a fine performance of the "little G" Beethoven Sonata which was recorded badly but still exists. My fondest memory was his interpretation clue in the middle movement by putting words to the last three note phrase which repeats in conversation with the two instruments, "tenderly." To this day I hear those words when playing or listening to the work.

I feel very good that we both were blessed with daughters that became fine world class musicians.

I saw Claude on one other occasion when he came to Los Angeles as the major solo artist for a Music Teachers National convention (I believe in the early 90's). He was still an elegant pianist and a lovely human being as we met over dinner.

Fun at Marlboro

It wasn't all music. Just a few miles from Marlboro there was a hilltop called Hogback. What a view! Three states! You were in Vermont, but you could also see New York and Massachusetts. The restaurant there served all-you-could-eat waffles with wonderful, natural Vermont maple syrup, which spoiled me forever for anybody else's maple syrup.

COMPETITIONS, VIOLINS AND TOURING
1952-1955

New York Town Hall debut review.
"keen feeling for color and drama..."

New York Times, October 9, 1952

Paul Whiteman gives Diana the keys to the car.
Winner of first radio, "Teen Talent Show" broadcast nationwide.
Fall 1952

Courtesy Family Archives

COMPETITIONS, VIOLINS AND TOURING
1952-1955

Paul Whiteman's Radio Teen Show, 1952

In 1952, Paul Whiteman started a new talent search radio show for teenagers. Whiteman was a famous jazz conductor, a discerning musician and had been a violinist.

The show went out over 200 AM radio stations; it was mostly pop talent with a back-up jazz band. It originated in Philadelphia over the Mutual Radio Network and WOR in New York. Whiteman called the Curtis Institute because he wanted a "class act" for the opening program. Jane Hill, the registrar, took the call. The producers called on Friday and wanted somebody for the following Monday.

Jane called me and asked if I wanted to go down. As I was in the Musicians Union, they would pay the normal union fee. I only had to play for three minutes. Of course I accepted. I think they paid me all of $22. But in those days I was getting $2 an hour from Curtis for accompanying, so $22 for three minutes looked pretty good.

The show's producers told me to play something very short and showy. I decided on Fiddle Faddle by Leroy Anderson, which had been written for the Boston Pops. The studio band arranged the piece for jazz combo accompaniment. We ran through the piece once. At the rehearsal, they said, "You know, that's a nice piece, but can't you play some sort of intro to show off your technique?" So on the spot I improvised some arpeggios as an introduction.

We went on live at 6 p.m.

They had a blues singer, an accordionist, a guitarist, and 3 or 4 other acts.

I didn't know until I was standing out in the hallway that the show was some sort of contest, but I soon became aware of what was at stake. As I was practicing the intro, I heard other performers standing around saying, "Hey, what are you going to do with the car if you win?"

My ears perked up and I said, "What car?"

They told me that the show was a contest and that if you received enough postcard votes from listeners within the week you could stay on the show. The prize for the first week was a Kelvinator refrigerator or freezer. If you stayed on six weeks by popular vote, you won a Nash Rambler, which was a car comparable to today's Ford Mustang.

The refrigerator was worth about $150 and the car about $2,300, which to me was a fortune.

So I went on air. I heard the announcer tell listeners to vote for the talent that they liked best, and the person who got the most postcards would continue on.

Postcards in those days were a penny. I came home to my mother and said, "You know, I could really use that car. If I sold the car then I would have the money to buy a violin." It would be $2,300 and besides I was getting paid $22 union scale. If I won the refrigerator, we could use the refrigerator or $150

So I bought myself a dollar's worth of postcards and voted for myself. I wrote some in red ink and some in blue, some back-handed and some left-handed Mother and Frances wrote some too. I had Veda Reynolds mail some when the Philadelphia Orchestra went to New York.

Lo and behold, I got a call Monday at noon the next week to come to the studio for the 6 o'clock broadcast that day. I had won.

I was already prepared for it because I knew I had sent in a lot of postcards and I hoped I wouldn't get caught. As time went on, other people were writing postcards for their kids.

So we started telling our friends. I bought maybe $5 worth of postcards and we spent all week filling them out. My cousins wrote postcards. Friends announced it at synagogues and clubs and it became the "Diana-Buy-a-Violin" Fund. My aunt in Florida was sending them as were my friends in Oregon–any place where they had one of the radio stations that broadcast the show. I don't think they even heard me. They were just writing postcards. And wherever the Philadelphia Orchestra went on tour–New York, Baltimore, Washington–Veda would take a packet of cards and mail them. So they received postmarks from all over the country.

I started getting a couple thousand a week. I am sure to this day that Paul Whiteman knew exactly what I was doing, as I was so far ahead of everybody else. By the last week I got 8,500 postcards. They didn't even count them, they just measured the stacks under each name.

So I won. Over a period of six weeks, I played a three minute version of Ziguenerweisen by Sarasate, Hejre Kati by Hubay and Czardas by Monti.

Then Paul Whiteman moved the show to New York. He had me come there to WOR where he presented me with the keys to the car.

He was on my side because he wanted me to win the car so I could get a fiddle. He knew I needed one. He was really sweet to me. A few years later he started a television version of the show and invited me to open that show again. But he fixed it so I couldn't win. This time it was by audience applause and he only gave me 4 tickets. Everybody else got 30 or 40. So I lost. But he gave me a $100 bond, paid my union fee and gave me a Helbrose wristwatch. By that time I had the violin that I had bought with my earlier winnings and he was very pleased.

Borrowed Violins: Guadagnini, Hill Strad

The year before I won the Naumburg Competition, I lost to Joyce Flissler from Juilliard, whose sister Eileen studied piano at Curtis. I was told that I lost by one point. There were 13 judges and one of their comments was that they thought my performance was fine but they didn't like the sound of the instrument I was playing. These were the days when I was playing on any instrument I could borrow.

In 1950, when I played with the National Symphony, I played on a Lorenzo Guadagnini, which was one step down from the J. B. Guadagnini I own now. They were members of the same family, but that one wasn't considered quite as good. I borrowed it from a friend of my mother, Sylvia Margolis, who had been a fairly successful concert violinist in Portland. She was quite ill, so her husband let me play it. It was a lovely sounding fiddle, but it wasn't brilliant. When I got out on the big stages, it didn't have a very big tone.

At the time, though he wasn't a judge, one of the guests at the 1951 Naumburg audition (when I lost) was Rembert Wurlitzer who owned the most distinguished violin dealership in the United States. He had a showroom and repair shop on 42nd Street in Manhattan. His head repairman, Sacconi, was a guru of violin repairmen. Many big artists in the East bought their violins from Wurlitzer; in the West, musicians like Heifetz usually dealt with Koodlach, both Sr. and Jr.

When I asked Rembert if I could borrow a violin for a short term, he told me that he felt that I should have won the competition, and if the difference was the instrument, he would make sure that I would sound my best for the next year's Naumburg competition. Most of the dealers would loan violins for two to four weeks, in part because the instruments needed to be played in order to sound their best when they were sold. In return for Wurlitzer's generosity, I used to help by playing instruments for potential buyers in New York.

The Naumburg Competition was to start in April and Wurlitzer lent me a brilliant early Stradivarius (1699), the Hill, in February. I had about two months to get acquainted with the instrument, which was much better than the usual week or so. Though I had the Hill Strad for the audition, I had a different Strad for my Town Hall debut, which I don't think was as brilliant. I really wanted that Hill. It was owned by violinist Dorothea Powers who subsequently purchased Kreisler's Stradivarius. All of the newspapers reported that she paid $85,000 for it. Violins were not as relatively expensive back then; they had not yet experienced the big jump in price. Powers's husband offered to sell me the Hill, valued at $23,000, for $17,000 cash. I tried desperately amongst my friends and relatives to raise the money for the violin, but I couldn't, so I missed out on that one.

Naumburg Competition, Town Hall Debut, 1952

I won the Naumburg by unanimous decision in the spring of 1952. The prize was a debut at Town Hall, which I played in October 1952.

When I gave my New York debut, I was accompanied by Elsa Fiedler, who became a dear friend.[1] Elsa was a very fine coach in her own right and was extremely helpful to me when I was trying out for the Naumburg. She was the official accompanist for the Naumburg competition and they paid for her services at rehearsals and auditions. However, Elsa and I got along so beautifully that I believe she gave me at least three or four times the amount of hours than they actually paid. This was typical of her generous spirit. Our warm relationship continued through the rest of her life.

As a result of my win, the hall and accompanist were paid for and the proceeds from the ticket sales were mine.[2] Usually, nobody came to these recitals other than parents, family members and the newspaper reviewers. I hated playing for an empty concert hall, so I decided I was going to fill the house with free tickets. I ended up sending out hundreds of invitations using names from dear friends like Mrs. Horace Stern of Philadelphia. The Friday Morning Music Club ended up renting a bus and coming to New York from Washington, D.C. I had almost a thousand people at my recital and a stage full of flowers.

Hettie Stern, whose husband Judge Horace Stern was the chief justice of the Supreme Court of Pennsylvania, was an amateur violinist as a youngster and a patron of the Philadelphia Orchestra. She was one of the group of women who adored Stowkowski and later Ormandy. Many lived on Rittenhouse Square, as Mrs. Stern did. Her apartment was the better part of a floor at the corner of 19th and Locust Streets. Mrs. Stern became a patron of mine, though she never offered me financial support. She was crucial in helping me get an audience for my New York debut at Town Hall by having me send out special invitations to a huge list of her personal friends. Some drove in from Philadelphia in limousines.

Mrs. Stern was a dear friend. When Ed and I were first married, she invited us to dinner. Judge Stern was about to retire from the Supreme Court and they had just celebrated their sixtieth wedding anniversary. After I left Philadelphia, I never saw her again.

At the time of my Naumburg recital, a nice evening gown cost about $300 which I didn't have. A friend of my mother, Johnnie Vincent, spoke to the owner of Milgrim's, one of the high-end boutique stores on 57th Street, off 5th Avenue. She told him that I needed a dress for my debut, and he sold us the one I wanted

---

1   Elsa was the sister of Arthur Fiedler, conductor of the famed Boston "Pops." Available in full as an archival recording housed at the Curtis Library; part of the performance is available on the commercial recording Sonatas.
2   I got a check for $19!

at cost; she paid for it.

One of the audience members was Paul Creston, who composed the Suite that I played on the program. We remained friends until his death.

I received wonderful reviews. Mr. Zimbalist then arranged for me to meet his manager, Marks Levine. Levine said to me, "It's fine that you had a nice debut, but if you want an important debut you'll have to perform another recital and pay us $10,000 to handle your publicity. Then we'll see if we can get you some concerts." It was such a racket and still is.

Michaels Competition, 1952 and Chicago Symphony Solo, 1953

In late spring 1952, right after winning the Naumburg, I competed for the Michaels Award in Chicago. The wealthy Michaels family decided it wanted to get an international name by running a competition. I still had the Hill Strad and for the finals I played the Tchaikovsky Concerto with the WGN radio orchestra. I came in second. The prize went to Sylvia Rosenberg, who was my replacement a couple of years later in The Gotham Trio. She and I were friends and she played very well. When Sylvia won and my second place was announced on the radio, the audience's gasps were loud enough to be audible on the recording.

The following morning, I received a telegram from a woman who said that she believed the judges made the wrong decision, so she sent me $1,000 which was the same amount as the prize. The other part of the prize for the winner was a performance as soloist with the Chicago Symphony Summer Series at Ravinia. The associate conductor of the Symphony, George Schick, was one of the judges. He said that while he couldn't change the decision, he would take me as soloist in the Symphony's Winter Series at Orchestra Hall. I performed on April 18, 1953. So I really came out a winner after all.

Community Concert Touring Anecdotes: 1953-fall 1955

In 1953, I signed a contract with Columbia Artists Management to tour with The Gotham Trio on the Community Concerts circuit. The pianist was Seymour Bernstein and the cellist was Ruth Condell (now Alsop).[3]

Izler Solomon's Violin, Glen Burnie, Maryland

In the fall of 1953, our first tour for Columbia was down the southeastern coast. I didn't own a violin and was still borrowing fiddles from Wurlitzer in New York.

---

3   The mother of Marin Alsop, conductor of the Baltimore Symphony.

I was desperate because I didn't have a violin to play on the tour. We had seven or eight concerts to play and Rembert wasn't able to loan me anything this time.

I called a conductor friend, Izler Solomon.[4] He had been a violinist but wasn't playing much anymore, and I knew he had a good fiddle. He was on tour conducting in California but his wife was at home in a suburb of New York City. I spoke to her, explained my need and asked if she would loan his violin to me. She called him long distance, and he said he would give it to me for this short tour.

This was a Friday, and I had to leave on Monday out of Philadelphia. Mrs. Solomon said that she would take the violin to Wurlitzer and let them check it. Then my friend Marie Sturla picked it up at Wurlitzer and gave it to Seymour in New York. He met me on the train in Philadelphia. Our first concert was in Glen Burnie, a suburb of Baltimore. I had never even seen the violin before and walked out on the stage that night and played the concert.

Experiencing the South: The Carolinas

After Glen Burnie we went to Fayetteville, North Carolina. We went all long distances by train. We rarely flew any place; it was too expensive and there were few commercial airports near these little towns anyway.

The main train, the Seaboard Express, went from New York to Florida. It was a nice train. I had ridden it a number of times to go visit my great-aunt and –uncle in Miami. But some of these little towns weren't regular stops. The trains only stopped if somebody had to get off or on. You literally flagged the train down, just like you would flag a bus or a taxi.

I was quite concerned because after we played a concert that night we had to get back on to get to the next town. Printed train schedules would have asterisks by the names of the towns where they had "flag stops." It was easy enough when you were on the train because you told the conductor and he would pull the brake switch and the engineer would stop the train. They would throw your luggage off and put a step down. They barely slowed down. It was quite an experience. I don't think they stopped more than 60 seconds.

I asked the conductor, "How are we going to get this train to stop and pick us up to go on to the next place?" He said in a deep southern drawl, "Well, now, don't you fret, honey. You just put your little foot out and we'll stop right 'thar.'" That is what happened.

Fayetteville was quite an interesting experience. We were "working white," the artist staying in a hotel. Young and inexperienced in southern societal norms, we made friends with people who worked in the hotel. For instance, we told our waitress, "Why don't you come to our concert? We will arrange for tickets for

---

4 Solomon conducted when I soloed with the Miami Symphony.

you." When we told the people who ran the series that we would like to bring this lady as a guest, they said, "Who is she? We'll be glad to have her." When we said she was the waitress in our hotel, they said, "Well, you know, this is a subscription series only, so we really can't allow individual tickets." We were very embarrassed when we had to go and explain to the waitress we were sorry but there weren't any tickets. She understood better than we did.

Until we got to the concert, we didn't realize that this was basically a debutante coming out party for the young belles of the area. They gave out programs and were dressed in formal evening gowns with long, white gloves. Their gowns were from Paris. My mother had made my gown and I was the visiting artist!

They were nice enough to us, but we were not terribly happy in the South of the 1950s.

I put my foot out and the train did stop. Our next stop was in South Carolina, which is really the most interesting part of this little southern tale.

We arrived in Beaufort, which is famous even today because it is the jumping off place for the big Parris Island marine base, a major training spot for young marines. They put recruits through such rigorous training. If you survived the training, the war was easy by comparison.

We were invited to visit the Marine base and observe. One of the tests trainers would do was put the men at attention and make them stand there for 2 or 3 hours with their legs and knees locked. Some of them would faint.

In those days almost everybody smoked. When I was there, the recruits were standing and couldn't move a muscle. The drill sergeant was walking around smoking a cigarette and blowing smoke in their faces just to tease them.

We, the Gotham Trio, were playing the first Community Concert Series concert organized by black people. The south was still segregated. There were "whites only" signs in restrooms, at drinking fountains and black people rode in the back of the bus. The schools were also segregated.

Community Concerts was doing a very forward-looking thing. They already had a white concert series in the town. The blacks organized their own series which, by the way, was written up in the "black section" of the newspaper. Even the newspaper was segregated. African Americans talk about the problems they have today. By comparison they just don't know.

We were the second concert of the new series but were the first white people to play there. The first artist had been a classmate of mine from Curtis Institute, a wonderful soprano, Theresa Green. She had been a winner of a Marian Anderson scholarship, which Anderson had established for young black singers.

We played in the black high school. Our hosts went to so much trouble to make us feel welcome. The auditorium had a real stage, but, for instance, they didn't have an artists' dressing room. So they set one up for us. People had donated furniture from their houses, such as a dressing table with a pretty little chintz flounce around it with a mirror, a carafe of water and a Kleenex box.

Today we get so much in hotels, people have no idea what it was like. In those days you got a bar of soap, a towel and toilet paper. I'm not sure they even had Kleenex; I think I used to carry my own.

On the Beaufort program, we played a nice arrangement of a Brahms Hungarian Dance, and somehow or another, my bow slipped out of my hand. It went sailing like an arrow out into the audience. One of the people caught it but didn't know what to do about it.

Meanwhile, Seymour and Ruthie were laughing hysterically, but they kept going. I sort of motioned to the people to hand me back my bow. Sure enough, we finished the piece together. Of course, we had quite an ovation on that one.

On the same program, we were playing a Brahms trio and became aware of the fact that there was a sort of humming and beat going on in the back rows. The people were picking up the rhythm. They were very discreet about it, but there was definitely a hum. You could feel the shuffle of feet as they kept time with us.

The black presenters were not able to entertain us "properly." They got one of the white teachers from the school to take us out because they couldn't go into a restaurant that they thought was suitable. The area was pretty poor. People had chickens in their front yards and vegetable gardens. I don't think it will ever be in the history books, but our trio was the first white group to play for a black concert series.

We stayed at a hotel that was just wonderful and had great food. It was American plan, so all the meals were included. We were treated like royalty.

While sitting in the lounge, some little old white lady came up to me. She said, "I saw your picture in the paper, in the colored section. You must come back sometime and play for us. We have our own series."

The waiters were white, but the busboys were black. The busboys would bring us second helpings. We were so hungry all the time. We were so young. Me especially. God, I could eat!

Pekin, Illinois

In our second year, we did a Midwest tour that included Pekin, Illinois, a small town in the southern part of Illinois which was famous because Senator Everett Dirksen was a native. He and former President Ford worked together back in the days when Ford was just a rookie congressman.

Seymour faced each piano on tour with fear and trepidation. He never knew what the condition would be. We arrived in Pekin and were having breakfast with the local Community Concerts representative. Seymour asked, "What kind of piano do you have?" The representative answered, "Piano? Gee, I wonder if Mr. Whateverhisnamewas who was responsible for having a piano hauled over from

Peoria did it. We usually have a Steinway shipped in. I had better check on that."

Sure enough, he came back very embarrassed saying, "You know, it was a good thing you asked because they forgot to order the piano." Fortunately the concert was the next night.

When the piano finally arrived at the high school, they discovered that a nine-foot concert grand was too big to come through the doors, so they had to hire a crane to bring it in through an upstairs window.

It was quite a sight watching that piano swing through the air on a pulley. It turned out to be a pretty nice piano, and the Steinway dealer actually sent a piano tuner along with it. But I have to wonder what it would have been like had it fallen.

A Well-Meaning Presenter

We just never knew what we were going to deal with. The local people were always trying to be very nice, and they would go overboard sometimes with un-intended consequences. This time, they had waxed the wood stage floor to a high polish so that it was like walking out on an ice rink.

When I walked onto that stage, I found that it was so slippery that I thought I was going to break my neck. So I took a bow, realized the problem, excused myself to the audience, and said I had to go find something to stand on.

As I turned around to walk off stage right I discovered that Seymour was walking off stage left because, as he took a bow and turned around, he discovered there was no piano bench! It was really strange as we walked onto the stage, took our bows and promptly left to find solutions for the stage problems.

A Pianist's Nightmare, New England

One time, in New England, we went to the concert and discovered to our absolute horror that the local presenter had borrowed the best piano in town from a lady who had it in her living room. It was an upright piano! We had to turn the piano around so that, though Seymour could not be seen by the audience, they could at least hear with the sound box facing them. Even with the lid off, it was totally inadequate.

St. John's, Newfoundland

We flew from Halifax, Nova Scotia across the ocean to Cornerbrook, which was on the west end of Newfoundland. The choice had been between a 24-hour ferry in early December in very rough seas with icebergs and a direct flight. We landed at Cornerbrook which was an interesting town, but smelled terrible. In fact, we were told that singers often had to leave because of the sulphur from a town paper mill.

We had checked our luggage. (That was back in the days when we used to trust our luggage to check-in, and besides there wasn't much overhead room.) I carried my violin onto these propeller planes, Ruthie's cello had a seat and Seymour was in charge of carrying the music briefcase. Sure enough, he left it on the airplane. As we were checking in at Cornerbrook he said, "Oh, my god, where's my music?"

In those days you walked off the tarmac and into the airport. Don't you know, he went running down the runway, waving frantically at this airplane, trying to make it stop so that he could get the music. Of course, it didn't stop.

The plane was going on to Gander. The airport employees wired ahead to Gander that the music should be taken off the plane to be flown back on the next flight. We were assured the music would arrive in time for the concert, which was the following day.

After we played in Cornerbrook we took a railroad train over to St. John's on the eastern end. We were to play two concerts there. Between Cornerbrook and St. John's there really wasn't much except a bunch of sheep and a few shepherds, a very rocky, flat, sagebrushy kind of country.

There used to be a famous cartoon in the newspapers called the Toonerville Trolley. It was just a single picture cartoon which looked like a dilapidated San Francisco cable car but was really a caboose.

The train we took was a narrow gauge railway that reminded me of the cartoon. It was big enough for people, but looked like something out of a wild west movie when the Indians come and "shoot 'em up." It had a narrow roadbed, so everything was just a little bit closer together. The bench seats barely would hold two people side by side.

It took 22 hours for the train to travel the distance because it went very slowly and made many, many stops. It was the only viable mode of transportation, other than flying between one end of the island and the other.

The sleeping berths were a little bit narrower and shorter than standard trains. Being 5'7", I could just barely fit. Seymour, at about 6'2", was wedged in like a sardine in a can.

On this long trip, they fed us nicely and everybody became friends in the two passenger cars. If sheep got on the track, the train would come to a stop and everybody would wait until they pushed the sheep off. The windows were open and we could lean out and talk to shepherds or farmers as we passed by.

About two-thirds of the way there, the train stopped again. There was some guy walking up and down the train yelling and when he got closer I realized he was yelling my name, "Is anybody there named Diana Steiner?" Pretty soon everybody in the train was saying, "Somebody out there wants you."

Sure enough, this young man wanted to say hello and see what I looked like. A supervisor for the telephone company that maintained both telephone and tele-graph lines across the island, he had flagged down the train just to meet me. He introduced himself and we talked for about 15 minutes. I never got over the fact that a whole train stopped just so some guy could talk to me.

When we got to St. John's, I discovered that he was the son of one of the lead-ing families. His father was Judge Higgins.[1] We were entertained at their home with a grand dinner.

In St. John's, our concerts were the cultural event of the year. There were maybe two or three artists on the series, so we were really the honored guests. We couldn't have been treated better and everybody entertained for us.

Being very English-oriented in Newfoundland, they ate their big meal in the middle of the day, which was fine. I remember it was the only time in my life I had ever been served moose steak. They cooked it very well done with onions and dark brown gravy. It was a little gamey but tasty.

Romance on the Way to Montreal

As part of our Canadian tour, we flew to Montreal. I had purchased a bunch of Irish Belleek ware to add to my mother's collection. There was a young man behind me getting on the plane and he offered to help by carrying the box of Belleek for me.

We got to talking and hit it off. He owned a factory that made shirts for Van Heusen, an American men's brand. When we arrived, we had dinner together and though I didn't usually pick up with men on tour, he just seemed okay. Then I went on my tour and that was that. We exchanged addresses.

After the trio finished the tour in the Maritimes, we rented a car and drove west. We had played in St. John's, Newfoundland but then we also played in St. John, New Brunswick. I remember we ended up driving 75 miles in a snow storm and were probably the only car on the road.

That was one of the things that began really to turn me off from touring be-cause we had to go by car so much. They just stuck you any old place and expected you to make your 250 miles a day and play a concert that night no matter what. It was barnstorming. It was difficult and the travel mostly unpleasant.

In any case, by the time I ended up back in Montreal, I was supposed to take a train home, but that night I got sick. I was in a hotel by myself and feeling

---

1   The reason the Higginses had been so personally interested in me was that they were close friends of the congregational minister Rev. Frederick Neal and his wife, the family that Mother, Frances and I had stayed with the summer I was 16 and lived in Kennebunkport, Maine, the now-famous home of former President Bush. The Neals knew I was going to Newfoundland and had told their friends, the Higginses.

really lousy. The next day I was supposed to sit up all night on the train ride home because, of course, I usually did that to save money. I really felt very friendless. I called the Van Heusen fellow up and I told him I was really feeling awful and had to get home. He said, "Don't worry about it. I will arrange the whole thing for you. I'll get you a state room. You just sleep all the way." He came and picked me up at the hotel, dropped me at the train, made sure I was comfortable, had the berth made up for me immediately even though they usually only made up the berth at night. It took all night to get back to New York where I had to change trains for Philadelphia. By that time I was better. But I never forgot him and his kindness.

The romantic part of it was that he wrote to me several times after that and even proposed marriage. He was a devout Catholic and I was not the least bit interested in marriage at the time. And I wasn't going to marry and live in Canada. Still, it was very romantic to be asked.

Punxsatawny, Pennsylvania

I remember almost all the towns I have played in. One of them was the famous Punxsatawny, where Punxsatawny Phil's shadow, or lack thereof, is consulted on Groundhog Day.

The day after our concert in Punxsatawny, there was a three-inch headline across the front of the newspaper. It said, "Steiner Hits a Winner." I remember Seymour brought it to me at the hotel and said, "Boy, did you get a headline!" When I first saw it I thought it was about me, but then I discovered the high school basketball star, who happened to be named Steiner, had made the headline.

We rarely got reviews or if we did we never knew because Columbia Artists never sent them to us.

Corning, New York and CAMI

CAMI seemed to go out of its way to make life difficult for us. According to our contract, they weren't supposed to be able to make us drive more than 250 miles the same day as a concert, but they hedged a lot. In this particular set of concerts, Monday through Thursday, we played two concerts in western New York and two in Pennsylvania. One was in Corning, while the other two were in Pennsylvania. The towns in New York and Pennsylvania were less than 100 miles apart in each state. But if you did it diagonally, which is the way they scheduled us, we had one in Pennsylvania, one in New York, then we went back to another one in Pennsylvania then back to one in New York. It was like doing a figure X, because we ate lunch in the same restaurant every day. The restaurant people thought we were crazy because we kept showing up, "Well, we're back." We crisscrossed back and forth through that town because they kept sending us 250 miles each way.

One thing about that trip was very pleasant. We went to the Corning Glass Works which had a wonderful museum on the history of glass that included items dating back to the Etruscans, with beautiful pieces of handmade glass from some archeological digs.

Another fascinating thing was that Corning Glass had made the largest telescope lens at the time for the Palomar Observatory in California. They had a replica; it was some three stories high.

During our tours those three years with Columbia Artists, our trio was paid $400 a concert for the three of us, and from that they took 20%. So we actually took home about $105 per person for each concert and then we paid for all our hotels, food and travel expenses.

In addition, the management would print the program for the year and supply it to the individual communities but they charged us for it. It was taken out of our salary checks. The irony was that we were supposedly hiring Columbia as our manager, but they were essentially hiring us as indentured servants because all the money went to management and whatever was left after they had taken their 20% and their expenses for phone calls and anything else, we got the little that was left. In fact, the first year we toured, CAMI spent so much money that was charged back to us, that we owed them over $1,000!

Teaching

One of the reasons I could afford to play concerts was because I taught a lot. This really earned my living. Though I had taught from age 14 in the neighborhood studio, starting in 1953 I was appointed to the faculty of the Settlement Music School in Philadelphia. I taught about 20 hours a week, mostly piano. I accepted violin students by audition only, but I could teach any level of piano. As Mother had rightly counseled, teaching was always a steady core career.

Concert with Yalta Menuhin, January 1955

During the Christmas holiday after I had been touring with the Gotham Trio for the third season, I finished the fall tour and went to Los Angeles to play a concert with Yalta Menuhin. My godmother Rose Herzog became friendly with Phil Kaghan, the director of a radio series from the Los Angeles County Museum of Art, which had only been on the air for a short while. He wanted to do a Beethoven Anniversary Series, an eight-week affair. They arranged for me to do a sonata recital with Yalta Menuhin.[2]

Ours was the first binaural broadcast. The concert was set up with one microphone broadcasting over AM and another over FM; that way, listeners who had two radios could sit between them. This produced an effect that was the precursor to the stereophonic experience. I stood near one mike and the other mike was near the piano. They had us play twenty feet apart to get some separation. This was a difficult arrangement for a sonata performance. We rehearsed a lot in order to be in sync. It was a historic broadcast. I have since looked at the program and discovered that a number of people on the series would become my acquaintances and friends when I moved to Los Angeles in 1960. These included USC professors and Curtis alums I didn't yet know about. It's funny that our pictures are together in the program booklet yet we didn't get to know each other until much later.

1955, My First Fine Violin: Gagliano

When I went to California that January 1955 to play with Yalta, I still didn't own a good violin, so my godmother Rose managed to borrow one from a local dealer for the concert. Though I had been working with Rembert Wurlitzer in New York who would lend me violins, I never seemed to be able to afford anything that I wanted or want anything that I could afford. The other dealer in Philadelphia, Moennig, seemed to be very high-priced, though I purchased my first good bow, a Lamy, there.

When I won the car on the Paul Whiteman Show, I got $1,700 for it after taxes. That was not enough money for a good violin. The average price for a violin that would be appropriate for someone at my level was about $4,500. My mother had her good violin, which Cesar Thompson had purchased for her: a Gragnani. The Gragnani was inadequate due to its small size, called an "Italian lady's full-sized" violin. It was worth a couple thousand dollars, so along with the money from the car, I had barely enough to purchase a better violin.

On that trip to Los Angeles, I met Benny Koodlach, Heifetz's and Piatigorsky's instrument dealer/repairman. Benny and I hit it off. He said he would try to find me something suitable. One day, he called me in Philadelphia to let me know that he had found a Ferdinand Gagliano which would be good for me. He wanted to know how much money I had. I told him I had the Gragnani and the $1,700, and he said that was enough. So I shipped Mother's Gragnani to him; he took it sight unseen. Then I sent him the $1,700 and I got the Gagliano. That violin stayed with me until the mid-1990s, when I sold it. I toured with it. It was in perfect condition, with no cracks, a solid violin with a beautiful, particularly rich tone on the G string. It was quite brilliant. When I auditioned for the major competitions,

---

2 The younger sister of Yehudi Menuhin.

sometimes I would borrow a Strad, but I won the National Federation of Music Clubs competition[3] on the Gagliano. It held me in good stead for many years. It was a fairly large violin, which might have contributed to its big tone. In any case, it was fantastic for me.

Only after Piatigorsky died, many years later, in 1976, Benny told me that he could break his silence. There was over a $1,000 discrepancy between what the violin was worth and what I was able to pay. Piatigorsky told him to take what I had and that he would make up the difference. Piatigorsky was that kind of man. He evidently did this for several other young, deserving and talented young musicians who were unable to afford instruments.

---

3 Won in 1959.

MARRIAGE, AWARDS, FESTIVALS 1956-1960

Review of Concert at National Gallery

"Ms. Steiner passed the test with flying colors. Technique proved virtually flawless and the clarity and sweetness of her tone were reminiscent of Zimbalist at his best."

Evening Star, January 25, 1960

"Both Ms. Steiner and Otto Herz are expert and thoroughly professional musicians. Their performances were intelligent and splendidly rehearsed."

Washington Post, January 25, 1960

Courtesy Family Archives

MARRIAGE, AWARDS, FESTIVALS, 1956-1960

"And What a Damn Good Decision It Was":
Ed and Diana in Love, 1956

Ed and I met on a blind date. I was the lowest thing you can be: a substitute for a blind date!

Frances was teaching at a junior high school for the spring semester of 1956. She was going on to her master's studies at Harvard-Radcliffe. Though she had received a full tuition scholarship she had to make enough money to pay for her room and board, so she taught school for a semester. In addition to her degree from Curtis, she had a teaching certificate as well as a bachelors degree from Temple University in Music Education.

Lenny (Leonard) Finkelstein, who was the science teacher at the junior high, became friendly with Frances. He asked Frances if she would like to go out with his friend, Ed, who was a doctor in the Navy and was coming in on leave from Germany. Lenny knew that Ed loved classical music, so a date with a musician seemed like a good idea. Ed was 27 at the time. Frances was 18, but Lenny didn't know that.[1] He assumed she was 23 or 24 because she was a certified teacher.

On the ship, Ed commuted back and forth from New York to Germany. He would come home for five days and usually see his folks and friends. The turn-around in Germany was shorter.

I had just come off my Columbia Artists concert tours. Along with teaching at Settlement School, I was playing a series of contemporary music concerts with the school's then director Arthur Cohen.

Frances turned down the blind date because she had a sort of "friend-boy" with a car who used to drive her to rehearsals or wherever she needed with her cello. In return she tried to be available for Saturday night dates. Ed was coming in on a Saturday night, so she suggested that Lenny have him go out with her sister. Frances told him that I was only a year older than her, because she was afraid Len would think I was too old as the "older" sister.

I had some boyfriends, but nobody in Philadelphia. I always had more time for dating when I went on summer vacation. So I accepted the invitation. It was to be Frances, her boyfriend, Ed, me, Lenny and his wife Leila.

That very day, Mother came down with pneumonia. She wasn't terribly sick,

---

1 Frances graduated high school at age 15 and had earned her bachelor's degree by 18.

but her doctor said she was going to need penicillin shots every six hours. She asked the doctor to put her in the hospital for 48 hours to be given the shots around the clock. She had insurance so the doctor agreed. This happened around four or five o'clock in the afternoon and we were supposed to meet for the date at six o'clock to go to a movie and then the Officers' Club at the Navy Yard.

Frances and her friend volunteered to take Mother to the hospital. There was no way to get hold of Ed and Lenny to cancel the date. So I waited for them even though we had never met.

That first date, I did what everybody did: I kept calling him Dick.[2] We went to see a French mystery movie which was very popular at the time. When we got to the movie, the only seats were in the second row, which for me was torture because of my astigmatic eyesight. We had no dinner and when I don't eat I get a headache. I sat there feeling just miserable and couldn't stand to look at the screen because it was too close.

But my date seemed kind of nice and sympathetic. I rather liked him. We went to the Navy Yard Officers' Club to go dancing and I told him I was just so hungry, I'd had nothing to eat, and was worried about my mother. They were only serving drinks, but Ed managed to scrounge up a sandwich to help me get rid of my headache. He must have thought I was really strange, but I guess he liked me too. We danced and talked a little bit and discovered that our mutually favorite composer was Brahms.

I don't remember if he asked me whether he could see me again or not that Saturday night, but on Sunday he called me and asked if he could come over. The doctors and nurses were putting on an evening of spoof skits at the University of Pennsylvania Hospital, Ed's alma mater, and he thought I might get a kick out of going. The interns performed all kinds of skits on doctoring and they were hilariously funny.

So he picked me up. Later, he took me over to meet his friend Sam's mother, Sara Karr.[3] I really liked her and thought she was just terrific.

I didn't meet his parents until several weeks later.

After the show, he took me home. By that time Mother was home from the hospital. I remember she was sitting there anxiously waiting to meet this new boy. He was very jolly with her. Of course, knowing him now, he hasn't changed a bit. He just looked over and told me she was going to be alright. I felt more confident.

I just had this feeling that I'd really like to see him again. On Tuesday I went to night school, which I was attending to finish up my degree by getting some credits at Temple University. I told Ed that I had to be there so we hadn't made plans that

2 Somehow the Dick from "Dickstein" stuck in people's minds. Even Ed's mother called her husband Dick, though his name was Abe.
3 Sara was a well-known antiques dealer, especially expert in Netsuke and Wedgewood. She started us collecting Japanese Netsuke miniatures.

night. When I came out of the class, somehow I had a premonition. I looked up and down the street and there was his car waiting for me. He always kids me about it because he says that I was looking for him. It was true. I was hoping against hope that he might be there.

Some of the sequence escapes me, but he took me to Pat's Steak House. He almost lost me on that. It was a dive, like Tommy's in L.A. In later years, I relaxed and began to appreciate the famous joint.

Ed came over once more, and I cooked dinner for him. I think I made, of all things, liver and onions. I was a pretty good cook. Why I ever bought calves liver for him I don't know. As it turned out he liked it.

At that point he had been home for five days, so he said goodbye and shipped off to Germany. I went back to my regular activities. He wrote me a letter from Germany which I got just before he arrived home again. He asked me if we could see each other again. I was so excited and really getting very, very interested. And I guess he was, too. Because, unknown to me, he got a beautiful gold chain on which to hang his Phi Beta Kappa key so that we could be pinned. He had decided to ask me to marry him when he returned.

He came over every day and we saw each other almost constantly. He followed me around to my rehearsals and came to one of my concerts. I was playing in a modern music festival and realized that he was really interested in what I was doing.

I guess it was the third of the five nights that we were together when he asked me to marry him. I told him, "Well, you know I'm not going to give up my violin career for you." He said he wouldn't even think of it, that he wouldn't want me to. So I said yes.

A few weeks later in June, my friend Sally Bridgeman[4] was getting married in Portland to Dale Gustafson and I was going to be one of her bridesmaids. I had signed up for eight weeks at Willamette University in Salem following the wedding. With two weeks for her pre-wedding festivities and eight weeks of summer school, Ed and I weren't going to see each other for quite a while.

He took me to meet his parents and I remember they were so adorable. They were all dressed up: Abe in his suit and tie and his mother in a navy blue silk dress and the two of them were sitting there very stiffly. I think they must have been more nervous to meet me than I was to meet them. They were very sweet and greeted me warmly.

On the last day of his leave, Ed and I went to New York to spend the day together because he had to be on the ship in the late afternoon. I remember walking up and down 42nd Street. We were talking about the fact that we really wanted to get married. It was then that he gave me his Phi Beta Kappa key.

He asked me to give him a picture of myself. All I had was the professional

---

4   Sally is my dearest friend, a friendship of over 75 years.

head shot that I got for my New York debut. He put it on his bureau. He tells me that when his mother saw my picture with the violin and asked him who I was, he told her that I was the girl that he was going to marry.

We decided not to tell people in Philadelphia because we were both going to be away.

We had known each other for such a short time. The sum total of it was the five days when we first met and the five days of his return from Germany. By then we had already decided to be married. It was kismet!

When I went out to Oregon, I remember talking to Sally's mother, whose husband was a doctor. I had real concerns about being married to a doctor only because my concept of a doctor was that they were never home. It seemed they were always out on house calls, because in those days that is what doctors did. The hours were just terrible. I didn't know how we would mesh his schedule with mine in the music world.

We met again after all those weeks apart and rapidly planned our wedding and honeymoon.

We've now been married for more than 50 years, which shows what a damn good decision it was.

NFMC Young Artists Award, 1959

Ed and I were married December 23, 1956. During the 1957-58 season, I was teaching a lot and playing some concerts though I had no management. In the fall of 1958, I decided to try out for the National Federation of Music Clubs' Young Artists Award. It was a very important competition because along with the cash prize came a number of exciting performance opportunities. It also brought an offer of management through NCAC.[5]

The requirements for the audition were intense. Competitors had to prepare two full concert programs of about 75 minutes, along with a couple of required concertos, contemporary American music, and a Bach solo suite. There was almost 200 minutes of music. I needed to know the music and also have the stamina to be able to play it. It took me four days in a row to be able to get through all the material. I practiced the works in rotation to learn it all.

As luck would have it, I got the chicken pox after the preliminary audition and before the semifinal. I was extremely ill, with a fever of 104 degrees, and was just miserable. NFMC does the first set of auditions within the state, the next by region and the final one was national. That year, the preliminary and regional auditions were both in Philadelphia. Philadelphia's region included New York, and many of the most formidable performers came from that area. The finals were held in San

5 National Concert and Artists Corporation.

Diego, California, as part of the 1959 convention.

I sailed through the first audition, but after getting the chicken pox I lost some of my stamina. Louis Vyner knew me from my jobbing around town, and he turned out to be one of the judges for the regionals. It came down to me and a girl from New York who was a good violinist. I didn't play my best that day, but he knew what I could do. I always felt that he swung it in my direction, which was very helpful. It wasn't that I didn't deserve it, just that it could have gone either way. These things happen.

So I went to the finals in San Diego. We had to supply our own accompanist or use theirs. I found an accompanist in Los Angeles who was willing to spend the week with me in San Diego at my expense. I stayed with my godparents, Ralph and Rose Herzog, in Westwood and rehearsed for a week with the accompanist. Among the people at the Convention who later became friends were the Paganini String Quartet members who performed and judged at the Convention. The Quartet included two Curtis alums: first violinist Henri Temianka and violist David Schwartz.

In San Diego, we went through two eliminations. I had a lot of auditioning experience and was at the top of my game in San Diego. The auditions were formidable. The judges could call for any part of a piece, though they gave us the option of starting with our first choice for the first of the two performances.

I played the Ravel Tzigane as well as the Glazunov and Tchaikovsky concertos, all part of my large repertoire. I won the competition.

The NFMC was a wonderful prize. I have stayed in contact with the national organization[6] and various affiliates throughout my life. The monetary prize was $1,000, which in the summer of 1959 was a lot of money. However, it cost me almost that entire amount to pay for my expenses and those of my accompanist, so there wasn't much left over. I did get to be soloist at the Brevard and Chautauqua festivals. The winners also went to Cincinnati and played in a major concert there. Unfortunately, the management contract I was offered was terrible. One of the first things I was asked when I met with NCAC in New York was who I knew who might want to take me as a soloist. My husband looked at the contract and said he wanted them to change some things. I think they were going to pay me $400 per concert and take 20% of that. They also wanted money up front for publicity, and I would have to pay for my own accompanist. It was even worse than the one I had several years before with Columbia Artists, despite the fact that I had just won another major prize. So Ed threw the contract back on the desk and said, "This is not a contract. This is an indenture to slavery." And we walked out. So that was the end of me and New York management.

I began managing myself and after twenty years of reasonable success doing

---

6 In 1959 there were at least 650,000 members.

that, I was able to use that experience to launch Marcia's career, managing her and her Debussy Trio, which I continue to do now in 2009.

1959-60 Concert Experiences as NFMC Award Winner

Several 1959-60 concert season engagements at which I performed as a result of winning the NFMC award stick out in my memory.

Brevard Festival, North Carolina, June 1959

I played the Glazunov Concerto with James Pfohl conducting at the Brevard Festival on June 28, 1959. This is probably the only performance I ever did in the pouring rain. It was an outdoor concert space with just a tin roof to protect performers and audience. The concert was being broadcast live, so we could not stop when there was a deluge. The rain virtually drowned out the music, so that the people in the back rows of the audience couldn't hear very well. The humidity also wreaked havoc on the bow hair, causing it to stretch. The rain didn't abate until halfway through the Concerto, whereupon the noise on the roof was replaced by a chorus of frogs. The festival took place in the hills above the Blue Ridge Mountains in North Carolina, so we were surrounded by quite a bit of noisy nature outside. The recording of this concert captures the sounds of the rain beating on the tin roof.

Little Rock, Arkansas performance, 1960

I had already had earlier experiences of Southern attitudes on race while on tour with the Gotham Trio. In January of 1960, I was engaged by one of the NFMC clubs in Little Rock. At this time, there was still a lot of tumult over de-segregation. At one point, I was driven by the hosting chairwoman to see both the black and white high schools in the city. The black high school was a much newer brick building than the white high school, and the woman's comment was, "I don't know why they want to go to our high school; theirs is much nicer."

Chautauqua, 1960, a Borrowed Stradivarius

I played on the Gagliano I bought after the Paul Whiteman Show for a long time, but as I matured and was doing more exciting performances, I found that every time I needed to play something very important I would still have to borrow a better violin.

Another major solo performance resulting from the NFMC award was when I played the Saint-Saëns Concerto in B Minor under the direction of Walter Hendl at the Chautauqua Festival in the summer of 1960.

I was very lucky. I had played the Brahms Concerto a few weeks before with the Germantown Symphony, a community orchestra outside of Philadelphia. A gentleman came up after the concert and told me that he had a Stradivarius he would love to hear me play. I found that hard to believe because he was dressed like a farmer and called it a "Strad-eee-varius." But the conductor, Vernon Hammond, told me that the man was very wealthy and he collected and owned thirty to forty violins. So I made an appointment to go see him. He showed me the Stradivarius and agreed to lend it to me when I told him that I was on my way to Chautauqua to perform and then to audition for Heifetz. Ed and I drove our little Ford across the country to Los Angeles to audition for Heifetz after Chautauqua, with no air conditioning and a Stradivarius in the car!

Heifetz was very impressed with the violin and said that he thought he remembered the instrument from his student days. Then, I had to bring the violin back to Philadelphia. Part of my agreement with the owner was that I would play it at a major performance where he could hear it. I had been engaged by Louis Vyner to play the Glazunov Concerto with the Lancaster (Pennsylvania) Symphony. So I brought the fiddle back, played the concerto, and returned the Strad. Then I was back on my Gagliano for the next few years.

A few years later, in 1963, when Heifetz recommended that I be engaged as soloist at a Hollywood Bowl concert, I again felt that my violin was inadequate. I called up the gentleman who lent me the Strad before and he was willing to lend it to me for a few weeks to play at the Bowl. The violin was hand-carried by an airline pilot, who brought it to me. I had to do the same thing to return it, so it cost several hundred dollars just to send the violin back and forth.

JASCHA HEIFETZ
1960

Jascha Heifetz greets Sallie at Dickstein home in Brentwood.
Summer, 1962

JASCHA HEIFETZ, 1960

Heifetz's Application for a Job at UCLA

Gregor Piatigorsky used to come to our home for dinner or just to sit and talk. He loved good listeners and was very fond of Ed and me.

During one of his visits, he told us about how Heifetz came to teach at the University of California, Los Angeles (UCLA). He said that he had been encouraging Heifetz to start teaching young people around 1957 or 1958. Grisha said that Heifetz had been coaching professionals occasionally, but he had never really taught on a regular basis.

Heifetz didn't realize that maybe everyone in the world didn't know his name. According to Grisha, Heifetz wrote a letter to the UCLA Music Department and said simply, "I am Jascha Heifetz. I would like to teach violin at your school." The low-level secretary who opened the mail at UCLA sent back a form letter thanking him for his application and informing him that there were no open positions at the time but they would keep his application on file. In typical Heifetz style, he picked up the phone to contact Chancellor Murphy of UCLA and by the next week he was offered a position on any terms he wanted.

Studying with Heifetz at UCLA, 1960

Heifetz set up a very unusual protocol for his master class at UCLA. During those first two years, he allowed students under the age of 21 to be what he called "performing students." They paid $500 or $600 for the 16-week semester starting in September. Then he had a "performing auditor" category for students from 21 to 25. Students over 25 were not supposed to play–they were only supposed to listen. I guess he thought students over 25 would be too set in their ways to teach.

When Ed and I decided to come to California to see if we wanted to live here, I wanted to take advantage of possible study with Heifetz at UCLA. I saw these categories and of course I had no interest in being an auditor, so I lied about my age since they didn't require a birth certificate. I said that I was 24½ so that I could get "performing auditor" status. At the time, performing auditors had to pay about $330 for the semester.

All performing students had to audition, so one was scheduled for me at the end of August before the class started. Ed and I had been traveling after the

Chautauqua Festival and I had a Stradivarius with me. I didn't practice for the three weeks of the trip, so I had about 48 hours to prepare for the audition.

When I went in, I knew Heifetz was strong on scales, so I had prepared both scales and concertos to play for him. We had a very interesting meeting because Heifetz was fond of testing the musician. He asked me how my hearing was. When I told him that I had perfect pitch, he immediately sat down at the piano to test that out. He asked if I could play the piano. I told him that I had been an accompanist at Curtis for many years. He then asked me to play the two hardest tuttis of the Glazunov Concerto to prove myself. At the end of that, he said I would be called. The next day I got the phone call informing me that I had been accepted.

A couple of weeks later, I arrived for the first class and the room was empty. Heifetz was nowhere in sight. I found him down the hallway at a stairwell. He asked me if anyone was there and when I told him that it was just me, he laughed. We then went into the classroom, we locked the door and he put paper over the peep window in the door so that no one could see. He told me that he hadn't accepted anyone else and that I would be the class. Of all of his students, I probably had the most undivided attention from him. From September through the end of January, on a twice-a-week basis, Tuesdays and Thursdays from 1-4, he worked with me exclusively. I was studying between 6 and 7 hours a week. At that time, he charged the seemingly huge fee of $100 per hour to private students and I was paying a pro-rated fee of about $3.30! After a couple of months, he decided he didn't want to bother to come to the UCLA campus, so he had me come to his private studio in Beverly Hills. It was a hexagonal building that had been built outside of his house on Linda Crest and that's where I took the rest of my lessons that year.

Heifetz's Teaching Philosophy

With the luxury of so many hours, I could bring him the equivalent of a full concert program each week. I would play a sonata, a concerto and two or three short pieces plus scales and Paganini Etudes on Tuesday. We would go through those and he would make suggestions. Then I was to go home, digest and practice it on Wednesday. On Thursday I would come back and play the whole thing all over again and if he was satisfied, we would move on. About 95% of the time he was satisfied with my incorporation of his suggestions and he would ask me to bring him something new for the following week. From Friday through Monday I would prepare the new program. I tried to go into repertoire that I hadn't covered much at Curtis.

Over the next few months, I managed to cover most of the Bach solo sonatas, both Prokofiev violin concertos and many short, encore-type pieces. I also prepared the Strauss and Saint-Saëns sonatas that he was famous for playing.

Heifetz's philosophy wasn't based in pedagogic methodology. He was Heifetz. He'd play for me. He was very thoughtful and thorough and would analyze a problem of fingering, for example, and make suggestions. Sometimes he would come to me on Thursday after a Tuesday lesson and suggest a new solution he had come up with in the time between. This was quite different from the style of other teachers I had known, such as Ivan Galamian, who had his way of doing things and would not accept any variation. Zimbalist's style was looser which I suspect was more typical of the Leopold Auer school. Auer's students were so talented that Auer just let them grow with only some necessary discipline.

Since I was already a well-established artist in my own right, Heifetz treated me not as a student but as a younger colleague. I really appreciated that and flourished. He could be very sarcastic in his corrections and he liked to test me often. I was pretty confident and could mostly hold my own. I admired him tremendously and was learning just by being around him and watching his mind work as he came up with solutions. His philosophy on violin playing technique was that you should try for it with gusto and if you missed now and then, that was ok. Of course, he was virtually perfect in his own performances.

Heifetz tended to play with a very strong grip on the bow. One of the exercises that he showed me was, instead of putting your thumb through the normal thumb hole, to put your thumb around the base of the frog and hold the bow almost like you would a tennis racket. He was a hard-ball tennis player, which was kind of unusual for a violinist, and he had a very strong grip. Consequently, when you were very close to him, the sound that he produced was a bit on the grainy side. But that was what gave him that marvelous, brilliant edge when he was in the concert hall. The graininess was lost within a few feet and all that was left was the sparkle and the brilliance.

In the Studio

Heifetz was a very well-rounded musician in every aspect, even though some people thought all he did was play fast. He had very little regard for what he called "musicriminologists." He didn't worry about Baroque performance practices and things like whether you started a trill from above or below. He started his on the note, no matter what kind of music he was playing. That said, I was surprised to find that he had done a lot of research into original scores. He would search for a wrong note quite diligently in original manuscripts.

His idea on fingering, which I found to be very effective, was that he showed a huge variety in tone quality by varying the fingering on repetitive passages. He would play repeats on a different string or in a different position so that it wasn't just loud or soft, but really had a change of quality.

Several times, he seemed to be puzzled by the manner of practicing and approach to learning that his students of the 1960s seemed to have. He echoed what Zimbalist had told me years before about being virtually petrified of the teacher who was god. Of course, for the Jewish boys in Russia, this was true. I experienced the same thing with my scholarship at Curtis every time I had a lesson. The kids of the 1960s just didn't seem to be that concerned. Not that they didn't try, but Heifetz had difficulty in relating to the current point of view. He would discuss this with me at great length and ask questions in a way that would help him to understand. He really wanted to understand students who had never been to conservatory under pressure as he and I had.

We had so much solfège and harmony, and we were all good pianists as secondary instruments. Heifetz and Zimbalist were excellent pianists and knew the repertoire. Both could sit down and accompany me the same way I would sit down and accompany them.

Heifetz was also a great student of art and well known as a stamp collector. He even traded stamps with Franklin Delano Roosevelt. One time he showed me his very extensive collection of stamps on musical subjects from all over the world. He had many albums that were beautifully organized.

It's interesting to me that Heifetz had a couple of kids of his own, and had a couple of wives, but he remained an extremely shy man. He was notorious for suing people, but when I first met him at UCLA he was literally hiding around the stairs because he didn't want to bump into a lot of other people. He did everything he could to be a private person, though in Los Angeles he was quite well known and recognized.

After 1960, Heifetz left and went to USC, where he started what was called "The Institute." He and Piatigorsky were put into some rarefied format where they held master classes, but they didn't count toward university credits.

By that time, I was expecting Sallie and had matriculated at USC, where I was working towards my doctorate. When Heifetz came, I wanted to work with him again, which I was able to do for a couple of years. Then the class got larger. I had been spoiled from my very special association with him. Despite the new situation, he always treated me well. He continued to listen to me and gave me several very special private lessons when I had concerts coming up, even after he left USC. He only stuck it out there a couple of years.

A Glimpse into Heifetz's Personality

Heifetz had a wicked sense of humor. For instance, one time I'd gotten a very fancy hairdo at Saks Fifth Avenue and really thought I looked like hot stuff. He didn't like my hairstyle and turned to me when I walked in the studio and asked, "Has your husband seen you?!" He had a very respectful relationship with Ed, and always seemed to admire the fact that we had a good marriage. When I had Sallie, he came to our house, knocked on the door, and handed Ed a beautiful bottle of aged cognac as a congratulations. I have a wonderful photo of him wearing a look of embarrassment as he held Sallie when she was about eight months old.

When Marcia was about five months old, we were involved in a terrible automobile accident on the Pacific Coast Highway. My back and neck were injured. I couldn't hold the violin properly for about five months or even turn my head for two months. Heifetz heard about it and called me. He wanted to make sure I was okay and said he was more than happy to send me to his own specialist if I wasn't satisfied with mine.

Heifetz was well known for his phone call style, which reflected his shyness. When he called people on the phone, he wouldn't say hello. We wouldn't hang up because we knew it was him. We would respond, "Oh, hello Mr. Heifetz, how are you?" and then he would answer with a laugh.

His relationship with Piatigorsky was particularly warm and friendly. Knowing Piatigorsky, I don't know how it could have been otherwise. Heifetz got into arguments with a lot of other people, though. For example, he had apparently been friendly with Zimbalist for a long time and there are even photos of them swimming together near Heifetz's Naples Island home near Long Beach. Later on, he and Zimbalist stopped speaking after some sort of misunderstanding. This was the difficult side of Heifetz's personality. Fortunately for me, he was never anything but friendly and generous to a fault.

During my semester at UCLA, he became concerned about my comfort with my chin rest. I told him I didn't like the one I had and never seemed able to find the right one. In typical Heifetz fashion, he considered the problem at home and came back the next lesson showing me what I would call a bouquet of chin rests, a beautiful array from his private collection, made of rosewood or ebony. He spread them out before me and asked which I would like. Because he had a reputation for being stingy, I assumed I would have to buy one from him. I chose a beautiful rosewood chin rest that was slightly higher than mine, which was what I wanted. He got a big smile on his face, and said he had thought that would be the one I'd want. And he gave it to me. It turned out that it was a hand-carved chin rest that had been made for Fritz Kreisler. Later on I had a duplicate made so that I could have one for each of my violins. That, again, just demonstrates the wonderful spirit Heifetz always showed me. I will always be grateful for the wonderful relationship that we had. After that, there was no other violin teacher that I could study with, and I never did.

Jack Benny Anecdote

My memories of Heifetz would not be complete without sharing this little example of his droll sense of humor.

Schoenberg Hall is the smaller concert hall at UCLA. It seats about 500 people—the perfect size for a solo violin recital. For this particular Heifetz recital, the hall was packed.

During the concert, he broke a string and had to walk off-stage to get a new one. When he walked back on stage, he made a funny quip which I don't remember, but it got quite a laugh from the audience.

All of a sudden, a gentleman in the fourth row stood up. It was Jack Benny. He said, loud enough for everyone to hear, "If he's going to start telling jokes, then I'm going to come up there and start playing the violin!"

LOS ANGELES MUSICAL COMMUNITY and a NEW FAMILY 1960-1969

Diana Steiner Hollywood Bowl Review

"Diana Steiner displayed commendable achievements in the way of a big tone and accurate technique."

Albert Goldberg, *Los Angeles Times*, July 27, 1963

Courtesy Family Archives

❧

LOS ANGELES MUSICAL COMMUNITY
AND A NEW FAMILY
1960-1969

Moving to Los Angeles, Summer 1960

When Ed and I arrived in Los Angeles, we stayed with my godparents, Ralph and Rose Herzog, for about ten days until we found an apartment. Ed began his first job at Kaiser Permanente in Hollywood. We lived in a nice apartment in Brentwood on Chenault Street. By January, we decided that we wanted to live in Los Angeles permanently and started looking for a house to buy. In the fall of 1960, I began my postgraduate studies with Heifetz at UCLA.

Minna Coe and the National Association of
American Composers and Conductors, 1960-61

Soon after I arrived in Los Angeles, I was contacted by Minna Coe. She happened to be an old acquaintance of Mother's from their Portland days, when Minna was a singer.

Minna's second marriage was to a wealthy man, Willard Coe.[1] Minna and Willard had a beautiful hacienda-style home in Pacific Palisades. Their home was particularly interesting because a previous owner had invited the famous Mexican artist David Alfaro Siqueiros to come and stay when he was having political problems in his home country. As a thank you to the family, he painted a gorgeous mural on the inside of the plaster fence in the front of their house. When the Coes died, their estate left the wall with its mural to UCLA who turned it down because it was too expensive to move. It stayed there for another ten or fifteen years until finally the museum in Santa Barbara managed to purchase it. They transported it to Santa Barbara where it sits now in front of the museum on State Street. Every once in a while we go up to visit it just because we loved the painting. Ed and I actually tried to buy the house from the Coe estate but were outbid; the Siqueiros was almost ours!

Minna used to host fantastic musicales and taught me how to do it. She could seat a hundred people in her large living room and would have a nice reception for

---

1 His family endowed the library at Mount Saint Mary's College and his sister was a nun there.

the attendees afterward. She liked to seek out young musicians and present them in private programs. She called them her protégés. When she heard that I was in town working with Heifetz, she got in touch and I became one of her flock.

As a patroness, she was very involved with the National Association of American Composers and Conductors (now NAACC). She got me involved and I was a member for many years, including as a member of its board. Through the NAACC I met composers like John Vincent, who at the time was chair of the Composition Department at UCLA. I also became acquainted with Mario Castelnuovo-Tedesco.

The other group with which I became very active was the Monday Evening Concerts, which was run by Lawrence Morton who was sort of the guru of contemporary music concerts in the Los Angeles area. He was well-known for the forward-looking series that he managed for at least 20 years. After he was no longer the head, it really lost the forward thrust that it had under his leadership. I performed at least twice a year on the series. Among many works, I played the Halsey Stevens Suite, Stravinsky works under the direction of Robert Craft and Schoenberg's Ode to Napoleon. Lawrence would sometimes couple the contemporary works with performances of major classical works. Some of the contemporary pieces we played were good and some weren't.

I also worked with Leonard Stein, who was one of the most knowledgeable people in contemporary music I've ever met. He certainly is a major figure in Los Angeles's history of 20th century music performance. I originally met him when I was preparing for a big competition in New York which required that contestants play a new piece by a University of California at Berkeley composer, Andrew Imbrie. Competitors had to learn it in ten days and it was a bear.

Leonard and I became good friends over the years. We played a number of performances together at the Monday Evening Concerts. I also met a pianist recommended by him, Michael Zearott, with whom I played a number of interesting programs on the Los Angeles County Museum of Art series, including the Hindemith Quartet for violin, piano, cello and clarinet. We also did the Fantasy Sonata for violin and viola by Arthur Benjamin with Michael playing the orchestra part on piano and Myra Kestenbaum on viola, a performance of which I am proud.

The early days with Minna and the NAACC got me off to a very good start in the city with a lot of very interesting musical connections.

Simon Ramo

Another interesting person I met through Minna and the NAACC was Virginia Ramo, and subsequently her husband Simon Ramo. He is the "R" in

TRW, a scientist and engineer. They were a very wealthy couple, and she gave lots of support to contemporary music.

Ramo was also an amateur violinist and he came to our house to play quartets once. Like most musicians, we did a lot of chamber music for fun, sometimes with all professionals and other times with good amateurs. We would get together and play in the evenings and have supper afterwards. One of those evenings, in the course of a conversation, he mentioned, "I know the name Steiner. I wonder if you're related to Ferenz Steiner." When I told him that Ferenz Steiner was my father, he was excited and related to me that he met my father in his home state of Utah, where my father taught and conducted before he met my mother.[2] When Ramo was a high school student and fairly competent violinist, he was trying to get a scholarship to attend university. My father was on the judging panel that awarded Ramo a scholarship, and that was how he was able to attend university in the late 20s. And 40 years later he was sitting in my living room playing chamber music with his judge's daughter!

Ed's Love of Music

The wealth of talent that became our family's circle of musical friends in Los Angeles was incredible. I felt embraced by the Los Angeles musical scene, as did Ed whose love of music pushed him to enjoy the experience in any way he could. He turned pages, listened, and balanced performances at rehearsals. He would be out front saying "The orchestra is too loud," or, "The microphone is not right." He has a superb ear and an unbelievable knowledge of music. He was happy to be a part of it, certainly adding to the richness of our relationship.

A New Home and a New Baby

In 1961, while I was working with Heifetz and Ed was practicing at Kaiser Permanente, we decided that we were going to make the move to Los Angeles permanent. By the late spring, when I completed my UCLA term with Heifetz, we discovered that I was expecting in December of 1961. We were living in an apartment and decided that it would be a good idea to look for a house, which would be better for us with a new baby.

In the early fall of 1961, I began my first semester at USC and was driving between Brentwood and USC on an almost daily basis, attending chamber music and music history classes. It got very difficult to do that and run around house-hunting. A realtor friend of my godparents did a lot of searching and found us an

---

2   There is a photograph of my father conducting at the Mormon Tabernacle in Salt Lake City in the Mormon Archives.

absolutely perfect home in Brentwood, which we still live in fifty years later. In today's world, it would have been considered a "fixer-upper," but it was a beautiful, custom-built, traditional, Mediterranean two-story. It was just perfect for us.

We put in a bid within two hours of seeing the house, on a Sunday. The next day, Monday, I was sitting in chamber music class with Gabor Rejto when a secretary came in to tell one of the students that she had to go home immediately because it was possible that her house had burned down. That was the opening day of the now infamous Bel-Air fire. As I was new to California, I was unaware of fire seasons, earthquakes, and the other natural disasters to which we have become accustomed. On my way home, as I was driving north on Sepulveda Boulevard, I saw huge clouds of smoke. I was stopped at Santa Monica Boulevard, south of where we lived near Sunset, and asked for identification and my home address because our apartment was within the fire area. I was able to go home and pack up a lot of our personal belongings in case an evacuation was necessary. At that time, the conflagration had started on the east side of the Sepulveda Pass, but within a few hours had jumped the canyon and was burning its way through Mount Saint Mary's College, about twenty blocks north of our apartment. The fire went on for days. As a result of this now historic fire, all of the insurance companies put a clamp on issuing new home insurance policies in the fire area. We were in escrow for the house. Luckily, an insurance dealer friend of my godparents worked very hard and since our house was two blocks south of Sunset instead of one block north, was able to get us an insurance policy. Otherwise, we never would have been able to get the mortgage and purchase our home.

That was in October and we moved in the day before Thanksgiving. I was only four weeks from my due date with Sallie. It was a pressured time, but we were lucky that it worked out so well.

On December 23, our beautiful Sallie was born. As luck would have it, it was two days before Christmas. Ed was on night duty at Kaiser Permanente, and the head doctor almost refused to let him take off to be with me during the birth. We laughed about the fact that the doctor said, "Ok, I will let you off this time, but don't make a habit of it!"

I was quite ill after the birth and the nurse I had hired called to tell me that she was unable to care for babies because she had gotten the flu. When I was released from the hospital three days later, I was very weak. My mother flew out from Philadelphia on 24 hours notice and stayed with me for the two weeks until I got back on my feet.

Sallie was such a beautiful, lively baby girl. She certainly was the answer to any new parent's prayers and dreams. We were now a real family.

University of Southern California Years

I made direct contacts with many musicians in Los Angeles. One of the most important was the renewed friendship with a Hungarian friend from my New York days, Gabor Rejto. He was Professor of Cello and Chair of Chamber Music at USC. When I decided I wanted to work toward a doctorate degree, Gabor invited me to attend USC in fall 1961 and additionally, join the conservatory faculty. As I attended classes in my seventh month of pregnancy I used to joke that I was the fertility symbol for the class during that first fall semester.

I had a bachelor's degree from Curtis, certified by the State of Pennsylvania, having completed all of my musical studies, as well as 34 academic units. I am the only person that I ever knew who attended three universities to earn 34 academic credits! One summer, I took five units at UCLA. The summer of 1956, when Ed and I got engaged, I earned ten units at Willamette University in Salem, Oregon–Mother's alma mater. In between, I attended night school at Temple University in Philadelphia. That last semester, just before we got married, I had to take twelve units to finish. Pennsylvania required a semester residency (12 units or more), so I used to go from 8 a.m. until 1 p.m. I could take any course I wanted, so whatever fit into those hours is what I studied. I took English literature, French, Latin American history, art history, and political science. I even took some homework on my honeymoon, though of course, I didn't do any.

The only way I managed to complete the work was by going to the classes and studying the textbooks on the subway–and Ed wrote all my book reports. He wrote one on France for political science, for which he had to clip New York Times articles for four months. When he had a drawer full of clippings, he wrote the paper. I got an A in the course and he got an A on the paper. For book reports, our deal was that I'd select the thinnest books available in each subject. Then Ed read the books and wrote reports. I knew French, so that posed no problem. Though they were considered advanced courses at Temple, I found them rather elementary compared to what I had learned years before. So that's how I managed to get my bachelor's degree.

When I applied to the doctoral program at USC, the music department accepted me at the doctoral level immediately. The faculty recognized my professional level and very much wanted me to attend. But the general admissions department evaluated my credits and admitted me as an entering sophomore because all of my Curtis music credits had been taken before I finished high school even though they were college-level equivalents. It took about six months for the dean of the music school, Raymond Kendall, to convince the administration that they had to accept my degree on face value, similar to what they did for people who came from Europe with conservatory degrees. It finally got straightened out, but for a while I was on a temporary basis.

In 1962, I continued working with Heifetz while I was a doctoral candidate. Heifetz was an entity unto himself and no credit was awarded for attending his classes. He had a couple of students in his class who were budding fine players. One was Glenn Dicterow; though still a teenager, he was dripping with talent.[3] Carol Zindel and Varujan Kojian also achieved considerable success.[4] I was the only student in the class studying for a doctorate at the same time.

For a DMA in violin, one of the requirements was two years of violin lessons. The violin department chair was Eudice Shapiro, a former student of Zimbalist at Curtis. She had graduated Curtis and was already a well-established concertizing violinist when I arrived as a child. We'd had much the same training, but after having studied with Zimbalist and Heifetz, there was no point in me taking more lessons.

I spoke to Gabor and asked him for advice. I told him I was particularly interested in contemporary music which I had less opportunity to explore thoroughly. (Zimbalist didn't care to teach anything past Sibelius.) I had studied Prokofiev and Stravinsky works with Veda, Heifetz, and on my own. I was very impressed by the courses that I'd taken on Bartok and Stravinsky with Halsey Stevens and Ingolf Dahl. I thought it would be interesting to coach contemporary music with them. Gabor said he'd see what he could do.

About a week later he said he'd arranged for me to major in performance of contemporary music on violin, which meant in essence I could take my "violin lessons" with Ingolf and Halsey. That was just wonderful because they respected me as an instrumentalist and I highly respected their amazing knowledge and talents as composers and composer-historians. So I decided to do my doctoral thesis on 20th century music for violin alone which allowed me total autonomy to work on my choice of material.

My thesis covered 1900-1965 and was completed with Dahl and Stevens as my thesis mentors. I analyzed some 65 works starting with Eugene Ysaye and I performed several of them.

Stevens had written the then definitive biography on Bartok. I visited his private studio several times and the shelves were lined with an extensive library of books on Bartok. Most were in the original Hungarian, which Stevens had learned, including notebooks, holographs and historical studies. It was a most amazing collection and the semester lectures he gave on Bartok at USC were truly outstanding.

Dahl was a true gem. I studied contemporary compositional analysis with him, which I had never delved into before. We began exploring orchestral tone poems of various composers and the music of Ingolf's passionate expertise: Stravinsky. He gave a detailed course on Stravinsky similar to Halsey's course

---

3 Glenn became concertmaster of the New York Philharmonic.
4 Carol was one of the students Heifetz had me coach on the side. She had a successful career in Portland, Oregon. Varujan (deceased) became conductor in Salt Lake City and Santa Barbara.

on Bartok. Dahl and I had a ball, especially when he would digress and play jazz piano which he did with such aplomb.

Once I was free to choose my topic of study, I took what were basically private lessons with each of these composers. These lessons were officially to be in 20th century performance practices, but they really became an exchange of ideas. I learned so much.

I performed Ingolf's Concerto a Tre for violin, cello and clarinet with cellist Larry Lesser and his cousin, clarinetist Dick Lesser. We coached the piece with Ingolf and performed it on a live broadcast on the Los Angeles County Museum series. Ingolf told me later that it was the best performance he'd ever heard of his piece. The recording is now in the Curtis library archives.

There were other special teachers and colleagues with whom I worked at USC. One of these was Alice Ehlers, a Baroque specialist and grande dame of the harpsichord. She gave me a different perspective on Baroque performance practices. I went through all of the Bach violin and harpsichord sonatas with her, which was enlightening.

I studied choral conducting with Jimmy Vail, who graduated Curtis around the time that I did. This was also new to me. The highlight of my brief choral conducting experience was Haydn's Creation. One of my assignments was to find a chorus to sing with during the semester. Luckily, the Brentwood Presbyterian Church choir was performing the Haydn piece. I observed rehearsals and sang with the choir, though I didn't sing in the concert.

One of Alice Ehlers's best students was Malcolm Hamilton, a fine harpsichord player. Then there was Brooks Smith, Heifetz's superb accompanist for many years.

One night Gabor and Brooks came to dinner at our home. Before dinner, Brooks and I decided to read through the Saint-Saëns Sonata, which Heifetz played so unbelievably. Gabor had never heard it before. The last movement is one grand perpetual motion and Brooks was used to playing it at Heifetz's tempo. I also liked to play it fast. I was too busy playing to notice, but Ed said that Gabor stood behind the piano watching the notes fly by in total amazement.

The Steiner-Berfield Trio

Frances came to Los Angeles for a visit in the summer of 1962 when Sallie was still a baby. We introduced her to several young men, two of whom proposed to her. She married one of them, Mervin Tarlow, a lawyer. As a result, she moved to L.A. and decided to go for her doctorate at USC too.

There we met a fellow DMA candidate, pianist David Berfield. We started playing trios together partly as a requirement for our DMA degrees, one of which was a chamber music recital. All three of us got credit for the work we did together. Greatly encouraged by piano professor John Crown, we formally became the Steiner-Berfield

Trio, and stayed together for almost 12 years, playing concerts and recording.

The Steiner-Berfield Trio also represented the State of California at the Kennedy Center in Washington, D.C. for the Bicentennial celebration in 1976. We played a piece by Gail Kubik, a composition professor at Pomona College. The Bicentennial presenters only took two groups from each state and we were the only classical group from California. Yvonne Brathwaite Burke, a Congresswoman from California who later became a supervisor on the Los Angeles County Board of Supervisors, introduced us to the audience. Amongst the attendees were the Catholic nuns that had befriended me when I won the Friday Morning Music Club competition in 1950. They had been in the audience when I played with the National Symphony at Constitution Hall and now they were there again.

David also accompanied me in solo recitals and on a couple of my recordings. Particularly satisfying were our concerts together at the National Federation of Music Clubs conventions in Albuquerque in 1969 and Portland in 1979. It seemed like every ten years the NFMC would ask me to come back as it did in 1989 with Marcia and The Debussy Trio in Fort Worth, and 1999 in St. Louis to play for my fortieth anniversary as a Young Artist winner.

Hollywood Bowl

Heifetz recommended me to be soloist at the Hollywood Bowl during the 1963 summer season. The L.A. Philharmonic manager called him wanting a violinist to play Tzigane on an all-Ravel program at the Bowl. Soprano Blanche Thebom and pianist Lorin Hollander were the other soloists, with André Kostelanetz conducting. All soloists were presented with red roses, some of which they graciously shared with the concertmaster. Albert Goldberg wrote an excellent review of my performance in the Los Angeles Times, but couldn't resist mentioning that I didn't share my roses (my hands were full with a borrowed Strad!).

Backstage after the performance, I was greeted by the president of the Mu Phi Epsilon sorority's L.A. alumni chapter, Sima Mannick. She invited me to join the local chapter, so I gained a group of warm, welcoming friends.

Years later, there was a Dean Martin-style roast held in honor of Albert Goldberg. For my segment of the roast, I decided that I was going to get back at Goldberg for his review. I went up and said, "Mr. Goldberg, I always appreciated the review you gave of my performance, but I was very concerned that you thought I was being stingy by not sharing my roses with members of the orchestra. Just to prove that I'm not, I've saved one all these years just to share with you." Then I pulled out a dead rose from underneath the podium and handed it to him. That got a big laugh.

Our Other Life: Foxhunting

Though the main focus of this story centers on music, I have been fortunate to partake of many other fascinating life experiences. The most important, as always, revolved around family and our activities together. In addition to the trips we took as a family, there was the exotic avocation which Ed enjoyed and in which we participated in various forms: English foxhunting. Ed became interested in this in the mid-sixties when an attorney friend with whom he worked, Louis Bell, invited him to go horseback riding. Louis was from upstate New York and was quite a proficient horseman. Ed told him, "I've never been on a horse. Where I come from, horses pulled garbage wagons."

Louis introduced Ed to a trainer and at first he rented a horse. Then before long, he was riding with the West Hills Hunt as a guest. West Hills was part of the American Foxhunting Association which is associated with the worldwide foxhunting groups. The sport is traditional in England and American foxhunters were located primarily in Virginia and other eastern states, where the sport was generally enjoyed by high society landowners. It was not a sport in which Jewish people usually participated.

The rules for foxhunting in the United States are similar to those in England. It requires formal dress in red coats that are called "pinks." People earned those by proving riding proficiency. Everyone else dressed in black, wearing jodhpurs, high hunting boots and riding English saddle. Ed became quite fascinated with the sport even though he had to learn quite a bit that first year. By the fifth year, though, he had earned his "pink."

Foxhunting season in California runs from November through April, when it begins to get too warm. There were lots of opportunities to ride in southern California in the 1960s through the 1980s, including in the Santa Monica Mountains and the San Fernando Valley. West Hills Hunt ran a formal hunt every Saturday morning that began at 7:00 a.m. This meant that the riders had to get their horses saddled before sunrise. Some had to trailer the horses for hours in order to get to the hunt site and were essentially up all night. Our trainer took care of Ed's horse, had him saddled to go, and then she would take care of the horse when the hunt was over.

The foxhunt was very colorful and exciting to watch. Spectators could follow by car on fire roads, though we had to be careful not to disturb the scent for the hounds. West Hills Hunt had a full-time huntsman whose job was to train and breed the hounds. The club had at least 36 pairs at any given time and others in training that were housed at Porter Ranch. As homes began to fill the area, the group had to keep moving the hounds farther and farther out. In the 1960s, one could foxhunt on ranches of at least 5,000 acres, including the Porter and Ahmanson Ranches and the area which is now Westlake and Lake Sherwood, all now full of homes.

The hounds are trained to follow by scent. Fox were scarce and became even scarcer as the inhabited areas began to encroach on the wildlife. Therefore, the prey was most often coyote. Coyotes are very "wily" animals, much like the cartoon character "Wile E. Coyote." They were hardly ever caught, though they enjoyed running and teasing the hounds. The riders essentially became spectators following the hounds. The huntsman would keep the hounds in control and let them run, using a horn and special calls that the hounds understood.

A sumptuous hunt breakfast took place after the riders returned, sometimes after three or more hours of riding. It was the responsibility of the members to take turns providing the meal. We served out in the open, sometimes on portable tables and other times on the hoods of cars. One of the most important items was the punchbowl. When the riders returned they were extremely thirsty; after they'd had soda and "kids' punch" they would then hit the real punch bowl, which included liquor.

Ed and I devised one of the more popular punch bowls. Our secret recipe mixed white wine, usually a German Riesling, and champagne in equal amounts, with a dash of Cointreau. For every six bottles of each, we used about a bottle of Cointreau, which smoothed it out and made it go down very easily. We poured this over lots of ice. It was considered bad form to run out of punch.

In addition to riding in the Los Angeles environs, where the hounds were kenneled, we also went once or twice a year to ride with Brooks Firestone, of the Firestone family and the Firestone vineyards, just north of Solvang, where we stayed for the weekend. There would be two hunts, a country square dance, a barbecue and a formal ball.

We rode in several other magnificent locations. These included Cota de Caza in San Diego county, the Lockheed Ranch near Palm Springs, and the Irvine Ranch in Orange County. These former ranches have all been totally taken over by housing, but at the time they were empty.

The first master of the hunt we knew was Harold Ramser, who owned a 5,000-acre ranch, Corte Madera, located between San Diego and the Mexican border. We used to stay east of San Diego in Green Valley and hunted on his ranch usually twice a year.

Another hunt was near Camarillo in Sycamore Canyon in Ventura County, which is now a state park. There's still plenty of space there, but the state passed a law banning dogs off a leash. You can't have foxhounds on a leash, so that was the end of that hunting ground

Over the years, Ed owned several fine horses. They had to jump pretty high fences, three- to five-feet, and wide ditches. His horses were 17-hand or better. We had a champion Appaloosa named Moonshine that was California high-jump champion for five years. A couple of times, we watched him participate in jumping competitions with other riders up at the Cow Palace near San Francisco.

Ed rode for 26 years with the West Hills Hunt and was honored for that fact. He was one of the few riders who stayed that long. Notable members over the years included former president Ronald Reagan and actor Burgess Meredith.

In addition to the regular foxhunts, there was an annual formal Hunt Ball. It was held alternately at the Beverly Hilton, Century Plaza, Beverly Hills and Beverly Wilshire Hotels. In fact, one time, the crazy guy who was running the Beverly Wilshire decided to make his entrance to the ball on a horse. He came in through the kitchen and rode the horse around the tables. Sallie and Marcia attended the hunt balls a number of times, which was an experience in itself. The balls always opened with bagpipers and Highland dancing and then proceeded to the regular dancing and a banquet.

It was a different life. It was a great relaxation and change of pace for all of us. We enjoyed the entire time as part of the club and made many great friends who continued to be friends for many years afterward. It was a spectacular experience.

1970S and 1980S

Frances Steiner, Conductor

1970S AND 1980S

House in Lincoln Beach, Oregon

Usually, Ed and I, the girls and Mother vacationed together in Oregon for several weeks in the summer. In 1969 and 1970, we stayed at Salishan Lodge. It was a great resort, but it was also expensive and not directly on the ocean. We always visited Mother's former violin student, Fay Mort, who owned a house in Lincoln Beach which was fifty feet from the ocean. We sat in her living room and it felt like being on a boat, without the seasickness! The girls could play on the beach and there were none of the problems they were exposed to on the California beaches, such as drinking and pot smoking. We appreciated the wholesome atmosphere. We could build bonfires and have weenie and marshmallow roasts on the beach.

We loved the area so much that Ed and I decided that we should try to buy a house in Lincoln Beach for our vacations. We called Fay to see if she knew a good realtor in the area. She told us that the house next door to her was for sale. She was certain that it was exactly what we wanted, and she was right. Even though the realtor had lined up several choices for us, we began escrow on the house within an hour of seeing it.

We have continued to enjoy the house at Lincoln Beach over the years and have brought our children and grandchildren there, so that four generations of the family have enjoyed this special place.

Margaret Hurley

Our family's friendship with Margaret Hurley, starting in 1971, was one of the rare coincidences of our lives in many ways because, as of the writing of this in 2009, at age 96, she is still a dear friend and surrogate grandmother. Her husband Joe was a distinguished illustrator and art director in the movie business; in fact, he won an Oscar nomination for his work on Alfred Hitchcock's Psycho.

In the early 1970s, when Sallie was at the Westlake School for Girls and Marcia was at the John Thomas Dye School, I hired Margaret Hurley to drive the carpool for me once a week. She was looking for something extra to do, as her children were adults, and luckily enough we found each other and she's been a true friend to all of us ever since.

Margaret became a wonderful companion and an influence on both the girls.

For instance, she encouraged Sallie as she began to show considerable talent in gymnastics. Sallie eventually became a prize-winner in the CIF (California Interscholastic Federation) division up through high school. Even though she showed considerable musical talent in her elementary school years, her natural leanings seemed to be more toward dance and gymnastics. Margaret's willingness to continue driving the girls was most helpful in allowing Sallie to continue.

In Marcia's case, Margaret drove her to harp lessons in Pasadena with Susann McDonald throughout those important formative years. Margaret was a willing and sympathetic pair of ears as Marcia progressed and coped with success and occasional frustration.

Guadagnini

By 1970, Ed was quite successful in his medical practice and we had enough money to buy a fine violin. Benny Koodlach found a J. B. Guadagnini for me in 1971. Benny had such a magic touch with setting a sound post, so that the instrument sounded better than in any other setting. He had worked for Heifetz and Piatigorsky for many years, and they were pretty picky. When I heard the violin, even though I thought I'd seen it before, it sounded fantastic. I virtually bought it on sight. That became my primary violin. I never let go of the Gagliano because normally you want to have a second violin. But it was difficult for me to switch back and forth because there was almost one-eighth inch difference between the two. I lent the Gagliano to a few people so that it would get played, but I wouldn't let it travel outside the city.

The Guadagnini was my best violin until I bought my Stradivarius in 1982 and I played a number of important concerts on it. From 1974 to 1979, all of my commercial recordings were done on the Guadagnini. Its sound is pure, rich, and beautifully balanced. Around the same time, my sister purchased a Guadagnini cello. The two instruments were made only about two years apart. When we played together, the sound was so beautifully matched; it was like having one grand instrument with eight strings.

Recordings

The last recording that I did with David Berfield was called Fantasie. The works are based on operatic melodies, including Carmen. I was particularly proud of that recording because I did it in one take. Normally recordings are spliced together from many takes. A couple of weeks after making the recording, I went to Philadelphia and played on a special program of former Zimbalist students at Curtis who had returned to pay tribute to him.

At that concert, Zimbalist sat in the front row of Curtis Hall, which was totally full. Only other Curtis students and alumni could appreciate the feeling of stepping onto that stage again. It is overwhelming and I was quite nervous. When I finished performing the Carmen Fantasy,[1] everyone applauded and then I dedicated it to Zimbalist. Remembering my student days, I said, "But as I stand here, I keep thinking that Zimbalist will say, 'That's nice, dear. But do it again.'" That's what he frequently said at my lessons.

Like all my recordings, the Fantasie recording is now on CD and MP3. David and I did several LPs in the mid-1970s which included some unusual repertoire: sonatinas by Sibelius and Français, the rarely heard Dohnanyi Sonata, and the Fantasy on Rossini's Othello by Ernst. I enjoy the thought that several of the current generation of recording violinists may have discovered these works from my originals as the pieces are popping up in new releases. They are repertoire gems that deserve notice.

Now the LP recordings are part of new remastered composite CDs of my playing.

Concertmaster

Around the 1980s, I became concertmaster of the Baroque Consortium, which was conducted by Frances and is now the Chamber Orchestra of the South Bay (COSB). I held the post for about 20 years and didn't stop playing with them until the late 1990s. It was the longest stretch I ever did as a member of an orchestra. When I first came to Los Angeles, I played in Henri Temianka's orchestra, the California Chamber Orchestra for a few years, which I enjoyed very much. In both groups, with six firsts and six seconds, it was almost like playing chamber music.

With COSB, we performed a huge repertoire of everything from Baroque to contemporary music. Though it can be challenging being the concertmaster of such a small group, the musical camaraderie makes up for it.

Curtis Alumni Association

Over time in Los Angeles, I was finding out that, even though Curtis was prestigious in musical circles, comparatively few people knew about Curtis while everyone seemed to know Juilliard.

In 1969, during one of Rudolf Serkin's Los Angeles area concert tours, he stayed at the Ambassador Hotel in the Wilshire District. He was to play a concert in Orange County, so Ed and I drove him there. During our drive I talked with him and convinced him that we should start an Alumni Association. I thought that more Curtis awareness would raise our professional standing. I wrote Serkin a long letter, at his request, detailing the need for an alumni association[2].

Soon after, Curtis decided to have a big celebration for its 50th Anniversary,

---

1 This was the Sarasate version that was re-arranged by Zimbalist.
2 See Letter to Serkin in the Appendices.

which was the 1974-75 academic year. The school's alumni records were on 5x7-inch file cards. The primary person who had maintained contacts was the former registrar, Jane Hill, who had run the school almost singlehandedly, from an administrative point of view, for a long time. She had her address book and joined forces with the two daughter-in-laws of the late Mrs. Curtis Bok Zimbalist to find the alumni. They became almost a private detective agency. I offered to help, so they sent me a couple hundred names of alumni who supposedly lived in the West to track down. Through my personal network, I managed to find a lot of people. Before we knew it, the "agency" had found approximately 1,500 of the 2,000 names on the list.

In its 85-plus years of existence, Curtis has only had some 3,500 total students. At any given time, the student body varied from 150 to 180 students depending on budgets and directors. It did drop quite a bit during the Second World War, when so many young men were drafted.

Unfortunately, there were some people we never located. It was easier to find the men, as we could often track them down through musicians' unions and networking. Active musicians, especially such a small elite group, tended to know each other. During my sleuthing out West, I discovered that I had been working with some people for up to ten years without knowing that they were fellow Curtis alumni. The women, however, were often more difficult to locate unless they maintained their maiden names in their careers—especially singers. Since singers didn't belong to the AFM,[3] we couldn't find them easily. It was a difficult job.

To get things started in the West, I gave a party in Los Angeles that was attended by over 45 alumni, many of whom hadn't seen each other in many years. They came from all over the west—British Columbia, Seattle, San Francisco and so on. We decided to establish Curtis Alumni Association West as a non-profit corporation which was greatly helped by Ron Steelman, a bass player-turned-attorney. Curtis arranged a three-day festival for the 50th in Philadelphia and approximately 900 alumni showed up. The numbers were amazing. Then we put on our own West Coast 50th Anniversary celebration because many couldn't go back east. This was in the spring of 1975, after the main affair in Philadelphia. A wonderful luncheon was attended by some 120 people in one of the private dining rooms at the Dorothy Chandler Pavilion. Among the guests were Zubin Mehta, conductor of the Los Angeles Philharmonic, and actor Efrem Zimbalist, Jr. Abram Chasins of WQXR and KUSC fame was co-master-of-ceremonies with me. Gregor Piatigorsky, who we didn't realize was seriously ill, did not attend.

Shortly after the anniversary celebration, Serkin retired as director of Curtis. The next year, John de Lancie became director. He had been the first president of the national Alumni Association.

---

3 American Federation of Musicians.

The West Coast organization took off with a flurry of excitement with me as president. My successor as president was Harlow Mills, who managed the Coleman Chamber Music Series in Pasadena. He was terrific as president and one of the finest gentlemen I have known.

We started holding regular meetings in Los Angeles and, among other activities, set up a student aid fund for West Coast students who needed help over and above the tuition scholarship while attending a school 3,000 miles from home. One of the young musicians we helped was violinist Mitchell Newman. He is a member of the Los Angeles Philharmonic and most recently the president of the Curtis Alumni Association West.

One of the events that I helped start was the Alumni Weekend at Curtis in Philadelphia. From the beginning, I worked with another alumna and friend, Edith Evans Frumin, a singer and a classmate of mine. Our aim was for Curtis alumni to stay connected and continue the good feelings fostered by the 50th Anniversary. As Edith was in Philadelphia while I was in L.A., we made a good team. Edith is the kind of person everyone would be lucky to work with–always willing, always capable, and one in a billion!

We also started honoring some of the less famous faculty during the alumni weekends. Major faculty, being big names in the music world already, were well-recognized. The secondary piano and theory teachers who worked with students daily, on the other hand, were sort of taken for granted. So Edith and I took advantage of these Alumni Weekends to honor them. Two of particular note were Freda Pastor Berkowitz, who was my first secondary piano teacher at Curtis. Then there was Martha Massena, another secondary piano teacher, and a few others who never would have "gotten a dinner."

Along with the dinners in honor of these teachers, we always tried to include a major concert. In 1982, a concert featured the Curtis Orchestra with Varujan Kojian conducting.

In 1983, Edith and I wanted to help the Orchestra make a trip to the Evian Festival. This time, Frances was asked to conduct an all-Brahms program. Cellist Ronald Leonard joined me in playing the Double Concerto.

My Stradivarius

The Double Concerto performance was a great opportunity for me to show off my recently purchased Strad, the "Imperator." Benny Koodlach, my violin guru, found the Strad for me. The instrument was one of the finest of the many I played. The ten years that it was part of my life was the culmination of a dream. Few are lucky enough to have such an experience.

Curtis Alumni Association, Continued

As in so many institutions, once things become formalized and administrative people set the agenda, events are not quite as much fun. Alumni Weekend is now a big Development Department affair and opportunity for fundraising. But it was a good idea and I'm glad we got it started. Those were the days when we could be creative.

Volunteering for Curtis became a big part of my life for 33 years. First, I was on the Alumni National Board and became liaison between it and the Curtis Board of Trustees for a year. After that I was appointed as a regular member of the Board of Trustees and served for about ten years.

After I left the Board of Trustees, the Overseers Board was established and I served on it for ten years. During my first ten years of service, I traveled from L.A. to Philadelphia two to three times a year. Sometimes Ed came too. Then, we could spend three or four days meeting with the couples that have been such a big part of our lives. They were Ed's friends from before and we've remained good friends as couples.

The group included Jan and Al Booker, Sunny and Sid Bruskin, Lenny and Leila Finkelstein and Jerry and Elaine King. We've all made it past our fiftieth anniversaries. It's been an amazing relationship. These couples all have children and grandchildren, and have stayed together with very rock solid marriages.

I supported the Curtis Board of Directors when it decided to replace John de Lancie. His successor was Gary Graffman, who remained for the next twenty years and was a fabulous director. The national Alumni Association was reconstituted into the organization it is today, which is extremely successful and very well-run. After about 35 years, the West Coast Alumni Association floundered because it is a lot of work and there was no one who had the time and energy to do what we did in the beginning.

The Board of Overseers was an interesting and very high-powered group of people: symphony managers, Curtis family legacies and educators. We brainstormed for two days and then sent reports to the Trustees with suggestions. Some were opposed to maintaining Curtis as a tuition-free school. That was ridiculous because when they were contemplating this, other schools including USC, Eastman, and Juilliard were giving living expense stipends in addition to scholarships to entice the best students. There is a finite number of highly talented students and if Curtis wanted to continue to attract them while maintaining an elite faculty, they had to make it financially attainable. We managed to avoid that even though it was brought up several times over the years. I think that this idea is no longer considered an option.

Adjunct Careers: Broadening the Horizon
Abram Chasins

In the 1970s and 80s, my broadcasting mentor and inspiration was Abram Chasins, who had put WQXR, the New York Times good music station, on the map by building up their library and producing programs of such distinguished quality. When he came to Los Angeles, he got in touch with KUSC which at the time didn't even broadcast 24 hours a day. They had a mixed bag of programming. The good music station at the time was KFAC-AM, a commercial station. Abram and Ed talked a number of times. Ed kept telling Abram that the station needed to broadcast 24 hours, which it eventually did.

Abram did a lot of personal interview programs and invited me to participate in them several times. He kept telling me, "You're good at this. Go out and do it yourself!"

Abram and I first crossed paths when I was 15 years old and a finalist for the New York Philharmonic youth concerts competition. Abram was the chair of the judging panel. I won that competition in the spring of 1948 and did not meet Abram again until the early 1960s, when he had retired and moved to L.A. to be classical music director of KUSC.

We were both attending a concert at UCLA's Royce Hall when I recognized him in the intermission crowd. I gathered my nerve and went up to him to see if by some outside chance he remembered me. To my amazement, he did and greeted me enthusiastically. From that moment on began a friendship that lasted until he died.

During those 20-plus years, he did a superb job for classical music radio in Southern California. He spearheaded the process for funding the station's antenna on Mt. Wilson that gave KUSC larger range. He donated his important collection of LPs to the station. He hosted many interesting shows in his own inimitable style and brought the caché of his years of success at WQXR, New York's ultimate classical music radio station.

His fund of musical knowledge was fascinating and deep. He inspired and encouraged me to try my hand at hosting and producing shows which I did at KUSC and KXLU. My greatest honor was to host and produce the 2-hour Chasins portrait over KUSC which was broadcast a few weeks before his death. I wanted him to know how much he was loved and respected by so many in the music world as spoken by former students and colleagues such as Jorge Bolet, Van Cliburn, Gary Graffman, Peter Nero and Roger Sherman. I know that he was very concerned that he would be forgotten by history. But his contribution to the music and performers in the 20th century is solid in the firmament.[4]

---

4 My thanks to Peter Rutenberg, then KUSC Program Manager for his advice in producing the AC show.

Radio Broadcast Host/Producer

As a broadcaster, I initiated a series of programs at KXLU-FM in Los Angeles, the radio station of Loyola Marymount University where I was on the faculty for a number of years in the 1970s and 80s as well. I produced and hosted a series called Air for Strings. The programs focused on various national and international competitions. I combined interviews with major musical personalities, and performances by winners on each of the string instruments. For instance, I featured the Coleman Chamber Music Competition, the American Harp Society and the Naumburg. I even did a show on the National Federation of Music Clubs when I was a judge in 1979 in Portland. The Air for Strings series is now housed in the Library of Congress.

Mehli Mehta on "Air for Strings"

I had met Mehli in Philadelphia in the early 1950s when he came as a young violinist from Bombay to study with Ivan Galamian, who, of course, I knew so well. Galamian introduced Mehli to me. He had just been recommended as a replacement second violinist in the Curtis String Quartet. Little did I know that less than 20 years later he would become an important part of our personal musical world. He had ended up in Los Angeles and become the musical director/conductor of the American Youth Symphony, among other posts. Marcia became principal harpist of the AYS, which proved to be a particularly important experience for her. Mehli and Marcia had a wonderful number of years performing together. They shared a rare and warm musical relationship, full of mutual respect.

Of course when I was doing Air for Strings, it was a natural choice to invite Mehli for an interview, as he was such an enthusiastic mentor of young musicians. Mehli reminisced about his early days in the United States. As he talked about his current AYS personnel, he mentioned how orchestras had changed their attitudes towards women and spoke of the large percentage of "girls" in his current orchestra. It reminded him of one of his earliest experiences in New York seeing a marquee advertising "Phil Spitalny and His All-Girl Orchestra featuring Evelyn and Her Magic Violin." Mehli was astounded at such a possibility and immediately went to hear the group. As he continued to relate the story, he said he couldn't get over the fact that the performance was so high quality. He admitted that he had brought prejudices with him that he had long since dropped.

Music Editing and Publishing

Another of my adjunct careers involved my editing music for students, which I started publishing. Again, I was lucky in that an honest gentleman, Herman Langinger of Highland Music Company, got me started in the publishing business. What I learned from him eventually allowed me to help Marcia start her own publishing company in the mid-1990s so that she could disseminate some of the many wonderful compositions written for her and her trio.

As a teacher of both violin and piano, I discovered very quickly that there was an unlimited repertoire for piano students at the beginning and intermediate levels. There were original short pieces or good arrangements of pieces by famous composers available for these students. There was nothing comparable for violin students. By the time they were ready for original pieces, Baroque music was all that was technically accessible.

I wanted to provide my students with an opportunity to play other periods of music at an easy, first-position level. I knew that most of them would not get much beyond that, so I planned to give them a nodding acquaintance with some of the major composers before they stopped lessons. This way they would understand and enjoy listening to the music when they attended concerts or listened to recordings.

I was very good at simplifying and completed two books of violin classics and two for string orchestra for publication with him.

In those days publishing was very work-intensive. I wrote everything out by hand, and then sent it to an engraver who had to make plates. The plates then had to be run by a printer who wouldn't accept an order for fewer than a thousand copies. It was a very expensive and time-consuming process. It took months to complete the first publications.

Now, we enter music on a computer, e-mail the file, or scan it and print the exact number we need. My first books were published in the early 1970s. In the last four decades, the whole music publishing business has changed more than it did in the hundreds of years since it was done with a quill pen on parchment.

Magazine Editing

I was Editor for Violin for the American String Teachers Association Magazine, for a couple of years and also Editor for Strings for the California Music Teachers Association Magazine for many years. It was a great opportunity to write on various musical subjects, like Air for Strings. Once again I frequently used the interview format to elicit the opinions of a number of colleagues and friends in the music world, highlighting subjects that I thought would be of interest to music teachers both locally and nationally.

Finding a Brother

The story of finding my half-brother, Carl, in the 1980s, seems to have come directly out of a storybook. My father had been married for a brief time in the 1920s to a woman in Los Angeles. They had a little boy and soon after, they were divorced. A few years later, in 1930, my father moved to Portland, where he met my mother. He never had any further contact with his son, at the request of the child's mother, though my father did send him support checks whenever he had the financial ability to do so.

In the early 1980s, Julie, the daughter of my first cousin on my father's side, Bernard Stark, was in high school in the San Fernando Valley. She and several classmates were chattering as girls do. One was teasing her about the fact that her handwriting was so very small. Julie fired back, "I inherited that from my grandmother Lillian." The girl who was teasing her asked Julie for her grandmother's name, and Julie replied, "Lillian Stark, but her maiden name was Steiner." The girl replied, "Oh, that's funny because my grandmother's name was Lillian Steiner Stark too." The girls went home and told their parents and when they started comparing notes, it began to look like there was a very close relationship.

At that point, Julie's mother Doris called me and told me she thought they had found my half-brother. She asked if she could put him in contact with me. We decided that it was definitely him. My mother had been trying to find Carl for a long time, but she had been looking for him under the last name of his stepfather. She had no way of knowing that he had kept the name Steiner.

Before we knew it, we set up a meeting. Frances and I met with Carl to see if we wanted to take steps to foster the relationship. Carl turned out to be a delightful man. He resembled our father very much. He was a teacher and counselor in the school system. We decided to become a family.

As luck would have it, a short time after that, Carl had a massive heart attack, which seems to run in the Steiner family (my father, Julie Stark's father, and so on). He almost died, but fortunately he was saved by modern medicine. He lived another 25 years, approximately.

My life story would not be complete without having a small part of this chapter devoted to the wonderful luck of being brought together as adults. We enjoyed each other's company and got to know his family during this special episode in our lives. Carl passionately loved music, probably a reflection of his musical genes.

TRIPS FOR FUN and MUSIC

Family trip to Alaska, 1978. Princess Cruise through the Inland Passage. This was the last major trip that included "Gracoo" (Elizabeth).

Courtesy Family Archives

TRIPS FOR FUN AND MUSIC

First Trip to Hawaii, 1974

The girls were quite young and Ed had just started a medical group company which decided to have a board meeting in Honolulu. So all of us, including Gracoo, went and had a marvelous time. In Honolulu we stayed at the Kahala Hilton and went surfing in Waikiki. After the board meetings were over, as a family we went to the Mauna Kea Hotel on the Big Island. It had just been built by the Rockefellers in order to stimulate tourism there because most people went to Honolulu and Waikiki. The Mauna Kea was built with virtually no concern for cost. Now there is row upon row of these marvelous resorts, but at the time the Mauna Kea was the only one. When we returned in 2006, it was still gorgeous. The rooms are palatial and beautiful, as is the setting.

Alaska, 1978

Mother, the girls, Ed and I went to Alaska on a Princess Cruise ship through the Inland Passage. We boarded from Vancouver, British Columbia, for a seven-day cruise.

One side trip that the girls, Ed and I took was on a seaplane from Juneau over the Juneau Glacier. We ended up at the foot of the glacier for an Alaskan salmon barbecue. Mother wasn't quite up to the plane trip, so she took the bus tour to the Mendenhall Glacier. Another day, we took the train from Skagway through the Klondike. The ship then went up through Glacier Bay. It was so cold that I had to go back inside the boat in order to have my hands work well enough to change the film in the camera. We also stopped at Sitka where we saw some of the traditional Russian dances.

Europe, September 1979

Our first trip to Europe as a family was in September 1979. Ed and I decided to keep the girls out of school so that we could take a super, month-long trip. I had never been to Europe before and we were comfortably well-off, so we decided to go five-star all the way. We started in England and spent the better part of a week in

London, staying at the Savoy Hotel on the Thames. Their restaurant is famous for serving huge roasts that are brought out on a cart and the chef carves at the table. We had an elegant suite with two bedrooms and a living room.

We saw the important attractions, including Buckingham Palace, the Tower of London, Westminster Abbey and Windsor Castle. We also attended a harp recital at Alfred Hall. Side trips included the Cotswolds where we stayed at the Lygon Arms, in Broadway. In our suite there, the girls' room was supposedly one in which Oliver Cromwell had slept. We also went to Stratford-on-Avon, Oxford and the site where the Magna Carta was written.

After that, we flew to Amsterdam, where we spent several days at the Europa Hotel which is right in the heart of the city. Side trips included the Zuiderzee, Delft, The Hague and a tulip festival.

After four days in the Netherlands, we took the train to Paris where we spent about a week. Then we rented a car and drove through Provence. First stop was at Chartres and its wonderful cathedral. We walked in on a Sunday morning and while I was looking up at the stained-glass windows, the organ started to play. It was a breathtaking experience.

Outside the cathedral, there were several traditional French bakeries with hundreds of baguettes hanging from little hooks. Local citizens would go in and emerge with a large baguette under the arm. We stayed at the Chateau d'Artigny for two nights before driving to Chateau d'Ige, where we had a suite again, which included a room in the castle tower. It is the closest thing I've seen to a real life version of Rumpelstiltskin's castle. The dining room in the basement was all in stone and had a huge fireplace. Set in the middle of vineyards, it was quite magical.

Then on to Les Baux and the famous hotel Oustau de Baumaniere. Here, French ruins sit atop ancient Roman ruins. We drove on to Santa Margherita di Ligure in northern Italy and from there on to Florence with a stop to see the Leaning Tower of Pisa. Then we spent several days at the Europa Hotel in Florence where luckily we were able to see the Medici exhibition being held in several of the palaces on both sides of the Arno River. Curators had collected Medici art objects from museums and private collections from around the world for this massive exhibition.

We stopped in Ravenna and saw its magnificent mosaics before heading to Venice, where we stayed at the Danieli, one of the most famous hotels on the Grand Canal. We were within walking distance of St. Mark's Square and the Doge's Palace. Fortunately, the weather was beautiful and there were no concerns about flooding.

We took a gondola to Murano and its fabulous glass factory. We were escorted at first like any other visitors. We were not interested in the first display room with items targeted to tourists. The salespeople kept taking us through successive rooms with items of increasing quality until we reached a room with beautiful wood paneling. We were offered champagne as they began to present gorgeous cut crystal and one-of-a-kind pieces. The items were shown like fine jewels: on black velvet pads. We ended up buying a couple of fairly large crates filled with pitchers, platters and glasses. We purchased not only the cut clear crystal, but also some of the pink crystal appliquéd with gold leaf and beautiful ceramic hand-painted decorations.

From Venice, we went to Milan where we spent the night before taking a flight home.

Japan, Summer 1982

During this family trip, we spent about three weeks in Japan and Hong Kong.

Our dear friends the Yoshinos, Atsuko and her daughter Naoko, took ten days out of their lives during our time in Japan to travel with us. Atsuko and Naoko are both concert harpists with distinguished careers. Naoko and Marcia first met while studying with Susann McDonald in Pasadena. We became close friends and renewed the friendship over several summers when Naoko and Marcia studied at Susann's harp workshops in California.

Our first stop was Tokyo. The Yoshinos took us to the Hakone district where they had a summer home and to the foot of Mount Fuji where we could climb as high as we wanted. As a party of six we had to take two cabs because they only held three passengers each. After touring the Imperial Palace, seeing a number of wonderful sights and enjoying wonderful restaurants, we traveled on the Shinkansen to Kyoto. There, we saw the Summer Palace. Coincidentally, there was a wonderful festival of Japanese handmade glassware. We also met a world famous ceramicist in his home where he treated us to a traditional tea ceremony.

A couple of days in Nara and a return to Tokyo rounded off our visit to Japan.

One of the outstanding experiences was a visit to the Mikimoto pearl showroom, a multi-story structure filled with magnificent pearls. Two stories were set apart for the company's museum, which exhibited some of the largest pearls in existence set in unbelievable jewelry with diamonds and other precious stones. I bought a beautiful set of Mikimoto pearls—I just couldn't resist!

We then went to Hong Kong, which was still an English protectorate. We had several days of wonderful shopping and dining, plus a trip to the Chinese border from which we could see the Chinese territories. And, of course, we had to visit several upscale registered Chinese snuff bottle shops to add to our collection.

Europe, Summer 1984

Marcia was in college at USC and we were deliberating on whether she should study in Paris during her junior year. The history of the contemporary harp world is French, so it made sense to consider study at the Paris Conservatory and perhaps at the Sorbonne. She and I went to Paris in July 1984 and spent a week perusing the situation. Marcia had already enrolled at the Académie d'Été in Nice, a summer extension of the Paris Conservatory. Veda was in Paris and arranged a hotel room for us about a block from her apartment near the Madeleine and, more importantly, a couple of blocks from Fauchon, the wonderful French delicatessen.

It was extremely hot during the week we stayed in Paris. When Marcia and I went to the Sorbonne, we realized that it was quite unstructured for one so young. Also, we had to consider the fact that Marcia was already extremely active performing in Los Angeles. What we discovered was that the tiny elevators like the one in Veda's apartment building could not accommodate Marcia with her harp. We didn't know how she would be able to get around even if she were able to obtain any concerts in Paris. The final decision was no.

In Nice, I stayed at the Meridien Hotel, the only air-conditioned hotel, which was great because it was over 100 degrees. Marcia stayed in the dorms which were arranged at a convent near the school. She had a lot of fun times, including a visit to the gambling houses in Monaco.

In Nice, Sallie came to join us. We rented a little Renault, which we used to say was the only air-conditioned car in Nice. It had very squeaky brakes, but Marcia, one of her English classmates, Sallie and I bopped around Provence, Monaco, and northern Italy. We did a lot of traversing of the Bas and Haute Corniche, enjoyed kir royales at the Hotel de Paris, ate at Roger Vergé's and visited the Chagall Museum.

After the Académie d'Été was over, Ed joined us and we flew to Rome, where a limousine with an English-speaking guide proved a great way to visit all of the attractions: St. Peter's, the Coliseum and the Sistine Chapel. While there, we took a great side trip to see the amazing historical site at Pompeii.

Courtesy Family Archives

Diana, age 3, poses in favorite
Shirley Temple dress.

Courtesy Family Archives

Ferenz hears Diana, age 18 months as
they pose for newspaper photo in
Portland papers.

Courtesy Family Archives

Diana's first recital, Steiner Studio students,
Portland, OR. Fall 1935.

Courtesy Family Archives

Diana with Maia Bang, famed
violin pedagogue, Winter, 1937.

Courtesy of the Curtis Institute of Music

Curtis Institute's Youngest, 1938/39, their ages range from 6-14. L-to-R Unidentified, Elliot Fisher, Nathan Goldstein, Seymour Lipkin, Gary Graffman, Bianca Polack, Diana Steiner, Rudulf Favaloro, Charles Libove, Hyman Bress, Robert Cornman and Margot Ros.

Courtesy Family Archives

Efrem Zimbalist,
personally autographed photo,
1939

Musical Courier, June 1, 1939

Courtesy Family Archives

Courtesy Family Archives

Marcel Dupré, French organist
in his studio with his daughter.
Photo autographed to Diana
after hearing her in Portland,

Courtesy Family Archives

Diana poses for Portland
papers before her debut,
September 30, 1940.

Courtesy Family Archives

Diana with Oregon Governor
Sprague before her Portland
debut, officially declared
"Diana Steiner Day"

Courtesy Family Archives

Diana and Frances at ages 12 and 7.

Courtesy Family Archives

Diana, Mervin Berger, and Joseph Plon, winners of Philadelphia Orchestra 1st Children's Concerts solo audition with conductors Eugene Ormandy and Saul Caston. September 1944

Courtesy Family Archives

Enid and Rachel Bok and Frances, winners of Philadelphia Orchestra Composition Contest, with Eugene Ormandy. Philadelphia Inquirer, Spring 1944.

Diana with conducting prodigy, Lorin Maazel, rehearsing for Philadelphia Orchestra Children's Concerts. The Evening Bulletin, January 5, 1945

Alexander Hilsberg and Mrs. Hilsberg on the Cunard Line "Parthia" (David Madison, assistant concertmaster in background) at farewell send-off of Philadelphia Orchestra leaving for 1st tour of any American orchestra after WWII.

Mme Tabuteau & Marcel Tabuteau, on the same ship.

String Section rehearsal for Curtis Institute 25th Anniversary concerts, Marcel Tabuteau conducting. 1st violins by stand: Jesse Cusimano, Marvin Morgenstern, Diana Steiner, Felix Sitjar, Michael Tree (Applebaum). 2nd violins by stand: Joseph Silverstein, Hyman Bress, Marilyn Woodruff and Jeanne Sandbank (?) and (?)

Courtesy Family Archives

Curtis Graduation, 1949.
1st row, 4th from left, Diana; 2nd row, l-r Judge Curtis Bok, Carlos Salzedo,
President of the University of Pennsylvania and ex-Governor of Minnesota, Harold
Stassen, Mrs. Zimbalist, Mr. Zimbalist, Isabelle Vengerova

Courtesy Family Archives

Elizabeth with Frances, who
received Mus.B from Curtis
Institute, May 1956.

Courtesy Family Archives

Diana surrounded by flowers at
NY Town Hall debut,
October 1952.

Diana with Jean Bedetti,
Tanglewood 1950.

Courtesy Family Archives

Courtesy Family Archives

Aaron Copland poses with
colleague for a relaxed photo,

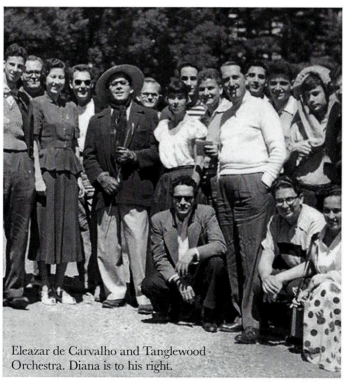

Eleazar de Carvalho and Tanglewood
Orchestra. Diana is to his right.

Courtesy Family Archives

Marboro
Musicians,
1951

Courtesy Family Archives

Courtesy Family Archives

Hermann Busch, Rudolf Serkin, Gary
Graffman, Marlboro campus.

Courtesy Family Archives

Louis Moyse and Marcel Moyse

Courtesy Family Archives

Nikki Busch (son of Adolf) starts violin
lessons with Diana, Philadelphia, PA.

Courtesy Family Archives

Naomi Reynolds (Young Artists Chairman, National Federation of
Music Clubs), Diana, and Ruby Voght (President, NFMC).
Probably 1960s.

Courtesy Family Archives

Izler Solomon, Guest Conductor, Miami (FL) Summer Pops Orchestra
with Mrs. Solomon and Guest Soloist, Diana. Summer, 1954.

Piatigorsky and Diana in his
Brentwood garden, 1960.

Courtesy Family Archives

Frances and
Piatigorsky in front
of Curtis, 1946.

Courtesy Family Archives

Abram Chasins,
Diana, Gregor
Piatigorsky, and
Henri Temianka
enjoy photos of
Curtis Institute
before the 50th
Anniversary
Reunion.

Courtesy Family Archives

Courtesy Family Archives

Diana backstage at the
Hollywood Bowl with
conductor André Kostelanetz,
July 1963.

Ed Dickstein on
champion Appaloosa
"Moonshine" riding to
hounds with West Hills
Hunt, mid-1960's.

Courtesy Family Archives

Courtesy Family Archives

Elsa Fiedler and Otto Herz on
Broadway in New York with
Diana, Sallie and Marcia,
1969-70.

Left: Leonard Bernstein talks with Diana &Milton Rock, Curtis Board of Directors Chairman as Freda Pastor Berkowitz looks on. (Philadelphia, 1968)

Courtesy Family Archives

Ed Dickstein and Diana with actor Efrem Zimbalist Jr. at Curtis 50th Anniversary celebration in Los Angeles, 1975

Courtesy Family Archives

Courtesy Family Archives

Above: Efrem Zimbalist 90th birthday celebration. Presentation by Diana of greetings from all Zimbalist students (Reno, NV 1980). L to R Philip Frank, Diana, Eudice Shapiro, A. Margaret (Stormy) Bok (founder's daughter-in-law and Curtis board member), Zimbalist and Vladimir Sokoloff (former Zimbalist accompanist).

Courtesy Family Archives

David Berfield, pianist of Steiner-Berfield Trio.

Courtesy Family Archives

Left: Calling All Girls magazine featured 3 young violinists making NY debuts in one weekend. Besides Diana, there was Karolla Muller and Camilla Wicks.
(Note: the photo above Diana is that of the Dionne quintuplets, a rare happening in those days).
February, 1942 issue.
Magazine now defunct.

Bottom left: Program of students of Efrem Zimbalist at Curtis, March 27, 1940.
(Diana first on program).

Bottom right: Program of New York Philharmonic presenting Diana as soloist at age 9.
February 24, 1942.

Courtesy Family Archives

Courtesy Family Archives

Above: Efrem Zimbalist and Ivan Galamian
write to Diana on her newly published books
for young violinists, January, 1973.

Left: Greetings from former
Mannes School (NY) violin
teacher, Paul Stassevitch.

20 décembre 1951
—Roma.

My dear Diana
It has been a joy receiving
your nice christmas post card.
Merry Christmas — Happy
new-year all sorts of
nice wishes — my best love
Jacqueline Ibert-gillet

Dear friends,
Your remembering my birthday
made me feel happy and grateful.
many thanks! They come so late
because of some health problems, but
it's getting better.
I was going to be on sending you many greetings, dear Diana and Ed,
your old friend
Rudi.

CHRISTMAS GREETINGS
Mario and Clara
Castelnuovo-Tedesco

Courtesy Family Archives

Top. Jacqueline Ibert note to Diana, December 1951, after performing together at Tanglewood in 1950.
Mid-page. Personal note to Diana and Ed from "Rudi" Serkin, late 1990.
Right. Personal greetings from composer Mario Castelnuovo-Tedesco.

THE THIRD GENERATION

3

THE THIRD GENERATION

"Dickstein played the presto at a fast and furious pace...more fluid in quieter sections, even heavenly in the exhilarating cadenza."

Daily Breeze (Palos Verdes, CA) March 11, 2009

"Richly characterized and sensitive."

Gramophone (London, UK) December, 2001

"Dickstein gives Bax's music a sense of direction, cohension & best of all, excitement."

The Harp Column, USA, May-June, 1999

Marcia Dickstein, soloist, Chamber Orchestra of the South Bay
Norris Theater, Palos Verdes, CA
Concerto for Harp by Mark Kuval. World premiere, March 8, 2009.

Courtesy Family Archives

THE THIRD GENERATION

Marcia and her Harp

In 1971 David Berfield, Frances and I played a series of concerts at USC, a month-long survey of the music of Maurice Ravel, including all of his chamber music and piano works. Amongst those pieces is the famous Introduction and Allegro; it's basically a harp concerto. Ed and I brought the girls to concerts in which I performed whenever possible and Marcia came to the dress rehearsal as well as the concert for the performance of the harp piece. She absolutely fell in love with the harp. She was also very much taken with Susann McDonald, the harp professor at USC who performed the Ravel with us. Marcia was just six years old at the time.

Unknown to me, Marcia had formed a very strong desire to learn the harp. This came out a few months later when she was practicing piano under duress. She had been taking piano lessons for three years and shown good talent, with a wonderful sense of rhythm. But children tend to want to play an instrument that appeals to them. Marcia announced she wanted to study the harp with Susann.

I immediately called Susann and told her that I wanted to bring Marcia backstage after her performance of the Gliere Concerto with the Santa Monica Symphony a couple of weeks later. I told Susann, "She's very little and very young, so you can tell her to keep studying the piano and think about the harp later." After the concert, when Susann saw Marcia's hands, she realized that Marcia had the physical attributes of a harpist. With a wink to me, Susann told Marcia, "Tell your mom to bring you for a lesson next week."

So then I had to go out and find a harp. At the time, the best harp for a little girl was the Lyon & Healy "Troubadour," a non-pedal harp. I managed to get one through a friend, because you couldn't just go down the street and buy one. We gave Marcia the harp for her seventh birthday and she began lessons with Susann. Within about a year, she was playing so nicely that I mentioned her talent to Henri Temianka, the conductor of the California Chamber Symphony. I suggested that she might be an interesting soloist for his children's concerts. He auditioned her and immediately took her. Then we had to find a piece that could be played with an orchestra by a seven-year-old, on a Troubadour.

I arranged Greensleeves for non-pedal harp solo with string orchestra. Temianka thought it was great.

Marcia continued her studies with Susann, making excellent progress, with the usual ups and downs. She seemed to revel in playing the harp. We took advantage of various opportunities to have her play with youth orchestras, in school programs and she even got a few Christmas jobs. Christmastime is a busy time for harpists.

Marcia continued her private lessons through high school. Though Susann had moved on to Indiana, Marcia was accepted at USC as a harp major. She entered college a year early, combining her senior year of high school with her first year at USC. As luck would have it, the university music department really needed her because after Susann's departure there were no harp students who could play the repertoire for orchestra, opera and other music in which harpists were needed. By that time, she was also principal harpist of the Young Musicians Foundation Orchestra and the American Youth Symphony. There were times when she was playing 40 to 50 concerts a year while attending university. This gave her an immense amount of experience, confidence and inspiration. It really set her up for an active career. She was used to being professional and learning things very rapidly.

Thanks to the years with USC, YMF and AYS, Marcia gained expertise and experience that opened an unusually wide range of performance opportunities in the Los Angeles music scene. These included principal and co-principal performances with the Los Angeles Opera, several symphonies, and hundreds of films and television shows.

As Marcia was completing her master's degree at USC and looking at career options, she decided that she really wanted to play chamber music, which was a very limited and difficult field for harpists, in part because of the lack of repertoire.

Classical harpists usually joined orchestras and there were very few positions open. For example, the Philadelphia Orchestra had only two harpists, Edna Phillips and Marilyn Costello, over a 50-year period. The other choice—touring soloist—was virtually impossible.

I had worked in the contemporary music scene from the time I moved to Los Angeles, so it was an easy jump for me to get involved with contemporary harp music when Marcia expressed an interest in having more high-quality chamber music written. That was how the Debussy Trio Music Foundation was born in 1988.

The Debussy Trio Music Foundation

Marcia established The Debussy Trio in 1987 with her USC colleagues flutist Angela Wiegand and violist Christopher Redfield. Angela and Marcia have subsequently been joined by two other fine violists, Keith Greene and most recently David Walther.

The Debussy Trio Music Foundation grew out of Marcia's dream of establishing a major repertoire for harp in chamber music and solo with orchestra. In the case of chamber music, there were only a few major works written in the early and mid-20th century. Debussy was the original inspiration to write for the harp as an equal partner in a trio. One of the best harp concertos ever written is by Ginastera. It was commissioned by Edna Phillips, my friend and Curtis colleague who had been the principal harpist of the Philadelphia Orchestra under Leopold Stokowski.

Until Marcia came along with her dedication and determination to have the harp considered a significant chamber music instrument, very little had happened since Debussy. It has been fascinating to watch her concept become an important segment of contemporary music. As a violinist I frequently think of how lucky I am that Brahms collaborated with Joachim. Otherwise there might not have been such magnificent Brahms works for violin. I believe that the same is true in Marcia's case as she has inspired, encouraged and prodded so many composers to rethink their approach to writing for harp. No longer is it background music and fluff. Composers now know there are infinite choices and there are and will be harpists that can play them.

While Marcia and I discussed various possibilities of how to go about commissioning and building this new repertoire, I came up with the idea of starting a non-profit corporation in order to qualify for grants, foundation contributions, and individual support for this new music.

It became evident that my allegiance had shifted away from violin music toward helping Marcia build this new harp repertoire. We have been very lucky. As of this writing, the Foundation has been in existence for almost 22 years and DTMF has funded many commissions and more than a half-dozen international competitions. Also, a large number of additional pieces have been written in hopes that Marcia and The Debussy Trio would play them because of the quality of their musicianship.

Salzburg Festival

We began making trips in connection with Marcia's musical activities that were added opportunities for family vacations. She was engaged to join the Los Angeles Philharmonic under Esa Pekka Salonen. We had some trouble with our airplane in Los Angeles and almost didn't make it. By the time we got to Paris we missed our connecting flights and had to stop in Zurich, from which we ended up taking a small plane to Salzburg.

Fortunately, Marcia made it to her rehearsal on Wednesday. Meanwhile, Salzburg was experiencing a hot spell which "never" happened there, so there was no air conditioning except in the concert hall. We had enough free time to explore the area, visiting many charming villages in the Bavarian Alps.

The concert hall in Salzburg is really interesting because it was originally a royal stable. The outside still looks like a stable, but the inside is magnificent, with beautiful wood and excellent acoustics. Unfortunately, Marcia couldn't continue to travel with us because she had return to Los Angeles to play at the Hollywood

Bowl.   Sallie, Ed and I went on to St. Moritz where we stayed a few days at the Badrutt Palace which was so beautiful and elegant. Then we took the Transalpine train which crosses the Rhine and the Loire headwaters. We then boarded the funicular to Zermatt. While there, Ed and Sallie rode the gondola to the top of the Matterhorn where it is possible to ski from Switzerland to Italy. I stayed in town and explored. It was a fascinating juxtaposition of time periods. The cabins looked just like the descriptions in the book Heidi which housed goats on the ground floor, but in Zermatt the lower floor had no goats and the upper floor had television. I loved Zermatt.

From there we went to Paris where we spent time with Veda Reynolds. Sallie then decided to fly to London to visit friends while Ed and I stayed at the Hotel Meurice where we had a penthouse suite with a spectacular view of Paris.

Sallie

Ed and I were so pleased that Sallie had the freedom to spend a little time with us and make this trip because she had been working so hard. She had graduated from the University of California at Santa Barbara and then had gone on to law school. She was then appointed as a law clerk to a wonderful judge, The Honorable Thomas Murphy, at the Superior Court level in Glendale. She spent two years clerking for him, which was a wonderful experience. We were always so proud of Sallie's ability to achieve her goals. She went on to practice various areas of the law. Several years ago, she found a wonderful niche for herself working for the federal government at the Department of Homeland Security.

Sallie always maintained her love for music, even though she didn't want a career in music. She has attended so many of the concerts that Marcia and I played. She seems to have enjoyed the enrichment that her early studies and innate talent provided. Ed and I are very fortunate that the girls have so many mutual interests, not the least of which are their families and wonderful children.

World Harp Congress Conventions
Copenhagen, 1993

Thanks to the formation of the DTMF, we were able to arrange and promote some interesting opportunities for the Trio. The first was playing in Copenhagen in 1993, where they performed pieces by American composers. DTMF hosted a musicale in Los Angeles which included the consuls general of the various major countries interested in our work. The Trio received a letter of commendation from the counsel general of Denmark.

Prague, 1999

The next big foreign event was the Trio's performance in Prague at the World Harp Congress in 1999. The Trio played the world premiere of Bruce Broughton's Tyvek Wood, which was supported by the National Endowment of the Arts and the Fund for US Artists at International Festivals. Also, I contacted the American Embassy in the Czech Republic and Ambassador John Shattuck decided to present the Trio in a private reception for invited guests at the ambassadorial residence. It was also attended by some of the leading harpists from the Congress. Bruce Broughton came from the United States to hear the performances of his work.

Geneva, 2002

The next trip, three years later in 2002, was the World Harp Congress in Geneva. The Trio was soloist with the Geneva Chamber Orchestra in the premiere of another DTMF commission: a triple concerto by Vince Mendoza entitled Turn-Out.

Ed and I were able to combine these trips, making them also family vacations. It was a lot of fun because during the Prague trip I was able to meet a cousin in Belgium, and during both trips, I was able to visit with my dear friend Veda in Paris. The trips were thus important for both Marcia's career and our family.

In Brussels, Ed and I were met by my cousin, Jacqueline Lion.[1] She drove us to a quaint inn near St. Armand de Fleurus, where she lived. It was near Waterloo, about 60 kilometers from Brussels. This was an amazing experience for me because all my life I had heard about this cousin who was exactly my age. We had a lovely time at her home, which is a converted 13th Century abbey.

On the way back from Prague, Ed and I stayed for a few days in Paris. We also had a stop in Amsterdam, where I met Curtis violin alumnus Isadore Lateiner. While there, I was able to explore my Dutch roots even more than I had before. In this instance, we were able to meet another cousin, Dr. Jack van Straaten, who had been located only recently through a family history search. Jack was found in a city registry in Amsterdam. He had us to dinner with his wife Carrie in a beautiful home a couple of blocks from the famous Concertgebouw Auditorium.

Other Notable Moments

The Debussy Trio's first major recognition came when it was a winner at the Carmel (CA) International Chamber Music Competition in 1989. In 1990, the Trio was chosen as "Young Artist of the Year" by Musical America Magazine.

The full list of awards and grants can be seen in the appendices, but certainly

---

1 Our mothers were first cousins.

one of the most satisfying was London's Gramophone Magazine's "Best Pick" (2001) for the Trio's recording 3 Friends.

In addition to the exciting premieres at the various World Harp Congress conventions, other major performances that deserve mention are: the Trio's performance at the Kennedy Center of Twelve Days in the Shadow of a Miracle by Lyle Mays; the world premiere of Andrea Clearfield's Dream Variations at the Disney Concert Hall in February 2009; and Marcia's premiere performance of a harp concerto by Mark Koval in March of 2009, with Frances conducting COSB. These are massive undertakings for Marcia, the Trio, the composers and the Foundation. In the case of the Koval concerto, Marcia spent almost two years working very closely with the composer on writing the harp part so that it would be an idiomatic, but spectacular, showcase for the instrument.

DTMF and its activities would not have been possible had it not been for the support of many wonderful donors, especially the original president, Thomas van Straaten and the current president David Hirsch, as well as board member C. Richard Neu and Virginia Ambrosini (Mrs. Neu).

A Multi-Faceted Career

Marcia has had the opportunity of working with some incredibly talented people in a variety of entertainment venues and media in classical, jazz, and popular music genres. She has played in numerous concerts under the direction of well-known conductors such as Michael Tilson Thomas, Mehli Mehta, and Leonard Bernstein. She has performed with Ray Charles, Sarah Vaughn, Dolores Hope, and Gene Kelly, and has recorded with Rosemary Clooney, and country music stars Vince Gill and Amy Grant.

In her many years in studio recording sessions, she has played hundreds of scores for movies and television shows. The list reads as a Who's Who, including composers Randy Newman (Toy Story I , II & III, Monsters, Inc., A Bug's Life), John Williams (A.I., Memoirs of a Geisha, 7 Years in Tibet), Mark Mothersbaugh (The Royal Tenenbaums {screen credit}), Don Davis (Matrix Trilogy), Bruce Broughton (Miracle on 34th Street), Joel McNeely (Tinkerbell), and James Horner (A Beautiful Mind, Troy).

Television credits include The Tonight Show, Star Trek, Diagnosis Murder, Murder She Wrote, Family Guy, American Dad, and Lost.

Teaching

Over the years, Marcia has analyzed and discovered techniques that helped create her individual sound and artistry. In working with students of all levels and abilities, she remains flexible in her approach, treating each student as an individual, addressing his or her needs.

Her training, of course, is in the tradition of Henriette Renié and Grandjany. I am always amazed at the depth and breadth of her analytical thinking for all aspects of performing on her instrument. I am sure this has contributed immeasurably to her work with composers, helping them to discover many possibilities, previously not explored.

Extensive thought has gone into her teaching philosophy and is reflected in her publications, such as Harp Warm-Ups– which is only the beginning. Also, her desire to be faithful to composers' original ideas has led to much research to bypass incorrect editions. The result has been scholarly editions of music by such composers as Arnold Bax.

Fatrock Ink

Early on, Marcia expressed a desire to disseminate the new music to an international group of harpists in particular and musicians in general. This would require more than just commissioning and performances. We decided it would be useful to start a music publishing company, which Marcia named Fatrock Ink. She was expending considerable energy attempting to build this repertoire and wanted to make sure that the music had a long lifespan and international visibility.

At first, we established a distribution relationship with Theodore Presser Company of Philadelphia, which lasted seven years. The then head of Presser, Tom Broido, was particularly helpful. We didn't make much money since the technology at the time was still so expensive.

Fortunately, the technology and related expenses have changed dramatically. When Presser was sold and no longer wanted to handle a niche market catalog such as Fatrock, we were able to go out on our own. It is now a growing international market.

Fatrock Ink will continue to flourish and bring this new group of compositions to the attention of the music world.

Third Generation: To Be Continued

Marcia has matured into a truly great musician and harpist. Her gaze is wide and dedicated. Her spirit of sharing her art with the world has encompassed such a wide area, not least of which is the over 22 years of presenting outreach programs with the Trio for over a quarter million children and families.

She shares her love of music, her artistic and educational philosophies with audiences, her children, students and many others. Her determination to preserve the environment for future generations means the sequel to this story should be ever more exciting.

CONCLUSION, 2009

I have related the saga of a hundred years of one family's three generations of women who were pioneers in the world of classical music. The first generation, Elizabeth, lived in a fairly primitive cultural situation in Oregon. The next generation, Diana and Frances, was able to take advantage of amazing educational opportunities which allowed access to some of the greatest musicians of the 20th century. The culminating third generation, Marcia, is still an ongoing story but unquestionably the result of the generations that preceded her.

None of this would have happened if not that "Mother Started It."

Courtesy Family Archives

Marcia at age 8 debuts with
California Chamber Symphony.

Courtesy Family Archives

Marcia at age 14 playing in
Portland, OR.

Courtesy Family Archives

Marcia with the first Central Coast Harp
Workshop at Cal Poly San Luis Obispo campus,
2004.

Courtesy Family Archives

Diana and Marcia in concert
for Mu Phi Epsilon Fraternity,
Los Angeles, about 2002.

World Harp
Congress, 1999.
Reception honors The
Debussy Trio at
American Embassy in
Prague. L-r, Angela
Wiegand, David
Walther, Marcia,
Bruce Broughton,
Ann Stockton,
Patricia Wooster,
Linda Wood Rollo,
Ambassador
Shattuck.

Courtesy Family Archives

Courtesy Family Archives

Above: The Debussy Trio
20th Anniversary.
Marcia Dickstein, harp;
Angela Wiegand, flute;
David Walther, viola.

Left: Mehli Mehta and Marcia after
her solo appearance with the
American Youth Symphony at Royce
Hall, UCLA. December 17, 1989

Courtesy Family Archives

Courtesy Family Archives

Judge Thomas Murphy with Sallie after he officiated at a private swearing-in ceremony, the day she became an attorney.

Courtesy Family Archives

The family celebrates en masse at Ed and Diana's 50th wedding anniversary.
Back row, l-r Keith, Sallie, Fred, Marcia.
Front row, l-r Grandchildren, Ed and Diana.

APPENDICES

Letter to Rudolf Serkin on Founding the Curtis Alumni Association   274

Discography
Commercial Recordings   275
    Diana Steiner   275
    Frances Steiner   276
    Marcia Dickstein   277

Archival Recordings   280
    Diana Steiner   280
    Frances Steiner   285
    Marcia Dickstein   293

Radio Broadcasts
"Air for Strings"   296
Other Broadcasts   298
"Portraits"   298

Publications
Music (Diana Steiner, Frances Steiner, Marcia Dickstein)   299
Magazine Articles (Diana Steiner, Editor)   301
California Music Teacher   301
American String Teacher Magazine   302
Miscellaneous   302

Major Concert Dates
Elizabeth Levy   303
Diana Steiner   303
Frances Steiner   308
Marcia Dickstein   310

Academic & Professional Credentials
(Elizabeth Levy, Diana Steiner, Frances Steiner, Marcia Dickstein)   314

꧁

LETTER TO RUDOLF SERKIN ON FOUNDING THE CURTIS ALUMNI ASSOCIATION

November 22, 1969

Dear Mr. Serkin,

It was good to hear from you. I am glad to know that you are considering the idea of an Alumni Association. I definitely am interested and willing to do whatever I can. It seems to me that an active group of Alumni could be helpful in supporting the school in many ways: encouraging talented students, advising and helping new graduates, perhaps eventually even funding projects that would not otherwise be included in the regular budget.

I am also quite sure that starting an Association will be a difficult task, the issue has been dead for so long. Enthusiasm and interest will have to be created in the old Alumni by making them aware of vital new outlooks and plans at Curtis plus the fact that it is healthy and necessary for the whole musical profession that Curtis be a center of learning that gives the artist and student a place other than the much publicized center in New York.

From a practical point of view, the first thing is to compile a mailing list of all former Curtis students that is as accurate and up-to-date as possible. Then, choose a small group of Alumni to formulate a set of objectives for the Association that can be presented to the whole as beginning plans and goals. Then, choose a group of former students from various periods of the school's history to pursue and persuade their fellow students and see how many can be interested in joining an Association. Once started it should begin to build momentum.

Ed joins in very best wishes and love to you and Mrs. Serkin.

DISCOGRAPHY

COMMERCIAL RECORDINGS

CDs and MP3s —all available through Fatrock Ink Music Publishers **www.fatrockink.com**

Diana Steiner

Sonatas

Diana Steiner, Violin; Elsa Fiedler and David Berfield, Piano

> Ernst von Dohnányi, Sonata in C# Minor- Op. 21
> Jean Sibelius, Sonatina- Op. 80
> Paul Creston, Suite for Violin and Piano
> Jean Françaix, Sonatina
> Paul Hindemith, Violin Sonata (1935)
> J.S. Bach, Partita No. 3 in E Major
> BWV 1006: Prelude & Gavotte

Fantasie

Diana Steiner, Violin; David Berfield, Piano

> Pablo de Sarasate/Efrem Zimbalist, *Fantasy on Bizet's "Carmen"*
> Henryk Wieniawski, Fantasy- *Op. 20 on Gounod's "Faust"*
> Heinrich Ernst, Fantasy- *Op. 11 on Rossini's "Othello"*
> Mario Castelnuovo-Tedesco, *Fantasy on "Figaro" from Rossini's Barber of Seville*

Encore

Diana Steiner, Violin; David Berfield, Piano

> Josef Suk, *Four Pieces - Quasi Ballata, Appassionata, Un poco triste, Burleske*
> Zoltán Kodály, *Adagio*
> Sergei Prokofiev, *Five Pieces*
> Jean Sibelius, *Devotion- Opus 77, No. 2 x, Souvenir- Opus 79, Berceuse- Opus 79*
> Pablo de Sarasate, *Introduction et Tarentelle- Opus 43*
> Karol Szymanowski, *Fountaine d'Aréthuse- Opus 30, No. 1*
> Aaron Copland, *Ukulele Serenade*
> Carl Engel/Efrem Zimbalist, *Sea Shell*
> Camille Saint-Saëns, *Havanaise- Opus 83*
> Marc Lavry, *Hora from Three Israeli Dances*

Live in Concert, Recorded at the Pequot Library, Southport, CT– November 7, 1959
Diana Steiner, Violin; Otto Herz, Piano

> Giuseppe Tartini, *Devil's Trill*
> Johannes Brahms, *Sonata in G Major "Rain"- Op. 78*
> Ernest Bloch, *Nigun (Improvisation from Baal Shem)*
> Aaron Copland, *Nocturne from Deux Pièces*
> Zoltán Kodály, *Adagio*
> Maurice Ravel, *Tzigane*
> Carl Engel/Efrem Zimbalist, *Sea Shell*
> George Gershwin/Jascha Heifetz, *It Ain't Necessarily So from Porgy and Bess*
> Fritz Kreisler, *Schön Rosmarin*

The following is available on MP3 only.
Ravel
Diana Steiner, Violin; David Berfield, Piano

> Maurice Ravel, Sonate for Violin and Piano

Frances Steiner

Available on LP
Ludwig von Beethoven, Trio- Op.36 (Symphony No. 2)
Steiner–Berfield Trio
Frances Steiner, Cello; Diana Steiner,Violin; David Berfield, Piano

Paul Hindemith, Sonatas for Cello and Piano
Frances Steiner, Cello; David Berfield, Piano

Marcia Dickstein — with The Debussy Trio

CDs and MP3s with * available through Fatrock Ink Music Publishers **www.fatrockink.com**

Art lies in the eye of the beholder (2009)*
Marcia Dickstein, Harp;
Angela Wiegand, Flute;
David Walther, Viola

> Sydney Hodkinson, *Skitter*
> Don Davis, *Slam Ahead*
> Paul Gibson, *Ritual Dances of the Divine Trinity*
> Don Davis, *'Til Human Voices Wake Us*
> Stephen Andrew Taylor, *Viriditas*
> Nicky Carligeanu, *Rondo*
> John Anthony Lennon, *Serpent*
> Bruce Babcock, *Springscape*
> Nimrod Borenstein, *Perpetua*
> David Lefkowitz, *Rage, Denial and Hope*

Three Friends (2001)*
Marcia Dickstein, Harp;
Angela Wiegand, Flute;
David Walther, Viola;
Suzanna Guzman, Guest Mezzo-Soprano

> Ian Krouse, *Trí Chairde (Three Friends)*
> Ian Krouse, *Tres Canciones Sobre Lorca*
> Bruce Broughton, *Tyvek Wood*
> Ian Krouse, *Cinco Canciones Insólitas*
> Ian Krouse, *Lullaby*

Music of Ian Krouse (2000)
Marcia Dickstein, Harp;
Angela Wiegand, Flute;
Keith Greene, Viola

> *Thamar y Amnón* (Koch International Classic)

Shadow of a Miracle (1996)*
Marcia Dickstein, Harp; Angela Wiegand, Flute; Keith Greene, Viola
> Lyle Mays, *In the Shadow of a Miracle*
> Jan Bach, *Eisteddfod, Variations & Penillion on a Welsh Harp Tune*
> Andrew Frank, *The Way You Hear It Is The Way You Sing It*

Augusta Read Thomas (1995)
Marcia Dickstein, Harp; Angela Wiegand, Flute; Keith Greene, Viola.
Soloist with Louisville Orchestra; Lawrence Leighton Smith, Conductor
> *Triple Concerto, night's midsummer blaze* (First Edition Recordings)

Baroque (1993)*

Marcia Dickstein, Harp; Angela Wiegand, Flute; Keith Greene, Viola;
Steve Erdody, Guest Cellist

Jean Marie Leclair, Triosonate in D Major– Op.2, No.8
Georg Philipp Telemann, Triosante No.5 in G Minor from *Six Trios*
Pietro Locatelli, Triosonate No.2 in B Major
Johann Gottlieb Graun, Triosonate in F Major
Georg Philipp Telemann, Triosonate in B Minor

Kumbosora and The Celestrial Harmony (1993)*

Marcia Dickstein, Harp; Angela Wiegand, Flute; Keith Greene, Viola

Roger Neill, *Kumbosora*
Dennis Davenport, *The Celestial Harmony*

Trios (1992)*

Marcia Dickstein, Harp; Angela Wiegand, Flute; Keith Greene, Viola

Vince Mendoza, Trio Music 5/90
Claude Debussy, Deuxième Sonate (for Flute, Viola and Harp)
Maurice Ravel, Sonatine

Eric Zeisl Chamber Music (1990)

Marcia Dickstein, Harp; Angela Schmidt (Wiegand), Flute; Keith Greene, Viola

Arrowhead Trio for Flute, Viola, and Harp (1956) (Harmonia Mundi)

World Premiere (1990)*

Marcia Dickstein, Harp; Angela Schmidt (Wiegand), Flute; Keith Greene, Viola

William Mathias, *Zodiac Trio*
Daron Hagen, Harp Trio
Michael Kibbe, *Trio- Opus 99*
Jacques Bondon, *Le Soleil Multicolore*

Marcia Dickstein — Featured Artist

Chamber Music for Harp by Arnold Bax (1998)*

Marcia Dickstein, Harp; Evan Wilson, Viola; Angela Wiegand, Flute;
Leslie Reed, English Horn; René Mandel, Violin; Natalie Leggett, Violin;
Simon Oswell, Viola; Timothy Landauer, Cello

Valse, *Solo Harp*
In Memoriam, English Horn, String Quartet and Harp
Fantasy Sonata, Viola and Harp
Quintet, String Quartet and Harp
Sonatina, Flute and Harp

Quilting an American Christmas (1997)

Roger Wagner Chorale, Jeannine Wagner, Conductor

19 Christmas songs (Chariot Records)

William Hall Chorale
Benjamin Britten, *Ceremony of Carols*

Available as MP3 only

Christopher Guardino, *Arabesque**

Marcia Dickstein, *From the Beginning**

Marcia Dickstein — Principal Harpist with Orchestra

Los Angeles Master Chorale
Grant Gershon, Conductor
Philip Glass, *Itaipu*

Los Angeles Master Chorale
Paul Salamunovich, Conductor
Dominick Argento, *Te Deum*

AT&T Presents Stormy Weather (1998)
Natalie Cole and Joni Mitchell, vocalists
They Can't Take That Away From Me (Natalie Cole)
Stormy Weather (Joni Mitchell)

Mothers and Daughters
Rosemary Clooney, vocalist
Multiple songs (Concord Records)

Ella Fitzgerald, vocalist
Multiple songs

Movies/TV Shows – Sampling from 300+
Toy Story I , II and III
A Bug's Life
Monsters, Inc.
Matrix Trilogy
The Royal Tenenbaums (screen credit)
Minority Report
A.I.
Memoirs of a Geisha
Horton Hears a Who!
Indiana Jones 4
7 Years in Tibet
Troy
A Beautiful Mind
Avatar
Princess and the Frog

ARCHIVAL RECORDINGS

Solo Recitals and Solo with Orchestra (Private Collection)
*indicates recording is in permanent collection at The Curtis Institute of Music

Diana Steiner

April 25, 1998 – Los Angeles, CA *
Mu Phi Epsilon Sorority Scholarship Concert
Diana Steiner, Violin; Marie Curea, Piano
> Vivaldi–Respighi, Sonata
> J.S. Bach, Partita in G Minor, Presto
> Jean Sibelius, *Souvenir*
> Jean Sibelius, *Berceuse*
> Marc Lavry, *Hora*

Late 1990s – Los Angeles *
Mu Phi Epsilon Program, Wilshire Ebell Theater
Diana Steiner, Violin; Marie Curea, Piano
> Antonín Dvořák, Sonatina
> Fritz Kreisler, *Recitative and Scherzo*
> Erich Wolfgang Korngold, *Much Ado about Nothing*

Late 1990's – Los Angeles, CA *
Mu Phi Epsilon Sorority Concert
Diana Steiner, Violin; Marie Curea, Piano
> Henri Vieuxtemps, Concerto in A Minor
> Marc Lavry, *Hora*

March 13, 1997 – Los Angeles, CA
Mu Phi Epsilon Sorority Concert
Diana Steiner, Violin; Marie Curea, Piano
> Edvard Grieg, Sonata in C Minor

October 13, 1995 – Los Angeles, CA
Mu Phi Epsilon Sorority Musicale
Diana Steiner, Violin; Marie Curea, Piano
> Samuel Barber, Concerto

September 30, 1990 – Northridge, CA *
Curtis Alumni Program, California State University, Northridge
Diana Steiner, Violin; Marcia Dickstein, Harp
> Camille Saint-Saëns, *Fantasie*

Mid 1980s – Los Angeles, CA *

Curtis Alumni Association West, St. Albans Church

Diana Steiner, Violin; Marcia Dickstein, Harp; David Berfield, Piano

Vivaldi-Respighi, *Sonata in D*
Max Bruch, *Scotch Fantasy*
Marc Lavry, *Sher, Yemenite Wedding, and Hora*
Antonín Dvořák, *Songs My Mother Taught Me*
Niccolò Paganini, *La Clochette*
Maurice Ravel, *Habanera*

November 1983 – Los Angeles, CA

Baroque Consortium

Diana Steiner, Jacqueline Brand, Yukiko Kumei, Violin Soloists;
Frances Steiner, Conductor

Antonio Vivaldi, *The Four Seasons*
Fall, Steiner
Spring, Kumei
Winter, Brand
J.S. Bach, Double Concerto (Steiner & Brand)

April, 1983 – Philadelphia, PA *

Curtis Symphony Orchestra,

Diana Steiner, Violin, Ronald Leonard, Cello; Frances Steiner, Conductor
Johannes Brahms, Concerto in D Major (the Double)

1981 or 1982 – Los Angeles, CA

Carson/Dominguez Hills Symphony

Diana Steiner, Violin; Richard Elgino, Viola; Frances Steiner, Conducting
W.A. Mozart, Sinfonia Concertante

February 15, 1981– Los Angeles, CA

American Youth Symphony, Wilshire Ebell Theater

Diana Steiner, Violin Solo; Mehli Mehta, Conductor
Camille Saint-Saëns, *Havanaise*
Béla Bartók, *Rhapsody, No. 1*

1978 - Los Angeles, CA *

Curtis Alumni West Musicale, Home of Eudice Shapiro

Jacob Krachmalnick, 1st Violin; Diana Steiner, 2nd Violin;
David Schwartz, Viola; Marie Fera, Cello; Dominick Fera, Clarinet
Johannes Brahms, Clarinet Quintet

1969 - Albuquerque, NM
National Federation of Music Clubs Convention
Diana Steiner, Violin; David Berfield, Piano
> Eugène Ysaye, *Ballad*
> Halsey Stevens, Suite for Violin Solo
> Camille Saint-Saëns, *Havanaise*
> Marc Lavry, *Hora*

Late 1960s - Los Angeles, CA *
Los Angeles County Museum, KFAC FM
Diana Steiner, Violin; Myra Kestenbaum, Viola; Michael Zearott, Piano
> Paul Hindemith, Sonata in E Minor
> Ludwig von Beethoven, Sonata #10, G Major
> Arthur Benjamin, *Romantic Fantasy*

1967 - Los Angeles, CA *
University of Southern California, Doctor of Musical Arts Recital, Hancock Auditorium
Diana Steiner, Violin; Frances Steiner, Cello; David Berfield, Piano
> W.A. Mozart, Trio in B Flat Major
> Leon Kirchener, Trio
> Johannes Brahms, Trio in B Major

July 1960 - Chautauqua, NY *
Chautauqua Festival Symphony
Diana Steiner, Violin; Walter Hendl, Conductor
> Camille Saint-Saëns, Concerto #3 in B Minor
> *1959 Young Artist, National Federation of Music Clubs Award Performance*

June, 1960 – Philadelphia, PA *
Philadelphia Invitational Recital
Veda Reynolds, Violin; Diana Steiner, Piano
> Johann Sebastian Bach, Sonata in E Minor
> Franz Schubert, Sonatina #1 in D Major
> Béla Bartók, *Romanian Dances*
> Sergei Prokofiev, *Two Melodies*
> William Kroll, *Banjo & Fiddle*
> Henri Vieuxtemps, Concerto #5 in A Minor
> Lili Boulanger, *Nocturne*
> Franz Schubert, *The Bee*

April 1960 – Bucks County, PA
Bucks County Symphony
Diana Steiner, Violin; Vernon Hammond, Conductor
> Johannes Brahms, Concerto in D Major

1960 – North Carolina

North Carolina Symphony
Diana Steiner, Violin; James Pfhol, Conductor
    Camille Saint-Saëns, Concerto #3 in B Minor

1960s – Los Angeles, CA*

Los Angeles County Museum, KFAC FM
Diana Steiner, Violin; Michael Zearott, Piano;
Lawrence Lesser, Cello; Richard Lesser, Clarinet
    Ingolf Dahl, Concerto a Tre
    Aram Khachaturian, Trio
    Darius Milhaud, Trio

1959 – Brevard, NC

Brevard Festival
Diana Steiner, Violin; James Pfohl , Conductor
    Alexander Glazunow, Concerto
    1959 Young Artist, National Federation of Music Clubs Award Performance

January, 1955 – Los Angeles, CA *

Los Angeles County Museum, KFAC FM
Diana Steiner, Violin; Yalta Menuhin, Piano
    Ludwig von Beethoven, Sonata #3 in G– Op. 30
    Ludwig von Beethoven, Sonata in F "Spring" Op. 24
    Ludwig von Beethoven, Sonata #2 in A– Op. 12

Mid-1950s – Marlboro, VT

Marlboro Festival
Diana Steiner, Violin
    Ludwig von Beethoven, Sonata "The Little G"
      (Claude Frank, Piano)
    W.A. Mozart, Concerto #5 in A Major
      (Festival Orchestra, Louis Moyse, Conductor)
    Sergei Prokofieff, Sonata #2 in D Major
      (Lawrence Leighton Smith, Piano)

1954 – Miami, FL

University of Miami Summer Pops Orchestra
Diana Steiner, Violin; Izler Solomon, Conductor
    Felix Mendelssohn, Concerto in E Minor
    Joaquin Nin, *Granadina*
    Antonín Dvorák, *Songs My Mother Taught Me*
    Fritz Kreisler, *Schön Rosmarin*

1952 - New York, NY *
Town Hall (Naumburg Debut Award)
Diana Steiner, Violin; Elsa Fiedler, Piano

> Paul Hindemith, Sonata in E Minor
> J.S. Bach, Prelude in E Major (3rd Partita)
> Felix Mendelssohn, Concerto in E Minor
> Paul Creston, Suite
> Zoltán Kodály, *Adagio*
> Maurice Ravel, *Tzigane*
> Engel-Zimbalist, *Sea Shell*
> Joaquin Nin, *Granadina*
> Aaron Copland, *Hoedown from Rodeo*

Spring 1952 - Chicago, IL *
Chicago Michaels Award Finals (broadcast nationally)
Diana Steiner, Violin, WGN Orchestra

> Peter Ilyich Tchaikovsky, Concerto 1st Movement

Date not known - Los Angeles, CA
Loyola Marymount Symphony
Diana Steiner, Violin; Pamela Highbaugh, Cello; Bogidar Avromov, Conductor

> Ludwig von Beethoven, Triple Concerto

Copyright 1945-46
Diana Steiner, Original Popular Ballads

> *In The Evening*
> *The Great White Way*
> *Some Day I'll Meet My Lover*
> *Ballad*

Compilation CD, Diana Steiner,
Archival Recordings, Ages 7-19: *

1940 - The Curtis Institute of Music
Zimbalist Students Recital, Casimir Hall

> J.S. Bach, Prelude in E Major (3rd Partita)

1942 - Town Hall, New York City
New York Philharmonic Young People's Concerts
Diana Steiner, Violin Soloist; Rudolph Ganz, Conductor

> Felix Mendelssohn, Concerto in E Minor (3rd Movement)
> Franz Schubert, The Bee (encore with pianist Otto Herz)

1949 – Carnegie Hall, New York City

New York Philharmonic Youth Concerts
Diana Steiner, Violin Soloist, Competition Winner

Igor Buketoff, Conductor
Felix Mendelssohn, Concerto in E Minor (1st Movement)

1952 – Michaels Award Finals

WGN Orchestra, Chicago – broadcast nationally
Diana Steiner, Violin Soloist

Peter Ilyich Tchaikovsky, Concerto in D Major (1st Movement)

Available on DVD

Early 1980s – Los Angeles, CA

Loyola Marymount University
Diana Steiner, Violin; Michael Cave, Piano

Mozart recital

Frances Steiner

March 1984 – Los Angeles, CA

Glendale Symphony, Los Angeles Music Center, Chandler Pavilion
Frances Steiner, Guest Conductor; Doc Severinson, Trumpet Solo

Gustav Holst, *Jupiter movement, The Planets*
Fisher Tull, *Concerto for Trumpet and Orchestra*

Diana and Frances Steiner (and Steiner/Berfield Trio)

September 16, 1990 – Los Angeles, CA

Chamber Orchestra of the South Bay Musicale
Diana Steiner, Violin; Frances Steiner, Cello; Leonid Gelfgat, Piano

Ludwig von Beethoven, *Trio in C minor*

1981–82 – Los Angeles, CA

Steiner & Curtis Friends, Chamber Music Party
Diana Steiner, 1st Violin; Mitchell Newman, Violin;
Francis Steiner, Cello; David Schwartz, Viola – et al.

Felix Mendelssohn, *Octet*

1976 – Fullerton, CA *

California State University, Fullerton
Diana Steiner, Violin; Frances Steiner, Cello; David Berfield, Piano

Gail Kubik, *Trio*
Felix Mendelssohn, Trio in D Minor

1970s – Los Angeles, CA

Los Angeles County Museum, KFAC FM
Diana Steiner, Violin; Frances Steiner, Cello; David Berfield, Piano

W.A. Mozart, *Trio in Bb*
Ludwig von Beethoven, Variations on *"Ich bin der Schneider Kakadu,"* –Op. 121A

1972 – Los Angeles, CA
University of Southern California Ravel Series
Diana Steiner, Violin; Frances Steiner, Cello; David Berfield, Piano;
> Susann McDonald, Harp
> Maurice Ravel, *Songs of Mallarmé*
> Maurice Ravel, *Introduction and Allegro, Harp, Winds, & Strings*
> Maurice Ravel, Trio, Violin, Cello, & Harp

March, 1966 – Los Angeles, CA *
Los Angeles County Museum, KFAC FM
Diana Steiner, Violin and Piano; Frances Steiner, Cello
> George Friderich Handel/Johan Halverson, *Passacaglia*
> Franz Schubert, *Arpeggione Sonata*

August 1964 – Los Angeles *
Los Angeles County Museum of Art, KFAC FM
Diana Steiner, Violin and Piano; Virginia O'Quinn, Violin; Meyer Bello, Viola; Frances Steiner, Cello; and Christina Carol, Soprano
> J.S. Bach, Sonata #3 – G Minor
> Arthur Honegger, Sonatina for Violin and Cello
> Franz Schubert, Trio #1 in B Flat Major
> Elinor Remick Warren, *Sonnets* for Soprano and String Quartet

1955 – Los Angeles, CA *
UCLA
Frances Steiner, Cello; Diana Steiner, Piano
> J.S. Bach, Solo Sonata in C Major
> Johannes Brahms, *Sonata in E Minor*
> Ernest Bloch, *Prayer*
> Listz–Popper, *Hungarian Rhapsody*
> Camille Saint-Saëns, *Carnival of the Animals: The Swan*

Date not known – Los Angeles, CA
Chamber Orchestra of the South Bay Musicale
Diana Steiner, Violin/Piano; Frances Steiner, Cello/Piano; Leonid Gelfgat, Piano
> Robert Schumann, Piano Quartet
> Camille Saint-Saëns, *The Swan*
> Marc Lavry, *Hora*

Available on DVD

1983 – Philadelphia, PA
Curtis Alumni Week, Curtis Symphony Orchestra
Diana Steiner, Violin, Ronald Leonard, Cello, Frances Steiner, Conductor,
> Johannes Brahms, Double Concerto in A Minor

Marcia Dickstein
Recital, Solo with Orchestra & Principal Harp

March 8, 2009 – Los Angeles, CA
Chamber Orchestra of the South Bay
Marcia Dickstein, Harp; Frances Steiner, Conductor
> Mark Koval, Concerto for Harp (world premiere)

December 3, 2006 – Los Angeles, CA
Chamber Orchestra of the South Bay
Marcia Dickstein, Harp; Nadine Asin, Flute; Frances Steiner, Conductor
> Mark Koval, Concerto for Harp (sneak preview)
> Mozart, Concerto for Flute & Harp

July 27, 2006 – Los Angeles, CA
Korn Hall, UCLA
I Palpiti; Guest Soloist, Marcia Dickstein, Harp
> Maurice Ravel, *Introduction and Allegro*

May 12, 2002 – Los Angeles, CA
Sundays Live, KMZT-FM
Dickstein and Friends: Marcia Dickstein, Harp; Philip Levy, Violin;
Timothy Landauer, Cello; Diane Alancraig, Soprano
> Camille Saint-Saëns, *Fantasy for Violin & Harp*
> Manuel de Falla
> Jean Françaix
> Vaughn-Williams, *Four Songs*

August 16, 1998 – Los Angeles, CA
"Sundays at 4," KUSC-FM
Los Angeles County Museum, Bing Auditorium
Dickstein & Friends: Marcia Dickstein, Harp; Paul Cohen, Cello:
Julie Gigante, Violin; Angela Wiegand, Flute; Evan Wilson, Viola
> Vincent Persichetti, *Serenade*
> Jacques Ibert, Trio
> Arnold Bax, *Fantasy Sonata*

February 25, 1997 – Thousand Oaks, CA
Symphony of the West, Thousand Oaks Performing Arts Center
Marcia Dickstein, Harp; Paul Fried, Flute
> Mozart, Flute and Harp Concerto

June 14, 1994 - Los Angeles, CA
KUSC-FM
Marcia Dickstein, Harp; Yehuda Gilad, Oboe
> Gunther Rafael, Sonatine
> André Caplet, *Divertissement à la Française*

March 1993 - Los Angeles, CA
Brand Library Recital
Marcia Dickstein, Harp
> J.S. Bach, Prelude in C Major
> Gabriel Fauré, *Impromptu*
> Benjamin Britten, Sonata
> André Caplet, *Divertissement à la Française*

March 1993 - Los Angeles, CA
Royce Hall, UCLA
Young Musicians Foundation Orchestra,
Marcia Dickstein, Harp; Lalo Schifrin, Conductor
> Alberto Ginastera, Concerto for Harp- Opus 25

December 17, 1989 - Los Angeles, CA
Royce Hall, UCLA
American Youth Symphony,
Marcia Dickstein, Harp; Mehli Mehta, Conductor
> Maurice Ravel, *Introduction and Allegro*

February 24, 1989 - Los Angeles, CA
University of Southern California
Marcia Dickstein, Harp; Angela Schmidt (Wiegand), Flute;
Anne-Marie Ketchum, Soprano
> John Anthony Lennon, *Ghostfires*

February, 1988 - Los Angeles, CA
Bovard Auditorium, University of Southern California
Marcia Dickstein, Principal Harp; USC Symphony; Daniel Lewis, Conductor
> Igor Stravinsky, Symphony in 3 movements

Christmas, 1986 - Mesa Verde, CA
Marcia Dickstein, Harp; Chancel Choir, Gregory Norton, Conductor
> Benjamin Britten, *Ceremony of Carols*

June, 1986 - Los Angeles, CA
Bovard Auditorium, University of Southern California
American Harp Society Convention
Marcia Dickstein & Joanne Turovsky, Harp; Larry Bunker, Percussion
> Bruce Broughton, *Toccata for 2 harps and percussion* (world premiere)

November 7, 1986 – Los Angeles, CA

Bovard Auditorium, University of Southern California

Marcia Dickstein, Principal Harp

> Reinhold Gliere, *Ilya Morametz* – Symphony #3

January, 1983 – Portland, OR

Chamber Music Society of Oregon

Marcia Dickstein, Harp; Eugene Raza, Conductor

> Claude Debussy, Danses Sacre et Profane

1974-1980 – Los Angeles, CA

First Archival CD

> *Greensleeves*, Solo with California Chamber Symphony;
> > Henri Temianka, Conductor (1974)
>
> Marcel Tournier, *Le Bon Petit* (about age 9)
>
> Hava Nagilah
>
> Naderman, Sonata (about age 12)
>
> Ned Rorem, *Sky Music*
> > American Harp Society Competition (Fargo, ND)
>
> Karl Ditters von Dittersdorf, Concerto, solo
> with Brentwood Symphony; Alvin Mills, Conductor

Date Unknown – Los Angeles, CA

Baroque Consortium

Marcia Dickstein Harp; Anne Diemer Giles, Flute; Frances Steiner, Conductor

> George Frideric Handel, Harp Concerto
> Howard Hanson, Serenade for Flute and Harp

Date Unknown – Glendale, CA

Glendale Symphony

Marcia Dickstein Harp; Sheridan Stokes, Flute

> W.A. Mozart, Flute & Harp Concerto

Marcia Dickstein – with The Debussy Trio

April 30, 2006 – Los Angeles, CA

"Sundays Live," KUSC-FM, L.A. County Museum, Bing Auditorium

Marcia Dickstein, Harp; Angela Wiegand, Flute; David Walther, Viola

> Roger Neill, *Kumbosora*
> Carlos Rodriguez, *De tiempo y agua y olas*
> J. Mark Scearce
> David Lefkowitz, *Rage, Denial, Hope*
> Bernard Rands, *Sans voix parmi les voix*
> John Anthony Lennon, *Serpent*
> Ian Krouse, *Tri Chairde*

July 10, 2005 - Los Angeles, CA
"Sundays Live," KUSC-FM, L.A. County Museum, Bing Auditorium
Marcia Dickstein, Harp; Angela Wiegand, Flute; David Walther, Viola
Karin Meshugian, Guest Mezzo-Soprano

>   David Walther, *A Two for One Trio* (broadcast premiere)
>   Ralph Vaughn Williams, *Three Songs*
>   Claude Debussy, Sonate for Flute, Viola and Harp
>   Paul Gibson, *Ritual Dances of the Divine Trinity*
>   Nicky Carligeanu, *Rondo*

June 1, 2003 - Los Angeles, CA
"Sundays Live," KMZT-FM, L.A. County Museum, Bing Auditorium
Marcia Dickstein, Harp; Angela Wiegand, Flute; David Walther, Viola

>   Don Davis, *No Exit*
>   Claude Debussy, *Deuxième Sonate*
>   Laura Karpman, *About Joshua*
>   Nimrod Borenstein, *Perpetua*

March, 2003 - Pasadena, CA
Dabney Hall, Cal Tech
DTMF 2002 Competition Winners
Marcia Dickstein, Harp; Angela Wiegand, Flute; David Walther, Viola

>   Nimrod Borenstein, *Perpetua*
>   Kevin Mayo, *Incantation #2* (world premiere)

January 6, 2003 - Los Angeles, CA
"Sundays Live," KMZT-FM, L.A. County Museum, Bing Auditorium
Marcia Dickstein, Harp; Angela Wiegand, Flute; David Walther, Viola

>   Don Davis, *No Exit*
>   Claude Debussy, *Deuxième Sonate*
>   Kevin Mayo, *Incantation #2*
>   Nimrod Borenstein, *Perpetua*

December 17, 2000 - Los Angeles, CA
"Sundays Live," KMZT-FM, L.A. County Museum, Bing Auditorium
Marcia Dickstein, Harp; Angela Wiegand, Flute; David Walther, Viola

>   J.A.C. Redford, *Water Walker*
>   Carlos Rodriguez, *De tiempo y agua y olas*
>   Mario Castelnuevo-Tedesco
>   Ian Krouse
>   David Long
>   Bruce Broughton, *Tyvek Wood*

December, 1998 – Los Angeles, CA
"Sundays Live," KUSC-FM, L.A. County Museum, Bing Auditorium
Marcia Dickstein, Harp; Angela Wiegand, Flute; David Walther, Viola

Nathan Currier , *Sambuca Sonata*
Bernard Rands, *Sans voix parmi les voix*
Todd Sickafosse, *Black is the Color*
Jean-Michel Demase, *Trio (1998)*
Sydney Hodkinson, *Skitter*

December 16, 1998 – Los Angeles, CA
"Sundays Live," KUSC-FM, L.A. County Museum, Bing Auditorium
Marcia Dickstein, Harp; Angela Wiegand, Flute; David Walther, Viola

Sidney Hodkinson, *Skitter*

June 22, 1997 – Los Angeles, CA
"Sundays at 4," KUSC-FM, L.A. County Museum, Bing Auditorium
Marcia Dickstein, Harp; Angela Wiegand, Flute; Keith Greene, Viola

Donald Crocket, *Short Stories*
Arnold Bax, *Valse*
Don Davis, *No Exit*

May 4, 1997 – Eugene, OR
Oregon Festival of American Music
Marcia Dickstein, Harp; Angela Wiegand, Flute; Keith Greene, Viola

Donald Crocket, *Short Stories* (world premiere)
Don Davis, *No Exit* (world premiere)

November 10, 1996 – Los Angeles, CA
"St. Paul Sunday," NPR Broadcast
Marcia Dickstein, Harp; Angela Wiegand, Flute; Keith Greene, Viola

Claude Debussy, *Deuxième Sonate*
Lyle Mays, *In the Shadow of a Miracle*
Ian Krouse, *Tri Chairde*

March 16, 1996 – Sedona, AZ
Marcia Dickstein, Harp; Angela Wiegand, Flute; Keith Greene, Viola

Claude Debussy, *Deuxième Sonate*
Roger Neill, *Kumbosora*
Lyle Mays, *In the Shadow of a Miracle*
Ian Krouse, *Tri Chairde*

January 7, 1996 – Los Angeles, CA

"Sundays at 4," KUSC-FM, L.A. County Museum, Bing Auditorium

Marcia Dickstein, Harp; Angela Wiegand, Flute; Keith Greene, Viola; Elayne Farone, Soprano

> Peter Schickele, *The Lowest Trees Have Tops*
> François Devienne, Duo
> Maurice Duruflé, Trio

January 29, 1994 – San Francisco, CA

First Congregational Church

Women's Philharmonic

The Debussy Trio, Soloist (Marcia Dickstein, Harp; Angela Wiegand, Flute; Keith Greene, Viola), Joann Falletta, Conductor

> Augusta Read Thomas, *Triple Concerto, night's midsummer blaze*

December 12, 1993 – Los Angeles, CA

"Sundays at 4," KUSC-FM, L.A. County Museum, Bing Auditorium Marcia Dickstein, Harp; Angela Wiegand, Flute; Keith Greene, Viola

> Paul Gibson, *Ritual Dances of the Divine Trinity*
> Arnold Bax, Sonatina
> Ian Krouse, *Tres Canciones Sobre Lorca*
> Roger Neill, Kumbosora

June 21, 1993 – Los Angeles, CA

John Anson Ford Theatre

Marcia Dickstein, Harp; Angela Wiegand, Flute; Keith Greene, Viola

> Georg Telemann, Triosonate
> Andrew Frank, *The Way You See It Is the Way You Hear It*
> Maurice Ravel, Sonatine

February 25, 1993 – Davis, CA

Cantrell Auditorium, University of California, Davis

Marcia Dickstein, Harp; Angela Wiegand, Flute; Keith Greene, Viola

Georg Telemann, Triosonate

> Arnold Bax, Sonatina
> Andrew Frank, *The Way You See It Is the Way You Hear It*
> Dennis Davenport, *The Celestial Harmony*
> Roger Neill, *Kumbosora*

April 2, 1992 – Carmel, CA

Marcia Dickstein, Harp; Angela Wiegand, Flute; Keith Greene, Viola

> Claude Debussy, *Deuxième Sonate*
> Vince Mendoza, *Trio 5/90*
> Maurice Ravel, Sonatine

February 9, 1992 – Chicago, IL
WFMT-FM, United Airlines Presents
Marcia Dickstein, Harp; Angela Wiegand, Flute; Keith Greene, Viola

> Vince Mendoza, *Trio 5/90*
> Claude Debussy, *Deuxième Sonate*
> Maurice Ravel, Sonatine

January 8, 1992 – Boston, MA
WGBH-FM
Marcia Dickstein, Harp; Angela Wiegand, Flute; Keith Greene, Viola

> Jacques Ibert, *Deux Interludes*
> Vince Mendoza, *Trio 5/90*
> Claude Debussy, *Deuxième Sonate*

February 2, 1992 – Philadelphia, PA
The Curtis Institute of Music, Perpetua Mobile Series
Marcia Dickstein, Harp; Angela Wiegand, Flute; Keith Greene, Viola

> Daron Hagen, Trio
> Claude Debussy, *Deuxième Sonate*
> Luigi Zaninelli, *Musical Fable*
> Maurice Ravel, Sonatine

February 9, 1991 – Laguna, CA
Laguna Chamber Music Series
Marcia Dickstein, Harp; Angela Wiegand, Flute; Keith Greene, Viola

> François Couperin, Concerts Royaux
> Claude Debussy, *Deuxième Sonate*
> Jacques Ibert, *Deux Interludes*
> Vince Mendoza, *Trio 5/90* (world premiere)
> Maurice Ravel, Sonatine

May 28, 1989 – Los Angeles, CA (first broadcast of the Trio)
"Sundays at 7," KFAC-FM, Barnsdall Park Auditorium
Marcia Dickstein, Harp; Angela Schmidt (Wiegand), Flute;
Christopher Redfield, Viola

> Pietro Locatelli, Triosonate
> Darren Hagen, Trio
> Mathias, Zodiac Trio
> Gabriel Fauré, *Pavane*

April 29, 1989 - Fort Worth, TX
National Federation of Music Clubs
Marcia Dickstein, Harp; Angela Schmidt (Wiegand), Flute;
Christopher Redfield, Viola

> Arnold Bax, *Elegaic Trio*
> Daron Hagen, Trio (world premiere)

September 7, 1988 - Los Angeles, CA
Dame Myra Hess Series, KUSC-FM, Cal Plaza Spiral Court
Marcia Dickstein, Harp; Angela Schmidt (Wiegand), Flute;
Christopher Redfield, Viola

> Jacque Bondon, *Le Soleil Multicolore*
> Georg Telemann, Triosonate
> Claude Debussy, *Deuxème Sonate*

February 18, 1988 - Fullerton, CA
California State University, Fullerton
Marcia Dickstein, Harp; Angela Schmidt (Wiegand), Flute;
Christopher Redfield, Viola

> Georg Telemann, Triosonate
> Claude Debussy, *Deuxième Sonate*
> Jacque Bondon, *Le Soleil Multicolore*

Available on DVD

Marcia Dickstein

December 16, 1999 - Burbank, CA
The Tonight Show (with Charlotte Church)

December 24, 1992 - Los Angeles, CA
Los Angeles Music Center Christmas Program
Soloist with Mansfield Singers
> Benjamin Britten, *Ceremony of Carols*

Composite:
> 1980 - Young Musicians Foundation Television Show
> 1983 - KOIN-TV, Portland OR
> Date Unknown - Barbara Mandrell Christmas Show
> Date Unknown - Jay Leno Show (with Andrea Bocelli)
> Date Unknown - Northridge Chorale and Orchestra (soloist)
> Date Unknown - Los Angeles Music Center Christmas Show

Available on DVD

Marcia Dickstein - with The Debussy Trio

July 2002 - Geneva, Switzerland
8th World Harp Congress
The Debussy Trio, Soloist (Marcia Dickstein, Harp; Angela Wiegand, Flute; David Walther, Viola), with Geneva Chamber Orchestra

> Vince Mendoza, *Turn-out* (world premiere)

July 21, 1999 - Prague, Czech Republic
7th World Harp Congress
Marcia Dickstein, Harp; Angela Wiegand, Flute; David Walther, Viola

> Bruce Broughton, *Tyvek Wood* (world premiere)
> Ian Krouse, *Tri Chiarde*

February 2, 1992 - Philadelphia, PA
The Curtis Institute of Music, Perpetua Mobile Series
Marcia Dickstein, Harp; Angela Wiegand, Flute; Keith Greene, Viola

> Daron Hagen, Trio
> Claude Debussy, Sonata
> Luigi Zaninelli, *Musical Fable*
> Maurice Ravel, Sonatine

May 19, 1991 - Flintridge, CA
The Debussy Trio Music Foundation Musicale
Marcia Dickstein, Harp; Angela Wiegand, Flute; Keith Greene, Viola

> Jacque Ibert, *Entr'acte*
> Claude Debussy, *Gollywog's Cakewalk*
> Luigi Zaninelli, *Musical Fable* (world premiere)

RADIO BROADCASTS

"Air for Strings"

Host/Producer Diana Steiner
A series of broadcasts over KXLU-FM
(Loyola Marymount College, Los Angeles, CA)
1979 – 1980

The focus of the series, broadcast on KXLU, was presenting young performance winners of national and international competitions with interviews of top professionals in related fields. The broadcasts have historical significance because of the famous interviewees and performers, many of whom are now major artists.

(listed in chronological order)

COLEMAN CHAMBER MUSIC COMPETITION
January 23, 1979 (Library of Congress ICD 39038)

Interview: Harlow Mills, Coleman Chamber Music Society
Performers: Tokyo String Quartet [K. Harada; A. Ikeda; K. Isomura; S. Harada] and Gagliano Quartet [Jacqueline Brand, Ida Levin, Paul Neubauer, Charles Curtis]

AMERICAN HARP SOCIETY
January 30, 1979 (Library of Congress ICD 39039)

Interview: Ann Stockton, President, American Harp Society
Performers: Marcia Dickstein, Tamara Bischoff, Joann Turovsky

NATIONAL FEDERATION of MUSIC CLUBS
February 6, 1979 (Library of Congress ICD 39040)

Interviews: Naomi Reynolds, NFMC National Young Artist Chair & Ronald Leonard, Principal Cello, Los Angeles Philharmonic
Performers: Charles Curtis, Cello, Neal Stuhlberg, Piano; Ronald Leonard, Cello; Pinchas Zuckerman, Violin; with Los Angeles Philharmonic

AMERICAN STRING TEACHERS ASSOCIATION
February 13, 1979 (Library of Congress ICD 39041)

Interview: Paul Rolland, Founder, ASTA
Performers: Katherine Jonke, Viola; Michaela Patsch, Violin

MUSIC TEACHERS ASSOCIATION of CALIFORNIA
February 20, 1979 (Library of Congress ICD 39042)

Interviews: Sybil Maxwell, Chr. MTAC-VOCE &
Arnold Steinhardt, Guarneri String Quartet, 1st Violin
Performers: VOCE winners, Melodia and Marakosh String Quartets; Guarneri Quartet
(Arnold Steinhardt, John Daley, Michael Tree, David Soyer)

THE DOUBLE BASS at ISLE OF MAN & LA PHILHARMONIC
February 27, 1979 (Library of Congress ICD 39043)
Interviews & Performers: Dennis Trembly, Co-principal, Los Angeles Philharmonic;
Oscar Hildago, USC; Nico Abondolo, Los Angeles Philharmonic Youth winner;
Rhonda Kass, Piano

GUITAR FOUNDATION
March 7, 1979 (Library of Congress ICD 39044)

Interviews only: Ronald Purcell, President, Guitar Foundation
Performers: George Vick, Charles Schwavenen, and John Holmquist

YOUNG MUSICIANS FOUNDATION
March 20, 1979 (Library of Congress ICD 39045)

Interviews: Barry Kimmelman, Chairman, YMF; George Kast, Artistic Chairman
Performers: Stacy Phelps, Violin; Cynthia Phelps, Viola; Nina Bodnar Horton, Violin

AMERICAN FEDERATION of MUSICIANS

CONGRESS of STRINGS
March 27, 1979 (Library of Congress ICD 39046)

Interviews: Louis Kievman, Chairman, Congress of String, L.A.
Performers: Irene Sazer, Violin; Richard Elegino, Viola; Steven Balderston, Cello;
Denise Dalgren, Piano

NATIONAL FEDERATION OF MUSIC CLUBS
April, 1979 (Library of Congress ICD 39047)
Young Artists Competition, Portland, OR

Interviews Only: Eleanore Schoenfeld, Judge; Christopher Rex, 1979 Young American
String Contest Winner; Leslie Parnas, Guest Artist, Cellist

MUSIC TEACHERS ASSOCIATION OF CALIFORNIA
W.W. NAUMBURG CHAMBER MUSIC AWARD,
1979 (Library of Congress ICD 39048)

Interviews Only: Robert Sutton, National President, Music Teachers National Association; Naumburg Winner, Sequoia Quartet; Miwako Watanabe, 2nd Violin; James
Dunham, Viola

JOHN DEALEY AWARD
April 9, 1980 (Library of Congress ICD 39049)

Interview: Mehli Mehta, Conductor, American Youth Symphony
Performer: Margaret Batjer, Violin

YOUNG MUSICIANS FOUNDATION
1980 (Library of Congress ICD 39050)

Interviews: Sylvia Kunin, YMF Founder & Exec. Vice-president;
Helen Peppard, Project Director.
Performers: Marcia Dickstein, Harp; Ida Levin, Violin

INTERNATIONAL COMPETITION WINNERS
1980 (Library of Congress ICD 39051)

Interviews: Irina Tseitlin
Performers: Irina Tseitlin, Violin; Nathaniel Rosen, Cello

OTHER BROADCASTS

"Portraits"
Host/Producer Diana Steiner

PORTRAIT OF ABRAM CHASINS
October 2, 1987 (Library of Congress ICD 39052)
KUSC- FM & NPR (University of Southern California)

Interviews : Jorge Bolet, Constance Keene, Peter Nero
Gail Eichenthal, Gary Graffman, & Robert Sherman
Performers: Abram Chasins, Jorge Bole, Gary Graffman, Constance Keene & Peter
Nero w/Arthur Fiedler & Boston Pops Orchestra

PORTRAIT OF EFREM ZIMBALIST
August 8, 1985 (Library of Congress ICD 39053)
KXLU - Loyola Marymount University, CA

Performers: Efrem Zimbalist, Roy Malan, Eudice Shapiro, Aaron Rosand and Diana
Steiner, Violins; Alma Gluck, Soprano
Accompanists: Eugene Lutsky, Marilyn Thompson, Brooks Smith,
David Berfield, Radio Luxemburg Orchestra

THE CURTIS INSTITUTE OF MUSIC 60TH ANNIVERSARY
KUSC 1984-85 (Library of Congress ICD 39054)
KUSC- FM & NPR (University of Southern California)

Abram Chasins and Diana Steiner, Co-hosts
Performers: Raphael Druian, Lynn Harrell, Peter Serkin, Diana Steiner, Anna Moffo and
Leonard Bernstein, Violins; George Szell, Piano

PUBLICATIONS

All Diana Steiner and Marcia Dickstein music and book publications
available through Fatrock Ink Music Publishers — **www.fatrockink.com**

MUSIC

Diana Steiner – Arranged and Edited by

Violin Classics Book I (Violin & Piano). Copyright 1972.

Violin Classics Book II (Violin & Piano). Copyright 1972.

Violin Classic, Angel's Serenade by Gaetano Braga. Copyright 1989.

Presto from String Quartet in G by Joseph Haydn. Copyright 1989.

German Dances by Joseph Haydn. Copyright 1997.

String Orchestra Classics Book I, Bach to Tchaikovsky. Copyright 1972.

String Orchestra Classics Book II, Bach to von Weber. Copyright 1979.

Greensleeves: Harp Solo with String Orchestra, Marcia Dickstein, Harp Editor; Diana
Steiner, String Editor. Copyright 1989.

Concerto for Flute and Harp, K.199 (2nd movement), Marcia Dickstein, Harp Editor;
Diana Steiner, String Editor. Copyright 2000.

Frances Steiner

Musicianship for the Classroom Teacher, by Max Kaplan and Frances Steiner.
Copyright 1966.

Six Minuets for Two Cellos, by Joseph Haydn, edited and arranged by Frances J.
Steiner. Copyright 1967.

Marcia Dickstein

Baroque to Romantic, Harp Solo pedal/non-pedal. Copyright 1998.

From the Beginning, Harp Solo pedal/non-pedal. Copyright 1997.

Harp Warm-Ups, Harp Solo pedal/non-pedal. Copyright 2008.

Occasional, Harp Solo pedal/non-pedal. Copyright 2009.

Arnold Bax Sonata (for Flute & Harp), Scholarly Edition. Copyright 2000.

Arnold Bax Valse, Scholarly Edition. Copyright 1995.

Concerto for Flute and Harp, K.199 (2nd movement), Marcia Dickstein, Harp Editor; Diana Steiner, String Editor. Copyright 2000.

Greensleeves: Harp Solo with String Orchestra, Marcia Dickstein, Harp Editor; Diana Steiner, String Editor. Copyright 1989.

MAGAZINE ARTICLES

California Music Teacher
(Official Journal of The Music Teachers Association of California)

Diana Steiner, Violin Editor

September/October 1982 – Vol. 6 #1
   "The Tradition of Efrem Zimbalist"

January/February 1983 – Vol. 6 #2
   "On Jascha Heifetz"

January 1984 – Vol. 7 #2
   "Style – The Dramatic Approach"

March 1984 – Vol. 7 #3
   "A Conductor's View of Auditions – An Interview with Dr. Frances Steiner"

September/October 1984 – Vol. 8 #1
   "Olympic Gold in Chamber Music"

January 1985 – Vol. 8 #2
   "The Bach Double Concerto Revisited"

March 1985 – Vol. 8 #3
   "You Are Out of Tune and it's Driving Me Crazy!"

March 1986 – Vol. 9 #3
   "A Stringed Instrument Gap"

Summer 1988 – Vol. 11 #4
   "Educating the Musician, Today and Tomorrow," An Interview with Larry Livingston, Dean of the University of Southern California School of Music

Winter 1992 – Vol. 15 #2
   "Duos, A Musical Treat"

Spring 1993 – Vol. 16 #3
   "Memories of Two Great Violinists (Nathan Milstein and Henri Temianka)"

American String Teacher Magazine
(Official Journal of The American String Teachers Association)

Diana Steiner, Violin Editor

Winter 1986, Vol. XXXVI, No. 1
    "Efrem Zimbalist: A Tradition, Today and Tomorrow"
    Veda Reynolds, Aaron Rosand and Eudice Shapiro

Spring 1986, Vol. XXXVI, No. 2
    "Developing the Secure Violinist" by Aaron Rosand

Summer 1986, Vol. XXXVI, No. 3
    "Violinistic Training – A Concertmaster's View" by Normal Carol

Autumn 1986, Vol. XXXVI, No. 4
    "Henri Temianka's Eightieth: Reminiscences with Diana Steiner"

Spring 1987, Vol. XXXVII, No. 1
    "Some Thoughts on Violin Playing" by Arnold Steinhardt

Spring 1987, Vol. XXXVII, No. 2
    "The Emerging Professional Violinist – Part 1
    (An interview with NancyBell Coe, Orchestra Manager, L.A. Philharmonic)"

Summer 1987, Vol. XXXVII, No. 3
    "The Emerging Professional Violinist – Part 2
    (Susan Wadsworth, A Concert Manager Speaks)"

Autumn 1987, Vol. XXXVII, No. 4
    "Learning from Heifetz"

MISCELLANEOUS

Strings, "Get It Right Up Front," (date unknown)

Violexchange Magazine, "An Interview with The Debussy Trio," 1990

Showcase, The National Federation of Music Clubs Magazine, Winter 61'- 62' – Vol. 61 #2
    "Time with the Master (on Jascha Heifetz)"

MAJOR CONCERT DATES

ELIZABETH LEVY
sampling

August 5, 1918 – Salem, OR
Elizabeth Levy Violin Ensemble
Oregon State Fair

July, 1926 – Philadelphia, PA
Sesquicentennial
Great Dome

July, 1926 – Philadelphia, PA
Sesquicentennial radio broadcast
WCAU

DIANA STEINER
sampling

In recital, as soloist with orchestra & on radio

August 27, 1939 – Greenbriar, WV
Greenbriar Music Festival Orchestra
Ferenz Steiner, Conductor

March 27, 1940 – Philadelphia, PA
Casimir Hall, The Curtis Institute of Music
Recital of Students of Efrem Zimbalist

September 30, 1940 (Diana Steiner Day) – Portland, OR
Civic Auditorium,
Edna Burton, Piano

February 23, 1942 – New York, NY
The Town Hall, Young People's Concerts
New York Philharmonic
Rudolph Ganz, Conductor

Other Recitals at Curtis Institute (list may be incomplete):
April 26, 1944
May 2, 1945
May 3, 1946
April 30, 1947
November 20, 1947
April 1, 1949
April 29, 1949 (Graduation Recital)
October 1, 1952 (New York debut preview)

January 6, 1945 – Philadelphia, PA
Academy of Music
The Philadelphia Orchestra Children's Concert
Lorin Maazel, Conductor

April 11, 1945 – Miami Beach, FL
Victor Hotel
American Jewish Congress

July 22, 1945 – Miami Beach, FL
Cosmopolitan Hotel
American Jewish Congress

July, 1948 – Kennebunkport, ME (several dates)
Music Meadows
Ruth Bradley, Piano

December 18, 1948 – New York, NY
Carnegie Hall
New York Philharmonic Young People's Concerts
Igor Buketoff, Conductor

February 28, 1950
Fidelity Great Music Television Series
Guy Mariner, Host

July 30, 1950 – Lenox, MA
Tanglewood Music Festival Orchestra
Serge Koussevitzky, Director

December 11, 1950 – Philadelphia, PA
Philadelphia Orchestra Youth Concerts
Benny Goodman, Guest Soloist; Eugene Ormandy, Conductor

January 19, 1951 – Washington, DC
Barker Hall, Winner's Recital
The Friday Morning Music Club
Elsa Fiedler, Piano

March 4, 1951 – Washington, DC
The Phillips Gallery
Elsa Fiedler, Piano

March 11–April 15, 1951 – Philadelphia, PA
WFLN-FM Young Artists Series

April 18, 1951 – Miami Beach, FL
Casablanca Hotel
Zionist Organization

Marlboro Music Festival – Marlboro, VT (list may be incomplete):
July 19, 1951
August 17, 1952
August 17, 1957
August 6, 1958

October 7, 1952 – New York, NY
Town Hall Debut
Walter W. Naumburg Winner
Elsa Fiedler, Piano

May 7, 1952 – Germantown, PA
Germantown Symphony
Arthur Cohn, Conductor

April 18, 1953 – Chicago, IL
Symphony Hall
Chicago Symphony Orchestra
George Schick, Conductor

September 27, 1953 – Washington, DC
The A. W. Mellon Concerts
National Gallery of Art Orchestra
Richard Bales, Conductor

June 25, 1954 – Salem, OR
Willamette University
Aurora Underwood, Piano

July 25, 1954 – Miami, FL
Dade Auditorium
Miami Symphony Orchestra
Izler Solomon, Conductor

1953-54, 54-55, 55-56 seasons
The Community Concert Association
The Gotham Concert Trio
Seymour Bernstein, Piano & Ruth Condell, Cello

January 5, 1955 - Los Angeles, CA
L.A. County Museum Services
KFAC - 1st live binaural broadcast
Yalta Menuhin, Piano

April 25, 1959 - San Diego, CA
NFMC Winners Concert
Horace Martinez, Piano

May 3, 1959 - Cincinnati, OH
NFMC Winners Concert

July 17, 1959 - Brevard, NC
Brevard Festival Orchestra
James Pfohl , Conductor

November 7, 1959 - Southport, CT
Wednesday Afternoon Music Club
Otto Herz, Piano

November 24, 1959 - Detroit, MI
Detroit Institute of Arts
Otto Herz, Piano

November 29, 1959 - Little Rock, AR
NFMC Concert Tour
Robinson Auditorium
Suzanne Waldbauer, Piano

January 24, 1960 - Washington, DC
National Gallery of Art
Otto Herz, Piano

February 6, 1960 - Redding, PA
Haage Concerts Series
Otto Herz, Piano

February 16, 1960 - New York, NY
Donnell Library Center
Otto Herz, Piano

March 30, 1960 – Akron, OH
Ohio Music Clubs Convention
Suzanne Waldbauer, Piano

April 29, 1960 – Falls Church, VA
NFMC Series
Otto Herz, Piano

April 30, 1960 – Doylestown, PA
Bucks County Symphony
Vernon Hammond, Conductor

July 17, 1960 – Chautauqua, NY
Chautauqua Festival Symphony
Walter Hendl, Conductor

July 27, 1961 – Boise, ID
University of Idaho Orchestra

April 29, 1963 – Los Angeles, CA
Monday Evening Concert Series
(25 years on series)

July 25, 1963 – Los Angeles, CA
Hollywood Bowl
Los Angeles Philharmonic Orchestra
André Kostelanetz, Guest Conductor

August 30, 1966 – Portland, OR
Mu Phi Epsilon National Convention
Frances Steiner, Cello; Sima Mannick, Piano

March 13, 1967 – Los Angeles, CA
University of Southern California
DMA Graduation Concert
David Berfield, Piano

April 20, 1969 – Albuquerque, NM
National Federation of Music Clubs Convention
David Berfield, Piano

April 20, 1975 – Los Angeles, CA
Los Angeles County Museum Series
(30 years on the series)

Oregon Chamber Music Society – Portland, OR
November 18, 1977
October 28, 1978
David Berfield, Piano

April 27, 1979 – Portland, OR
National Federation of Music Clubs Convention
David Berfield, Piano

September 15, 1980 – Los Angeles, CA
Baroque Consortium
Diana Steiner, Concertmaster, 1980–1995

February 15, 1981 – Los Angeles, CA
Wilshire Ebell Theatre
The American Youth Symphony
Mehli Mehta, Conductor

May 3, 1981 – Los Angeles, CA
Loyola Marymount University Orchestra
Bogidar Avramov, Conductor

April, 1983 – Philadelphia, PA
Penn's Landing Auditorium
Curtis Institute Symphony Orchestra
Ronald Leonard, Cello & Frances Steiner, Conductor

March 6, 1983 – Dominguez Hills, CA
California State University, Dominguez Hills
Carson/Dominguez Hills Orchestra
Ronald Leonard, Cello

For later years, see "Archival Recordings."

FRANCES STEINER

Compositions performed

April 6, 1945 – Philadelphia, PA
Philadelphia Orchestra; Eugene Ormandy, Conductor
Winner, Philadelphia Orchestra's Children's Composition Competition, for Country Dance

Solo with Orchestra and Chamber Music Groups

March 31, 1951 – Philadelphia, PA
Academy of Music
Philadelphia Orchestra Children's Concerts
Alexander Hilsberg, Conductor

July 27, 1958 – Marlboro, VT
Marlboro Music Festival
Eugene Istomin, Piano

1965 – New York, NY
Town Hall Debut Recital

March 21, 1971 – Los Angeles, CA
Royce Hall, UCLA

Conductor, Musical Director

1974–present – Palos Verdes, CA
Chamber Orchestra of the South Bay (previously Baroque Consortium)

1975–1978 – Compton, CA
Compton Civic Symphony

1977–2008 – Carson, CA
Carson-Dominguez Hills Symphony

January 15, 1977 – Los Angeles, CA
Dorothy Chandler Pavilion, Los Angeles Music Center

April 11, 1978 – Oakland, CA
Winner of the Conductor's Guild Prize
American Conductors Competition

April 17, 1983 – Philadelphia, PA
Symphony Orchestra of the The Curtis Institute of Music

April 26, 1984 – Maracaibo, Venezuela
Maracaibo Symphony

March 10, 1984 – Los Angeles, CA
Dorothy Chandler Pavilion, Los Angeles Music Center
Glendale Symphony

April 20, 1985 – Santo Domingo, Dominican Republic
National Symphony Orchestra

February 15, 1986
Texas All-State High School Symphony Orchestra

May 9, 1986 – San Francisco, CA
Bay Area Woman's Philharmonic

1987–present – Los Angeles
Southwest Youth Music Festival
Festival Orchestra

April 11, 1987 – Billings, MT
Billings Symphony

April 11, 1988
Washington–Idaho Symphony

1991
Montana All–State Honor Orchestra
July 5, 1995
Wisconsin Chamber Orchestra

May 18, 1997 – Glendale, CA
Glendale Symphony

March 2005
California All–State Honor Orchestra

October, 2003 – Nizny Novgorod, Russia
Sofia Chamber Orchestra

MARCIA DICKSTEIN
sampling

Solo with Orchestra, Recitals, etc.

December 17, 1989 – Los Angeles, CA
American Youth Symphony
Royce Hall, UCLA
Mehli Mehta, Conductor

March, 1993 – Los Angeles, CA
Young Musicians Foundation Orchestra
Royce Hall, UCLA
Lalo Schifrin, Conductor

December 4, 1999 – Glendale, CA
Alex Theater
Glendale Symphony
Sydney Weiss, Conductor

Chamber Orchestra of the South Bay – Palos Verdes, CA
January 19, 2003
December 7, 2003
April 30, 2005
December 3, 2006
March 8, 2009
Norris Theater
Frances Steiner, Conductor

With The Debussy Trio

April, 1989 – Fort Worth, TX
National Federation of Music Clubs Convention

December 19, 1989 – Portland, OR
Marylhurst College

July 3, 1990 – Houston, TX
University of Houston

March 8, 1991 – Boise, ID
Boise Chamber Music Society

February 2, 1992 – Philadelphia, PA
The Curtis Institute of Music
Perpetua Mobile Series

November 16, 1992 – Eugene, OR
Vanguard Series, University of Oregon

July 1993 – Copenhagen, Denmark
World Harp Congress
National Radio Broadcast

November 10, 1994 – Costa Mesa, CA
Orange County Performing Arts Center

1994 – Louisville, KY
Soloist with Louisville Orchestra
Lawrence Leighton-Smith, Conductor

March, 1995 – Washington, DC
Kennedy Center

March 14, 1998 – Honolulu, HI
University of Hawaii

July 21, 1999 – Prague, Czech Republic
7th World Harp Congress

July 22, 1999 – Prague, Czech Republic
American Embassy

July 30 & August 3, 2001 – Los Angeles, CA
Hollywood Bowl

February 23, 2002 – Boise, ID
Boise State University

July 25, 2002 – Geneva, Switzerland
8th World Harp Congress
Geneva Chamber Orchestra

September 29, 2002 – San Luis Obispo, CA
Cal Poly Performing Arts Center
March, 2003 – Pasadena, CA
Dabney Hall, Caltech

February 1, 2004 – Seattle/Tacoma, WA
Northwest Sinfonietta
Christopher Chagnard, Conductor

March 14, 2004 – Los Angeles, CA
El Camino College

October 1, 2004 – Victorville, CA
Victor Valley College

April 17, 2005 – Downers Grove, IL
Artists Series

July 8, 2005 – Redlands, CA
Redlands Bowl Summer Music Festival

April 13 & 15, 2007 – Los Angeles, CA
South Bay Chamber Music Society Series

May 22, 2007 – Berkeley, CA
Berkeley Chamber Performances

February 7, 2009 – Chicago, Il
Lyon & Healy Artists Series

February 22, 2009 – Los Angeles, Disney Hall
Los Angeles Master Chorale
Grant Gershon, Conductor

Other Chamber Groups

1983– present, Los Angeles, CA
Los Angeles County Museum of Art Series

1991 – Santa Fe, NM
Chamber Ensemble of Santa Fe

February, 2007 – Los Angeles, Santa Barbara, San Marino, CA
Camerata Pacifica Series

Principal harpist

1977–89 – Carson/Dominguez Hills Symphony
Frances Steiner, Conductor

1980–90 – Young Musicians Foundation Orchestra
Lalo Shifrin. Neal Stuhlberg & Myung-Whun Chung, Conductors

1983–90 – American Youth Symphony
Mehli Mehta, Conductor

1983–89 – University of Southern California Symphony,
David Lewis, Conductor et al.

1985–90 – Pasadena Symphony
Jorge Mester, Conductor

1989 – present – Glendale Symphony

1985, 86–88 – Los Angeles Institute Orchestra, Hollywood Bowl
Leonard Bernstein, Director; Michael Tilson Thomas, Andre Previn, Sir Charles Grove,
Leonard Slatkin, Yuri Temirkanov, Edo de Waart and Otto Werner-Mueller, Conductors

1990 – Los Angeles Philharmonic (Alternate)
Esa Pekka Salonen, Conductor

1980– present – Chamber Orchestra of the South Bay
Frances Steiner, Conductor

Co-Principal harpist

1987– present Long Beach Symphony, CA

1987– present Los Angeles Music Center Opera
Placido Domingo, Director

1991–92 – Hollywood Bowl Orchestra
John Mauceri, Conductor

1992, 93 & 94 – Fairbanks, AK
Alaska Music Festival

ACADEMIC & PROFESSIONAL CREDENTIALS

ELIZABETH LEVY

ACADEMIC
1915-24 – Academic & Music Studies, Willamette University, Salem, OR

1924– Mus.B (Violin), Ithaca College, NY

PROFESSIONAL
1920s-1938 – Various Official Positions, Oregon Music Teachers Association

1938-40 – Certification Chairman, Oregon Music Teacher Association

1950s – President & Other Official Positions, Philadelphia (PA) Music Teachers Association

DIANA STEINER

ACADEMIC
1972 – M.M. (20th century violin performance), University of Southern California

1957 – Mus.B. (violin), The Curtis Institute of Music

1949 – Diploma (violin), The Curtis Institute of Music

PROFESSIONAL
May 5, 2001 – Alumni Award, Curtis, Philadelphia

1982 – Master Teacher Certificate (National), National Music Teachers Association

FRANCES STEINER

ACADEMIC

May, 1969 – Doctor of Musical Arts (cello, conducting), University of Southern California

May, 1958 – M.A. in music, Radcliffe College (Harvard University). Composition study with Walter Piston and Randall Thompson

April, 1957 – Fontainebleau School of Music with Nadia Boulanger

May 12, 1956 – Mus. B., The Curtis Institute of Music

April 1, 1956 – Danforth Graduate Fellowship, Radcliffe College

February, 1956 – B.S. in Ed. (music), Temple University

PROFESSIONAL

1962–65 – Faculty, Music Dept., Brooklyn College, Brooklyn, NY

1966–67 – Faculty, Music Dept., Fullerton College, Fullerton, CA

1967–2004 – Professor of Music, California State University, Dominguez Hills, Carson, CA

2004–present – Professor of Music emeritus, California State University, Dominguez Hills, Carson, CA

MARCIA DICKSTEIN

ACADEMIC

June, 19 – M.M. (harp), University of Southern California

June, 19 – Mus.B (harp), University of Southern California

PROFESSIONAL

Adjunct Professor

    1993 –present, California State University, Long Beach

    2000 –present, Cal Poly, San Luis Obispo

DIRECTOR/TEACHER

2002–present, Central Coast Harp Workshop

INDEX

A

Air for Strings 230, 231, 273, 296
Alchin, Carolyn 4
Ambrosini, Virginia 264
America Federation of Musicians 297
American Harp Society (AHS) 145, 230, 288, 289, 296
American Jewish Congress 119, 304
American String Teachers Association Magazine 141, 231
American Youth Symphony (AYS) 230, 260, 281, 288, 297, 308, 310, 313
Antheil, George 99
Apap, Gilles 133
Auer, Leopold 62, 66, 94, 203

B

Baltimore Symphony 153, 177
Bang, Maia 94, 96, 239
Barber, Samuel 99, 119, 280
Baroque Consortium 225, 281, 289, 308, 309
Bedetti, Jean 141, 245
Beecham, Thomas (Sir) 143
Bell, Louis 217
Benny, Jack 206
Berfield, David 141, 215, 224, 250, 259, 275, 276, 281, 282, 285, 286, 298, 307
Bergman, Elma 151
Berkowitz, Freda Pastor 99, 227
Bernstein, Leonard 99, 142, 143, 146, 264, 298, 313
Bertolami, Vivian 127
Betti, Adolfo 4, 82
Bird, Winifred 22
Blaustein, Barbara 145
Blaustein, Jacob 145
Bolet, Jorge 229, 298
Borisoff, Josef 4, 67
Boston Symphony Orchestra 140, 141, 142, 143, 144, 145, 146, 158, 173, 176, 293, 298
Boulanger, Nadia xiii, 315
Braun, Edith Evans 98
Brevard Music Festival 195, 196, 283, 306
Broido, Tom 265
Broughton, Bruce 264, 277, 288, 290, 295
Brown, Elaine xiii
Browning, John 167, 168
Brussels Conservatory 14
Buchsbaum, Ben 43, 44
Buchsbaum, Kathryn Wolf 44

Buketoff, Igor 127, 285, 304
Burgin, Richard 143, 144
Busch, Adolf 122, 163, 164, 165, 166, 168, 246

C

Carmel (CA) International Chamber Music Competition 263
Casals, Pablo 166
Castelnuovo-Tedesco, Mario 210, 253, 275
Caston, Saul 118
Celibidache, Sergiu 144
Chamber Orchestra of the South Bay (COSB) 225, 257, 285, 286, 287, 309, 313
Charles, Ray 264
Chasins, Abram 127, 226, 229, 248, 298
Chautauqua Music Festival 98, 195, 196, 197, 202, 282, 307
Chicago Symphony 177, 305
Clearfield, Andrea 264
Cliburn, Van 167, 229
Clooney, Rosemary 264, 279
Coe, Minna 209
Cole, Orlando 116
Columbia Artists Management Inc. 128, 153, 165, 167, 177, 184, 185, 191
Condell, Ruth 177
Constitution Hall 151, 216
Copland, Aaron 141, 142, 146, 245, 275, 276, 284
Costello, Marilyn 260
Craft, Robert 210
Curtis Alumni Association 153, 225, 226, 227, 228, 273, 274, 281
Curtis Institute of Music, The 5, 91, 96, 97, 111, 116, 144, 173, 280, 284, 293, 295, 298, 303, 308, 309, 311, 314, 315

D

Dahl, Ingolf 214, 215, 283
Daley, John 297
Davis, Don 264, 277, 290, 291
Davis, Meyer 118
Debruyn, Gertrude 12
Debussy Trio Music Foundation vii, 108, 260, 295
Debussy Trio, The vii, xiii, 77, 167, 216, 260, 261, 263, 277, 289, 292, 295, 302, 311
de Carvalho, Eleazar 141, 245
de Lancie, John 226, 228
Dickstein, Ed xii, 6, 108, 134, 135, 143, 146, 147, 160, 166, 170, 171, 176, 189, 191, 193, 194, 195, 197, 201, 209, 211, 213, 217, 218, 223, 225, 233, 235, 249, 250, 259, 262, 263, 270
Dickstein, Marcia xiii, 11, 78, 79, 134, 135, 167, 196, 205, 216, 219, 223, 224, 230, 231, 233, 237, 238, 249, 257, 259, 261, 262, 263, 264, 265, 267, 268, 269, 270, 277, 278, 279, 280, 281, 287, 288, 289, 290, 291, 292, 293, 294, 295, 296, 298, 310, 315
Dickstein, Sallie 78, 79, 135, 153, 160, 199, 204, 233, 249, 270
Dicterow, Glenn 214

Director (Nagel), June 6, 68, 76
Druian, Rafael 99
Dupré, Marcel 241

E

Ebann, William 108
Ehlers, Alice 215
Epinoff, Jackie 128

F

Fiedler, Arthur 176, 298
Fiedler, Elsa 176, 249, 275, 284, 304, 305
Flesch, Carl 131
Flonzaley Quartet 4, 82
Francescatti, Zino 107
Frank, Claude 166, 167, 169, 283
Friday Morning Music Club (FMMC) 151, 176, 216
Friendly, Joan 104
Frumin, Edith Evans 227

G

Galamian, Ivan 127, 131, 203, 230, 252
Ganz, Rudolph 107, 284, 303
Geneva Chamber Orchestra 263, 295, 312
Gerle, Robert 140
Gilels, Emil 132
Gill, Vince 264
Glazer, Esther 145
Glendale Symphony xiii, 285, 289, 309, 310, 313
Goldberg, Albert 207, 216
Goode, Richard 169
Goodman, Benny 152, 304
Gormé, Eydie 6
Gotham Trio 177, 179, 185, 196
Graffman, Gary 136, 169, 228, 229, 246, 298
Graham, William Wallace 21, 22, 25, 26, 28, 31, 32
Grant, Amy 264
Greenbriar Resort Music Festival 98, 303
Greene, Keith 260, 277, 278, 291, 292, 295
Green, Theresa 119, 179
Guarneri String Quartet 297

H

Hadassah 80
Hagen, Daron 99, 278, 293, 294, 295
Hambro, Leonid 127

Harrington, David 133
Heaton, Nancy 128
Heifetz, Jascha 84, 94, 99, 127, 128, 139, 175, 186, 197, 199, 201, 202, 203, 204, 205, 206, 209, 210, 211, 214, 215, 216, 224
Hertz, Alfred 89, 96
Herzog, Rose 185, 195, 209
Herz, Otto 106, 107, 132, 189, 276, 284, 306, 307
Higdon, Jennifer 99
Hilsberg, Alexander 119, 120, 121, 157, 243, 308
Hirsch, David 264
Hoffman, Irwin 145
Hofmann, Josef 5, 96, 98
Hogg, Margaret 6, 63, 65
Hope, Dolores 264
Horner, James 264
Horszowski, Mieczyslaw 98
Hume, Paul 149, 151
Hurley, Joe 223
Hurley, Margaret 223, 224

I

Ibert, Jacqueline 137, 144, 253
Ibert, Jacques 137, 144, 145, 146, 287, 293, 295
Imbrie, Andrew 210
Istomin, Eugene 157, 166, 169, 308
Ithaca College 4, 32, 39, 314
Ito, Toshiya 127

J

Janover, Gertrude van Straaten 39
Jones, Franklin 107, 108, 109
Jones, Ruth Bradley 35, 66, 107, 108, 109, 126, 304

K

Kaghan, Phil 185
Kelly, Gene 264
Kestenbaum, Myra 210, 282
Kojian, Varujan 214, 227
Koodlach, Benny 175, 186, 224, 227
Kostelanetz, André 216, 307
Koussevitzky, Serge 140, 142, 143, 146, 149, 304
Koval, Mark 264, 287
Kreutzer, Rudolph 95
Kroll, William 139, 282
Kronos Quartet 133
Krouse, Ian 289, 290, 291, 292, 295
Kuerti, Anton 169

L

Langinger, Herman 231
Larson, Sylvia 45
Lateiner, Isadore 263
Lawrence, Steve 6
Leschetizky, Theodor 107
Lesser, Dick 215
Lesser, Larry 215
Leventritt Competition 163, 167
Levin, Abe 44
Levy, Ben 16, 17, 21, 25, 26, 27, 30, 31, 35, 43, 44, 46, 51, 67, 81
Levy, Harry 13, 16, 17, 26, 27, 32, 41, 43, 45, 46, 67, 68, 81, 125,
Levy, Solomon 11, 12, 13, 16, 40, 45, 47, 68, 81
Levy, Wolfe 11, 12, 39
Liege University 12
Lincoln Beach, Oregon 6, 75, 134, 223
Lion, Jacqueline 263
Lipkin, Eleanor 167
Lipkin, Seymour 167
Los Angeles Philharmonic 135, 158, 226, 227, 261, 296, 297, 307, 313
Loyola Marymount University 6, 230, 285, 298, 308
Luboshutz, Lea 98, 167

M

Maazel, Lorin 118, 304
Mannes School 100, 106
Marlboro Music Festival 117, 122, 145, 146, 161, 163, 165, 166, 167, 168, 169, 170,
283, 305, 308
Marymount School 6
Massena, Martha 122, 227
Mays, Lyle 264, 277, 291
McDonald, Susann 224, 237, 259, 260, 286
McNeely, Joel 264
Mehta, Mehli 226, 230, 264, 269, 281, 288, 297, 308, 310, 313
Mehta, Zubin 226
Mendoza, Vince 263, 278, 292, 293, 295
Menotti, Gian Carlo 99, 119, 122
Menuhin, Yalta 185, 186
Menuhin, Yehudi 70, 103, 186
Michaels Award 177, 284, 285
Mills, Alvin 289
Mills, Harlow 227, 296
Mitchell, Howard 151
Moiseyev Ballet 132
Morini, Erica xii, 136
Mort, Fay 6, 33, 51, 63, 64, 65, 85, 123, 223

Mosher, Tilly 46
Mothersbaugh, Mark 264
Moyse, Blanche Honegger 163, 169
Moyse, Louis 163, 166, 246, 283
Moyse, Marcel 163, 168, 246
Mu Phi Epsilon Sorority 108, 109, 216, 280, 307
Murphy, Thomas (Hon.) 262, 270
Music Teachers Association of California 80, 231, 296, 297, 301

N

National Association of American Composers and Conductors (NAACC) 209, 210
National Federation of Music Clubs (NFMC) 108, 151, 187, 194, 216, 230, 282, 283, 294, 296, 297, 302, 307, 308, 311
National Federation of Music Clubs (NFMC) Young Artists Award 194, 297
National Symphony Orchestra 107, 133, 151, 175, 216, 309
Naumburg Award 107, 128, 153, 167, 175, 176, 177, 230
Neeley, Marilyn 140
Neu, C. Richard 264
Newman, Mitchell 227, 285
Newman, Randy 264
New York Philharmonic 94, 106, 107, 118, 126, 146, 214, 229, 284, 285, 303, 304
Nixon, Marni 145

O

Oistrakh, David 132
Oregon Music Teachers Association 4, 5, 31, 33, 92, 95, 314
Ormandy, Eugene 118, 131, 141, 152, 153, 176, 242, 304, 308
Orsini, Tom, 30

P

Parker, Louise 119
Pepper, Joe 127
Persinger, Louis 96
Pettibone, Lillian 6
Pfohl, James 196, 283, 306
Philadelphia Orchestra 43, 65, 107, 117, 118, 120, 121, 131, 132, 133, 135, 141, 142, 144, 146, 152, 153, 174, 176, 260, 261, 304, 308
Philadelphia Orchestra Children's Concerts 121, 304, 308
Philadelphia String Quartet 133, 134, 155
Phillips, Edna 260, 261
Piastro, Mishel 95
Piatigorsky, Gregor v, 116, 117, 119, 155, 157, 158, 159, 160, 186, 187, 201, 204, 205, 224, 226, 248
Piatigorsky, Jeptha 160
Piston, Walter 315
Portland Symphony 4, 5, 51, 52, 67, 71, 72, 92, 95
Powell, Maud xii

Primrose, William 116, 117

R

Ramo, Simon 210, 211
Redfield, Christopher 260, 293, 294
Rejto, Gabor 212, 213, 214, 215
Reynolds, Veda xiii, 99, 120, 121, 127, 129, 131, 132, 133, 134, 135, 136, 139, 146, 174, 214, 238, 262, 263, 282, 302
Richmond Symphony 98
Rochberg, George 99
Rosand, Aaron 127
Rose, Leonard 157
Ross, Hugh 145
Rutenberg, Peter 229

S

Salonen, Esa Pekka 261, 313
Sayre, Robert 141
Schick, George 177, 305
Schmoll, Rudolph 94
Schneider, Alexander ("Sascha") 145, 166, 167, 168
Schwartz, David 135, 195, 281, 285
Senofsky, Berl 165, 169
Serkin, Irene 166, 169
Serkin, Peter 166
Serkin, Rudolf 117, 122, 161, 163, 165, 167, 168, 170, 225, 226, 246, 253, 274
Settlement Music School 185
Shefeluk, Marie 127
Shu, John 137
Sigma Alpha Iota 6, 33, 80, 109, 141
Silverstein, Joseph 127
Sitjar, Felix 127, 128
Smith, Brooks 215, 298
Smith, Lawrence Leighton 167, 277, 283, 311
Sokoloff, Eleanor 99
Sokoloff, Vladimir ("Billy") 99, 127
Solomon, Izler 177, 178, 247, 283, 305
Soyer, David 297
Speciale, Rosalie 109
Spencer, Delta 5, 67
Stage Door Canteen 118
Starr, Susan 169
Stassevitch, Paul 100, 106, 252
Steelman, Ron 226
Stein, Edna 22
Steiner, Carl 232
Steiner, Elizabeth Levy xii, xiii, 1, 3, 4, 6, 7, 9, 11, 13, 14, 15, 16, 17, 18, 19, 20, 21, 22,

23, 25, 26, 27, 28, 29, 30, 31, 32, 35, 37, 39, 40, 41, 43, 45, 46, 47, 49, 51, 52, 53, 54, 55, 56, 57, 61, 62, 63, 64, 65, 66, 67, 68, 69, 72, 75, 76, 77, 78, 79, 81, 82, 83, 84, 85, 105, 106, 107, 108, 113, 114, 115, 116, 119, 122, 123, 125, 126, 152, 174, 179, 183, 185, 186, 191, 192, 212, 213, 223, 233, 235

Steiner, Ferenz (Franz) xii, 4, 5, 29, 35, 37, 40, 44, 45, 46, 47, 51, 52, 53, 61, 63, 64, 66, 67, 70, 152, 211, 239

Steiner, Frances xi, xii, xiii, 5, 7, 79, 87, 101, 104, 105, 106, 108, 113, 114, 115, 116, 117, 118, 119, 121, 123, 125, 126, 155, 157, 158, 159, 166, 174, 183, 191, 192, 215, 221, 225, 227, 232, 242, 248, 259, 264, 267, 273, 276, 281, 282, 285, 286, 287, 289, 299, 301, 307, 308, 310, 313, 315

Steinhardt, Arnold 297, 302

Stein, Leonard 210

Stern, Hettie 44, 104, 176

Stern, Horace 44, 104, 176

Stern, Isaac 139

Stevens, Halsey 210, 214, 282

Stewart, Reginald 153

Stokowski, Leopold 261

Stringart Quartet 133

T

Tabuteau, Marcel 117, 120, 121, 243

Tanglewood Music Festival 139, 140, 141, 142, 143, 144, 145, 146, 147, 151, 157, 158, 163, 167, 170, 304

Tarter, Lena Belle 6, 31, 32, 33, 34, 46, 61, 85

Tatton, Jesse 132

Taylor Foster, Hortense 6, 51, 52, 62, 277

Temianka, Henri 195, 225, 248, 259, 289, 301, 302

Theodore Presser Company 265

Thomas, Augusta Read 167, 277, 292

Thomas, Michael Tilson 264, 313

Thompson, Cesar 4, 14, 22, 28, 32, 33, 34, 82, 186

Thompson, Marilyn 298

Thompson, Randall 315

Tree, Michael 297

Trepel, Shirley 169

Tuttle, Karen 117

U

University of California, Los Angeles (UCLA) xi, 4, 34, 134, 153, 155, 158, 201, 202, 204, 205, 206, 209, 210, 211, 213, 229, 286, 287, 288, 309, 310

University of Oregon 34, 51

University of Pennsylvania 153, 192

University of Southern California (USC) 134, 140, 186, 204, 211, 213, 214, 215, 228, 237, 259, 260, 288, 297

V

Vail, Jimmy 215

van Beinum, Edward 158
van Straaten, Alexander 5, 13, 15, 41, 42, 43, 44, 47, 52, 83, 103, 105, 116, 119
van Straaten, Harry 12
van Straaten, Herbert 126
van Straaten, Herman 12, 13, 14
van Straaten, Jack 263
van Straaten, Jacques (Jacob) 12, 39, 40
van Straaten Levy, Dientje (Diana) xii, 3, 4, 11, 12, 13, 15, 16, 46, 67, 68, 70, 72, 77, 79, 81
van Straaten, Maurice 12, 14, 15
van Straaten, Thomas 264
van Straaten, Willem 12
Vaughn, Sarah 264
Vincent, John 134, 155, 210
Vincent, Johnnie 122, 176
Vogelgesang, Frederick "Freddie" 98
Vyner, Louis 195, 197

W

Walther, David 260, 269, 277, 289, 290, 291, 295
Warfield, William 107
Whiteman, Paul 171, 173, 174, 186, 196
Wiegand, Angela 260, 269, 277, 278, 287, 288, 289, 290, 291, 292, 293, 294, 295
Williams, John 264
Winkler, Elizabeth Levy 11, 39, 40, 47
Winkler, Oscar 40
Wise, Rabbi Jonah B. 61, 84, 103, 104
Woodruff, Marilyn 128
World Harp Congress 135, 262, 263, 264
Wurlitzer, Rembert 175, 177, 178, 186

Y

Young Musicians Foundation Orchestra 260, 288, 310, 313
Young Musicians Foundation (YMF) 260, 294, 297, 298
Ysaye, Eugene 214, 282

Z

Zayde, Jascha 127
Zearott, Michael 210, 282, 283
Zighera, Bernard 145
Zimbalist, Efrem 66, 69, 70, 84, 94, 96, 98, 99, 111, 113, 116, 119, 121, 122, 127, 128, 131, 132, 157, 167, 177, 189, 203, 204, 205, 214, 224, 225, 226, 240, 250, 251, 252, 275, 276, 284, 298, 301, 302, 303
Zimbalist, Efrem, Jr. 226, 250
Zimbalist, Mary Louise Curtis Bok 97, 98, 112, 226
Zindel, Carol 214